NEVER WORK WITH ANIMALS

The unfiltered truth
of life as a vet

GARETH STEEL

*This book is dedicated to the unspoken heroes of
animal welfare: veterinary nurses*

HarperElement
An imprint of HarperCollins*Publishers*
1 London Bridge Street
London SE1 9GF

www.harpercollins.co.uk

HarperCollins*Publishers*
Macken House, 39/40 Mayor Street Upper
Dublin 1, D01 C9W8, Ireland

First published by HarperElement 2022
This paperback edition published 2023

1 3 5 7 9 10 8 6 4 2

© Gareth Steel 2022

Gareth Steel asserts the moral right to be
identified as the author of this work

A catalogue record of this book is
available from the British Library

ISBN 978-0-00-846661-9

Printed and bound in the UK using 100%
renewable electricity at CPI Group (UK) Ltd

CONTENTS

INTRODUCTION

First of all, a warning. I've been a qualified vet for almost twenty years. I've enjoyed it enormously. I have also been challenged and humbled by my profession. I've found vets are much misunderstood by the general public and I'm seeking to redress the balance here. I've tried to be as candid as possible throughout and there is much to criticise. You may be surprised by bits of this book, and it isn't suitable for the younger reader. The overarching concept throughout is to inform and provoke thought. Unfortunately, that means grappling with some difficult, uncomfortable and even distressing issues. There are some high highs in this book, and some low lows; they reflect the reality of what it is like for the vets, nurses and support staff who care for our animals.

Second, an explanation. This book is a product of communication, or at least, the lack of it. TV abounds with veterinary series and documentaries searching for the extreme, the entertaining and the further boundaries of veterinary medicine. We are also blessed with the excellent and entertaining *All Creatures Great and Small*: a book, subsequently adapted into television series that have inspired many a veterinary career. There are shark documentaries, series about wildlife veterinarians and even a programme called *Penguin A&E*. I'm not sure what a penguin accident and emergency department would look like, but it seems an unsound proposition for a small business. However, rarely, in any of these, is someone presented with a bill. What is lacking in many of them, in my opinion, is realism. That's not to denigrate these shows; they often have admirable goals. However, the primary goal is to entertain within the limitations of television. It is extremely hard to accurately convey someone's thoughts or feelings via TV. Especially so when they are complex or nuanced.

It was recently noted in the veterinary press that almost no other profession has a higher chance of people entering it with a romanticised concept of their future employment. This book seeks to fill the information void. At the same time, I want to drag you around a rollercoaster of adventure, mistakes and successes, and hopefully have a little fun en route.

This book is for anyone, but especially the aspiring vet, the pet owner who wants to know what their vet is really thinking, anyone with an interest in science, and my fellow professionals for whom I'm trying to speak, however imperfectly. If anyone thinks they recognise themselves, or their practice, they're mistaken. It's not me, it's not you, I was never there and please don't phone to check.

Third, a caveat. Had there been a vote in vet school for 'Person Least Likely to Write a Book on Veterinary Medicine', I like to think I would have won outright. I'm not the best vet in the world, I'm very often not even the best vet in the room. I'm not a specialist, though I have worked in emergency-specific clinics. I've worked all over the UK, in many different practices and with most domesticated species. I've worked with some creatures who have fallen some way short of household-pet suitability. This is not a work of clinical excellence, nor a reference text. I've left in medical mistakes that I've made and older treatment protocols that have become outdated. I've deliberately avoided referencing scientific papers or articles. Veterinary medicine and science in general is constantly evolving, and what is 'correct' at the time may not be in the future. My opinion will change with the evidence. For the curious I recommend you do your own research.

I don't want to gloss over our profession. Rather, I want the public to have as honest an account as possible. Vets already enjoy enviable levels of public trust. I suspect this will only be increased when the challenges involved are unveiled.

With that in mind I've taken steps to anonymise everyone, human or otherwise, with the exception of myself. Locations are deliberately approximate, clinic names omitted, and patient confidentiality respected. For owners, keepers, riders, farmers and the interested, I want to give you a glimpse into the lives and minds of your veterinary advisors. Maybe it'll increase your empathy for them, maybe it'll make you change to another vet. If what you do involves some thought, I'm glad I could help.

If the Royal College of Veterinary Surgeons feel that any particular passage warrants my being struck off, know that I am prone to exaggeration and am a notorious liar, so that bit is probably not true. But it happened.

Scientific Statements

Don't be so sure.

Always consider the possibility that you are wrong.

What assumptions have you made?

What does the data *not* tell you?

Do not mistake the absence of evidence for evidence of absence.

1

BULL-HEADED

After five years of university, I had proven myself to be a fairly mediocre vet student. I only had myself to blame, but, despite this, I'd just managed to land my first job at a six-person mixed practice in Northern Ireland. My family had generously donated their ageing estate car to me in which to make my way around the beautiful countryside. Armed with the enthusiasm and knowledge of a fresh-faced graduate, I was determined to save myself and my patients from catastrophe. Like many students starting their first job, I was full of both confidence and doubt in my own abilities. The exact ratio of one to the other changed on a minute-to-minute basis. And so it was that I found myself on a farm in a corner of the UK with the mission of shooting a bull. Not, you might think, a natural mission for one tasked with saving fluffy things and bunnies. However, there are darker regions of veterinary medicine that not even Batman would willingly enter into. My boss was an unashamedly 'no nonsense' kind of guy and mentoring was not a word that tripped off his tongue. In his defence, I was pretty poor at asking for assistance and we were so busy there was little time for teaching or training.

What had happened was that a young male cow, or a bull, as we professionals call it, had broken a leg. Due to the size and weight of the animal, along with technological and budgetary constraints, treatment was out of the question. It could still go into the food chain and end up as burgers, but it could not be transported to a slaughterhouse with a broken leg for welfare reasons. In essence this left only one option. We would have to shoot it, drain it of blood, and then the farmer would transport it to the meat factory.

Enter man with gun. Now, at this point in my career, my knowledge of firearms was based on war movies and being briefly trained to shoot a polar bear using a rifle. However, I was armed only with a single shot .32 revolver and grim determination. I should also mention several complicating factors. The bull was murderous and running around the field frothing at the mouth with its broken leg flailing around, presumably adding to its anger. The farmer was terrified of the bull, and I had opted to bring along a girl I knew from vet school. We'd recently met for a drink, and she'd suggested coming to see practice. We were a year apart in age and I will confess that I had a not-very-secret crush on her.

Just getting near the 'patient' felt like going to war. There was definitely a sense of having to be 'up for it'. The plan was to drive into the field in a JCB digger and get to within small-arms range of the bull in the digger's protective shell. Okay as far as it went. I would then dismount and quickly dispatch the bull with maximum manliness, and return; hopefully doused in the kind of post-combat pheromones that female veterinary students are powerless to resist.

Unfortunately, the bull had other plans. On dismounting, I found that it simply stared at me as I approached it – easy so far. However, once he judged that I was sufficiently far from my yellow, digger-based safe room, he charged me. So, I found myself sprinting in my wellies back towards my not-to-be girlfriend, uttering: 'Shit, shit, shit, shit, shiiiiit!'

I tried this guileless approach a few times. No luck. Then I hit on an idea. What if I put down some delicious cow snacks, waited for him to have a nibble, then shot him in the head? Well, we tried that. The bull gingerly approached and dipped his head to the perfect angle to catch a lovely .32 round right in the sweet spot; he began to eat. I was some distance away, and figured I had to get within five metres to have any chance of a clean kill. I cautiously approached, the bull watching me with one eye. I took aim, in the fashion all fans of American cop dramas would have found familiar, and waited for my sights to settle on the correct spot.

Bang! I fired a shot.

Moo? The bull looked up, curious as to what the odd noise was. At first, I thought I'd missed, but then he developed a bit of a nosebleed. Once satisfied that any oddity had passed, he continued to eat, unabashed …

Bang!

Moo?

Bang!

Moo?

Bang!

Moo!?

By now I had miserably failed to impress the girl in the JCB, and the farmer was only more terrified. It was unclear to him what the greater danger was, should he step out of the JCB: the bull or my ineptitude.

The bull had a fairly severe nosebleed, but it certainly wasn't going to be dying anytime soon. I mean, my pistol was supposed to be put almost next to the skull and fired. It had not been designed with this scenario in mind. Time for plan C. There was nothing else for it, I had to get close. So, with some trepidation, and still hoping to salvage a peck on the cheek at some point (from the girl), I approached the bull. He watched while happily munching away, until he judged I was sufficiently committed, pawed the ground once and gave chase. I did a 180 and made for the JCB. I reached it, as yet unscathed, but with him hard on my heels. There was no hope of getting in quickly enough to avoid injury, so I was forced to run around the back, and he followed. He was faster, but I could corner better. We entered a comedic chase around and around a bemused farmer and horrified veterinary student, while they watched, agog.

Even in my somewhat compromised state I realised this couldn't go on indefinitely; eventually one of us would tire, likely me. Then I would be crushed or trampled to death and be unable to collect my meagre pay cheque. So, I put on a final burst of speed, rounded the back wheel, got as far as the front wheel, and stopped. The bull rapidly rounded the back wheel and I managed to get off an instinctive shot. He dropped immediately, more or less at my feet.

Moo?!!!

He had been a worthy opponent and it was with some sadness that I secured his feet to the bucket of the digger with chain, got the farmer to lift him off the ground and punctured his carotid artery with a scalpel, allowing his mindless, comatose bulk to spill its lifeblood on the ground. My job was done, and I could leave.

There was some awkwardness at the car. My companion was pretty hardy, but there was no doubt that I had failed to provide the kind of nurturing learning environment that universities seek to foster.

I mean, the lesson from the day was pretty much 'sometimes shit gets real'.

We cleaned up, packed up and made for the next call, for which we were massively late. As I drove along the main road, I realised that I couldn't recall what I'd done with the gun. I pulled over under the pretence of 'checking something'. I rapidly rifled through the boot, checked under the seat in the small plastic case in which I kept the revolver between murders and eliminated the back seat as hiding places. I'd say that this all looked nonchalant and casual, but it did not. As I glanced up towards the front of the car and my passenger's puzzlement, I caught a glimpse of my gun, casually laid on the outside of the windscreen against the wiper. I'd only driven 20 miles along the main road with a pistol displayed on the front of my car – nothing to draw any attention.

I replaced the pistol in its secure, rickety, plastic box, impossibly concealed from criminal types under the passenger seat, and drove us to the next call.

This was life as a young vet in mixed practice.

I have to say that sometimes I made my job harder than it needed to be. There were four young vets at the practice, and we all showcased this same problem to varying degrees. Each time I went to a call, I felt the pressure to solve the problem in front of me. I still lacked the experience and confidence to know when to admit defeat or ask for help.

Here's the reality: I should have phoned the police and described the situation and the danger the animal presented. They would have been compelled to send a marksman with a suitable rifle. There would have been a delay, but there's no doubt it was the safer option. It hadn't even occurred to me. I just got on with it, as bull-headed, stubborn and determined as, well, a bull. University had left me knowledgeable, but not wise.

I have to say that I had been warned. At the start of calving and lambing season, spring, my boss had given us a pep talk: 'It'll be hard, sometimes you'll work all day, all night, then all the next day. You'll be exhausted and irrational at times, and it wouldn't surprise me if one of you either shagged or knocked out one of the others.'

He had been right in many respects. We worked a two in five rota. This meant that in any given week we each did one night 'first on call'. That is to say, the practice's phones would be diverted to our mobile phone, and any emergency would be ours to deal with. In addition, one further night would be our 'second on call'. This meant that, should the first vet be too busy or too far away from a call, we might be pressed into service. The same system applied to weekends. One in five you would be 'first on', another one in five, you'd be 'second on'.

We also got one half-day off per week. On paper.

Now, for those of you who are mathematically astute, you will have already worked out that we were not working under the tender care of the EU working time directive. Signing out of it was kind of how you got a job. Even the suggestion it might be applicable would have been met by derisory laughter. You simply could not be a rural vet and stay within 40-odd hours a week. In fact, it was not unusual to break that by Wednesday evening and then go on to work another 60 hours. I once sat down and worked it out. Calculated hourly, I was being paid just over the minimum wage.

On top of which I had neither shagged nor knocked out anyone since starting the job.

But it was a vocation! I was engaged in my life's passion!

Eh, well, that wasn't quite true. I mean a typical day went something like this. I'd arrive from my flat upstairs a few minutes late. It was perfectly possible to get up 15 minutes prior to work and be on time. But I just had to have a second cup of tea. I'd then pick up my 'TB' folder for the day. TB or tuberculosis is the scourge of cows throughout the UK. It is caused by a micro-organism that is, to date, rather hard to definitively detect in a non-lethal fashion and can survive in its victims for years prior to causing overt symptoms. It can also affect humans, hence the testing. In my TB folder would be a list of farms that I would have to visit for the purposes of driving TB from existence. The plan was simple. We tested all cattle annually. If they were negative, then: Woohoo! If they were not, well, that was bad. Very bad, especially if you were the cow in question.

Now 'TB testing' sounds quite scientific and sterile. Nothing could be further from the truth. The idea was to test each cow by:

1. Clipping two patches of hair approximately one to two inches in diameter on the cow's neck, one above the other, perhaps six inches apart.
2. Measuring and noting the thickness of cow skin at both sites using small and antique-looking brass callipers (they're the kind of thing you'd imagine a fashion model uses to measure body fat).
3. Injecting 'avian' tuberculin, intra-dermally (within the skin), at the top site.
4. Injecting 'bovine' tuberculin, intra-dermally, at the bottom site.
5. Coming back on day four (first visit is day one) and measuring the thickness of cow skin at the two sites, then working out the difference from day one.
6. If there was a greater increase in skin thickness at the bottom (bovine tuberculin) site compared to the top then: Moo?!

Now please bear in mind that all of this must be done on each and every animal. Some of them would rather not have been tested and said as much. Or at least kicked the nearest person in the genitals. There would normally be anywhere from four to four hundred animals per farm to be tested and anywhere between 0.25 and three people to help you achieve your aim. A lot of our farmers ran small and rather ramshackle affairs. It was not uncommon to have to chase animals down on foot, jam them behind gates and then test them. It wasn't unusual to be presented with an animal housed in a small pen, looking as though Satan himself had possessed it, and be expected to somehow unambiguously ascertain its disease status.

It certainly wasn't uncommon to be accused of 'giving me TB'.

'Eh?'

'You gave me TB!'

'Eh?'

'You fucking come here with your fucking callipers and, just like that, I've got TB!'

'Eh, well, you see …'

'Don't fucking, "Eh, well, you see …" me!'

'Eh?'

I have, before now, watched a cow walk around a corner 100 metres away and spotted a lump on its neck the size of a melon. I mean, I made a show of measuring it, but given that a 5-mm-size increase in skin thickness meant death, no amount of innovative calliper work could really positively rule out TB. If the bottom skin lump's increase is bigger by even a little, the cow is classified as a 'Reactor'.

I've been toe to toe with a farmer over this. I honestly thought I'd have to hit him before he hit me. He wasn't happy about the outcome of the test. It's fair to say he was a very unpleasant individual. If he hit me and grounded me, I'd be very vulnerable and there'd be no help coming any time soon. I had no idea what he might do if he got the upper hand. In the near past a farmer had been prosecuted after he knocked a female vet to the floor and tried drowning her in a puddle. Fortunately, in my case, despite his clenched fists, furious expression and the spittle hitting me in the face from his angry diatribe, he backed down.

I understood, or at least, thought I did. Farmers whose herds were found to have TB could have all their animals slaughtered. Some of these people had spent generations building up a herd. Some grown men were visibly distraught that their favourite cow, the one they'd helped give birth in the middle of the night as a teenager, was condemned to die.

It wasn't just the slaughter. They'd face months of restrictions in which they could neither buy nor sell cattle. Re-test upon re-test could be visited upon even those farms whose animals had only been IRs (Inconclusive Reactors). All the while their livelihood was under threat. Some simply killed themselves.

In the meantime, wildlife reservoirs went largely ignored. Non-production animals such as deer, and famously, badgers, could carry and spread the disease. However, no one was injecting them in the neck. In addition, there was widespread public objection to badger culling. Now, no one wants to kill animals unnecessarily. Especially the average vet or farmer. But I think it's fair to say that when your national disease prevention strategy has the kind of holes in it through which one could comfortably pilot a super-tanker, we have a problem. Science should be independent of politics. The answers to complex problems are rarely simple and just as rarely popular.

He wasn't a vet, but Prussian general and military theorist Carl von Clausewitz said it best: 'Two qualities are indispensable: first, an intellect that, even in the darkest hour, retains some glimmerings of the inner light which leads to truth; and second, the courage to follow this faint light wherever it may lead.'

Happily, I hear a vaccine is soon to be trialled. I hope that will save future vets the calliper work, and future farmers the conflict with badgers. Anyway, the morning would usually consist of driving from farm to farm, injecting unwilling subjects in the neck, twice. Assume the odd accusation of being in league with the government or the devil, which are believed to be part of the same organisation by many farmers. Maybe chuck in a few kicks to the shin and perhaps a little shit in the face courtesy of a wayward, faeces-covered tail. Call that lunch.

Generally, the latter would either be non-existent (maybe a drink of water out of the welly-washing tap?), or some generic shop sandwiches, eaten while driving to the next life-lesson.

The afternoon would consist of 'calls'; making your way round the various sick cases that had been reported to the office in the morning. An emergency might cause a diversion from even the all-important TB eradication strategy or a rearrangement of things. But largely you'd make your way from one place to another logically. Now, I was not a local; getting from A to B meant steering one-handed while glancing at an Ordnance Survey map or clutching a mobile phone to one ear and listening to directions. Satnav was still in the future. In among the cows, sheep, horses and other 'large animals' we visited, we also found the time to offer an hour or two of appointments in our clinic for 'small animals', pets as you might know them, in the morning and again in the evening. Calls and clinics would wind up around 6 o'clock. Once the practical work was finished it would be time for a cup of tea in the office while dealing with any paperwork, then call it a day. Unless you were on call. In which case, you'd just keep doing calls, sometimes all night. Then the sun would come up and you'd start again. Never mind, tonight's a night off. You could be in bed by 7 o'clock, dreaming about having a poo-free life.

Unless … you're second on call?

2

TESTING! TESTING!

Testing for tuberculosis was a huge part of our income as a practice. It allowed us to have six or so vets and made the on-call rota just about bearable. Without it, we'd probably have had three vets. Since we had to provide 24-hour coverage by law, that would have placed us in an unenviable position. As it was, we could just about maintain some semblance of a normal life, even if it was impossible to be a regular attender at any club, activity or relationship.

Farmers could choose which practice carried out their TB testing, and because that practice was often their own vet, there was an obvious conflict of interest. Occasionally farmers would use the income from testing as a bargaining tool. If they didn't get what they wanted, they'd threaten to use another practice, impacting our financial viability. This led to a strange dynamic. In theory, when attending a TB test I was a representative of the government and carrying out the test work on their behalf as an impartial scientific observer. In practice, clients would, for convenience, ask for a variety of veterinary tasks to be carried out during the test. In addition, they'd probably have you out on the farm before long in a private capacity.

I had heard of a few colleagues who went out to a TB test and found either Reactors (Rs) and/or Inconclusive Reactor

(IRs). This suggested the animals had either been exposed to tuberculosis or might even have active disease. The farm should have been placed under immediate restriction in order to protect both human and animal health. However, a phone call to the practice from an irate farmer would summon the boss to go and 'check' their measurements. Supposedly, 're-measurement' would sometimes take place and Rs would become IRs, and IRs would be miraculously cured. Perhaps some of these cases were the correction of overzealous measurement by someone newly qualified and terrified of a mistake. But I think it would be a little credulous to accept this excuse in every situation. In any instance, the farmer might go from losing their whole herd to merely having to re-test in a couple of months, maybe even to being cleared to continue buying and selling cattle. Yes, if it truly was TB, it would likely get picked up at the next test, when it would be even more obvious as more animals would almost certainly positively react. That would be an easy rationalisation to make for anyone downgrading a result. But in the meantime? TB was being spread. Young vets were being undermined and put in near-impossible circumstances. What to do? The law was being broken. Theoretically there was only one course of action: become a whistle-blower. Self-doubt and peer pressure can make fools of any of us. Loyalty to the practice and colleagues, fear of being made to look stupid, fear of the future in a small profession in which you're seen as a 'tell-tale', reluctance to ruin a farmer's livelihood – who knows how we would each handle it?

Just this sort of thing happened to me. I mentioned earlier that I'd ended up nose to nose with a farmer. I'd visited his farm that day to read his TB test. On my return to the practice, bad news had clearly beaten me back. Mr Jenkins was not happy. He'd called me up hill and down dale on the phone. The office manager was too embarrassed to use the same adjectives as he'd employed, and could only bring herself to spell things out using the phonetic alphabet. Since she was also a special constable, it came quite naturally.

'Well, Gareth, he was very rude. Apparently, you're an arrogant Charlie – Uniform – November—'

'Okay, okay, thanks Jules, I think I get it,' I interrupted.

'Oh, that's not all though,' she continued. 'He said you were a Scottish Tango – Whisky – Alpha—'

'Yep, yep, I get the picture.' I tried to turn off the tap of adjectives.

By now she was enjoying herself. With a wry smile I was subjected to most of the remainder of the alphabet arranged into the whole gamut of insults available to the average citizen and a few specific to farming or pertaining to the marital status of my parents at the moment of my birth. Mr Jenkins had also suggested that I was the antagonist, rather than himself. I'm not sure what my reason for becoming the aggressor would have been. TB testing was important, but undeniably dull. The idea that I was so passionate about disease eradication that I would engage in a one-man, super-hero-like crusade against innocent farmers was as laughable as it was inaccurate.

A government vet from the Department for Agriculture and Rural Affairs (DEFRA) had attended the first day of my TB test on Mr Jenkins' farm. Since we were in an area of the UK considered low risk, TB tests were only carried out every four years. There was a relaxed air about the whole process, a sense that a clear test was inevitable, and we were really just indulging the government in its whimsy. Ben, the guy from the government, seemed to feel the same way.

The animals were in a barn with a race (a corridor made of fencing) leading off from one corner. Access to the race was from a pen, and the race led to a crush, which would allow us to restrain each animal in turn and carry out the necessary test. There were a couple of extra farmhands to make things smoother. Ben was there to supervise things and really didn't have to lift a finger. But in an act of generosity or boredom, he offered to fill out my paperwork. I'd shout the animal's ear tag number to him, followed by the thickness of its skin at the two injection sites. He'd kindly annotate the correct boxes with the correct millimetres. Mr Jenkins was minimally involved; we were clearly an inconvenience, but he was polite enough. However, day one is not when the results come out. That happens on day four.

My second visit was quite different. The cattle were still in the same barn, but the handling facilities, the pen, the race, the crush – all gone. Mr Jenkins met me on his own, and his mood was aggressive from the start. Initially he subtly tried to dissuade me from even examining the animals.

'I've had a look myself,' he said. 'Hardly a lump on them.'

It wasn't so unusual to have someone start the conversation this way. Often it was just a sign of genuine worry at the outcome. But this was different.

'Ah, great stuff,' I said. 'Shouldn't take us long then.' I tried to keep things light, but I had a job to do.

Mr Jenkins' next ploy, after he'd failed to dissuade me from examining the animals, was simply to make it too hard to do so. As I made my way to the barn, I noted the lack of handling facilities. The barn was open at the front and the cattle contained by five bar gates about a metre high. There were forty or so in this batch, all milling around in the straw behind the gates.

'There you are, see, nothing on them,' he said.

'Well, we'll have to take a look. Where's the crush?' I enquired.

'Ah, we had to move it over to the other farm to get the worming done; haven't had time to bring it back,' he replied. I could see a slight smirk forming on his face.

'Well, I'll need to check them myself. I'm sure you're right, but you know the drill.'

'No problem, there they are; check 'em yourself.' The smirk was there again.

He was well aware that the test protocol meant I had to check the injection sites on each animal individually. Mr Jenkins was already in breach of his obligations. He was required to provide adequate handling facilities and staff to facilitate the test. I could refuse to conduct the examination, phone the relevant government department and inform them of his recalcitrance. Then it would be someone else's problem. Instead, I let my rising irritation get the better of me. I needed my paperwork from the previous day and some small callipers to get the test done. I tucked my clipboard and paperwork into my cotton stock coat; the fabric and my outer leather belt held it securely in place. The callipers I held in my hand. The all-important pen, said to be mightier than the sword by many who've never actually been in a sword fight, was in my top pocket. It was also, in fact, a pencil. Damp and pens don't mix. In addition, I grabbed a tin of orange spray paint I carried for marking animals; it would allow me to highlight who I'd already victimised and concentrate on those cunning enough to avoid me thus far.

I climbed on top of the gate and swung a leg inside.

'What are you doing?' asked Mr Jenkins, clearly surprised.

'Reading the test,' I replied.

The animals were tightly packed in. None of them wanted to be anywhere near me; it was like being back at high school from a social point of view. As soon as I got in, I was crushed against the gate. It was painful, but not particularly dangerous. However, if I got knocked to the ground in among the cattle, it would be very dangerous. Once I was down, the animals would probably close the space and I'd struggle to get back up. If they panicked, kicked me, stood on me or stampeded, I'd almost certainly be severely injured.

I had a plan. The animals would force themselves into a corner with their backsides facing me. This is a natural reaction to a perceived threat. It's both safety in numbers and clever use of the weapons available to them. By getting headfirst in a corner the animals protect many of their vulnerabilities, and only the animals at the rear are in immediate danger. They also have their trump card, two powerful back legs that allow them to lash out with injurious effect. I'd start at one end and get right up against my target. Then I'd gradually work my way up their left side until I could reach their neck; not too far forward, or they'd run backwards and away from the group. I'd stay midway up their body and reach forward to the neck. If there were no lumps, I'd mark them with orange paint then shoo them backwards out of my way. If I felt lumps, I'd get out my callipers, do my best to measure the skin, then pull out my paperwork and record the results. They too would then receive the glorious orange mark, proof that I was making progress.

Some animals had horns, a handy addition to their suite of anti-vet equipment. Cattle can be quite adept at using their horns as weaponry. As I approached their neck, they'd glance at me out of the side of their eye. Knowing that I was too far away to satisfyingly impale, they'd just keep watching, until … I came into range. Then a sideways swipe of their head would bring their horns flying towards me. Little stubby horns are very painful. The big sharp ones … they might be fatal. Even properly restrained, horns are dangerous. Over time I'd developed the only defence I could come up with. I'd reach out and place my hand on the end of the horn. I would close my hand around the point, making a fist with my thumb pointing towards their head. It gave me enough leverage to have half a chance at fending off an incoming blow. If I miscalculated and the strike landed, at least I would end up comically punching myself in the face, rather than receiving the tip of a horn to the eyeball or brain.

The first couple of animals had no lumps. I glanced over my shoulder to speak to Mr Jenkins, but he was nowhere to be seen. I suppose if they found my mushy, wet, poo-covered corpse later today he could always claim ignorance. As I ran a hand along animal number three's neck, the reason for Mr Jenkins' attitude came into sharp relief. There was a large lump at the lower injection site, about the size of half an apple. Conversely, the top site had minimal swelling. To recap from earlier, the top site was injected with avian tuberculin. The bottom site was injected with bovine tuberculin, the disease we are searching for. In both instances the tuberculin is a refined protein that stimulates the animal's immune system. The stimulus provided is like that generated by the pathogens themselves. The lumps at the top sites reflected routine exposure to *Mycobacterium avium* or 'bird TB'. However, lumps at the bottom site reflected exposure to *Mycobacterium bovis* or 'cow TB'. Cow TB is a zoonosis; it is capable of infecting humans.

According to the World Health Organization, TB is one of the top 10 causes of death worldwide. But that's mostly *M. tuberculosis*; why are we worried about *M. bovis*? Well, in the 1930s in the UK around 40 per cent of cattle were infected with cow TB and approximately fifty thousand new cases of human infection were recorded annually. The main route of transmission was via unpasteurised milk. In fact, some cases of cow TB in humans these days are in the older population who have had dormant *M. bovis* infection that has re-emerged as they age. The pasteurisation of milk, inspection of meat and the testing and culling of infected animals has all but eliminated the transmission of cow TB to humans. It's still a controversial subject though, especially in relation to the culling of wildlife reservoirs of disease, and badgers specifically. There have even been cases of cats acquiring cow TB. The entire strategy around the disease in the UK is a hotbed of debate between farmers, vets, scientists, government, animal rights groups and conservationists.

This animal at least was a Reactor. As I awkwardly, dangerously, but steadily worked my way from animal to animal it became apparent the problem was significant. About 25 per cent of the animals were Reactors. Potentially, the biggest issue was that the area was meant to have a low incidence of cow TB. I had thought Mr Jenkins was just a difficult person who wanted to make my life harder for the sake of it. In fact, he knew there was a big issue and had been hoping to cover it up. As I sprayed my last orange mark and satisfied myself I'd read the test to the best of my ability, I pulled out my mobile phone. I had to notify the government department as soon as possible. Unfortunately, I had no reception. I sighed, stared at my wellies and steeled myself. I knew what I had to do. I had to go to the farmhouse and notify Mr Jenkins that he was under restriction from this moment forth. It was highly likely his herd would be slaughtered in its entirety. I'd also have to use his phone to contact the practice and DEFRA. There was going to be some fallout from this.

I approached the farmhouse with some trepidation. Upon my knocking, Mr Jenkins came to the door; I could see by the look on his face he already knew what was coming. I tried to pass him the appropriate form, notifying him of the restrictions. As I began my slightly apologetic explanation, he swatted the paperwork aside.

'I'll be out in a minute,' he spat, before disappearing back inside.

I tried to relax, but I too knew what was coming. My heart rate soared, and I could feel adrenaline flooding my system. It was classic fight, flight or freeze. However, flight wasn't an option. Freezing would be weird initially and difficult to maintain. I'm not a human statue. I was left with accepting a confrontation and hoping it didn't turn violent.

Mr Jenkins reappeared, dressed in his working attire. He wasn't much taller than me; I was confident I could hold my own if it really came to it. His two farmhands appeared behind him. They were much bigger than me; if push came to shove, I was well and truly outmatched.

'I'm sorry, it's not great news, Mr Jenkins …' I began. I could at least try to defuse the situation.

'Save your fucking apologies,' he began. 'You've got no idea; I've been farming here since I was a kid – I left school at fourteen to work here. My family has been here for a hundred and fifty years. Who the fuck are you? Some fucking posh twat who fancied a crack at being a vet. We got wiped out by Foot-and-Mouth a few years ago, because of fuckers like you. I'm not having it again.'

He kept getting closer and closer until his face was practically touching mine. I stole an occasional glance over his shoulder. The lads behind him were a fair bit behind him. They were there out of solidarity, but they didn't want to be involved any more than I did. Mr Jenkins' fists were clenched as he leaned towards me.

My animal instincts were shouting, 'Hit, him. Hit him now. If he knocks you down, you might not get up, he might not let you up, this is self-preservation, HIT HIM NOW!'

'Mr Jenkins …' I began, reaching out to put a hand on his shoulder. It might console him, it might not, but it would keep him at arm's length.

He slapped my hand away. 'Don't fucking touch me! Do you know what this means? That's it, the whole herd will go. I'm sixty-five, I'll never rebuild it.'

'Mr Jenkins, I do understand, I do.' I tried to be conciliatory. However, the undeniable truth was that I didn't. Sure, I knew the rules, I understood the logic of limiting the spread of disease, but I didn't understand. How could I? I was about to get schooled.

Having slapped my arm away, Mr Jenkins was face to face with me again. I sincerely hoped he wasn't a closet TB sufferer himself. At this rate DEFRA would be taking me along with the cattle.

'Understand, do you? Let me explain it to you. These animals are my product; now I can't sell them. I'll get compensated, but I've lost my replacement heifers (the young females and future mothers in the herd), so the next generation is gone as well. I've got no cows! And that's this farm. What about the beasts at the other steading, eh? They'll be restricted as well. I can't sell them either. That means I have to feed them. There's not enough grass and without the money from this lot, I can't afford feed over the winter. So, they'll have to go too, or starve to death. My nephew is just starting to work up here. He's planning on taking over after me. Well, that's done. I can't pay him, so no doubt he'll be off somewhere, to get a job some wanker like you can't snatch from him. I might as well just sell the lot and walk into the burn down there.' He pointed to the rapidly flowing river, 50 metres beyond the barn.

I opened my mouth to say something, but there was nothing to say.

'Yeah,' he said simply as we made eye contact. He held my gaze for an uncomfortably long time, though it was only seconds. Then he turned his back and stormed off into the house. As suddenly as it had begun, the confrontation was over. I was left looking at his two farmhands. As I caught the eyes of one of them, he just shrugged, offering a slight smile that was half enjoyment at my dressing-down and half apology. As the two of them drifted off, I made my way to the tap, disinfected my kit, washed my wellies and waterproofs, and stuck everything in the car. I figured that asking to use the phone in the farmhouse was no longer an option; I would have to call from the office. The drive back to the practice gave me plenty of time to mull things over and I spent it deep in thought …

* * *

'Oh yes, he really doesn't like you ...' Jules continued, and as she finished her blow-by-blow account of Mr Jenkins' phone tirade, it became apparent that he'd demanded my boss, Charlie, come out and re-examine my work. This was entirely inappropriate, and Charlie did not officially or legally have the power to change anything. To be fair to Charlie, he made it clear his visit would be a sympathy call, nothing more. I still resented it. It bothered me for the rest of the day. I had a difficult relationship with Charlie for several reasons. Some were undeniably my fault, some his, but we did not get on.

Charlie phoned me that evening. 'We've got a big problem ...' he began.

The problem wasn't me, and it wasn't him, it was that Mr Jenkins' farm was riddled with TB and there wasn't supposed to be any. Over the next few weeks, we would test other farms in the area and have similar results. As DEFRA and ourselves started to test and speculate as to what was going on, the origins of the local outbreak came to light. Many of the local farms had been wiped out during the Foot-and-Mouth outbreak in 2001, entire herds slaughtered. As they'd received compensation, some had folded and given up farming. Others had chosen to restock. Many had bought animals from the southwest of England, a known TB hot spot. It was likely that the real culprits weren't the local badgers, but the local farmers. They'd no doubt purchased animals that had been tested, but the tests weren't 100 per cent and some infected animals had slipped through the net. It would take weeks, months, even years of testing, restrictions and culling to get on top of the outbreak. I had to tell many more local farmers that their herd would be taken from them.

Each time I felt for them; some I considered friends. They'd shown me kindness when I'd first appeared as the 'new vet'. I'd eaten at their tables, been offered flasks of coffee, munched on homemade sandwiches and even flirted with the occasional daughter who had popped out to ascertain what this new vet looked like and whether he was worth getting to know. I can confirm that for the most part the answer was a resounding no. I'd been in occasional tight spots with some of them. Spend time with anyone in a hazardous environment and you can't help but either permanently fall out or develop a bond of trust, even with those you don't like on a personal level. I recall one farmer who slipped and fell in among some young, excited cattle milling about. I rushed to grab him, pulling him to the edge of the pen until he could get on his feet.

'Not everyone would have done that, you know?' he said.

'What was I going to do? Leave you there until you got crushed?'

'Still though …'

From that day forth, he treated me differently. I was no longer a sort of junior partner when I stood on his farm. Regardless of any professional difficulties, he accorded me the respect of an equal. It was heart-breaking to visit him, do my duties for DEFRA, and give him the same news so many of his neighbours had already received. His reaction stood in stark contrast to that of Mr Jenkins. As I delivered the bad news, he reached out and placed a hand on my shoulder.

'It's not your fault, you know?' he said. That simple phrase meant a lot coming from him.

The guy was a born and bred farmer. When his herd had been slaughtered after Foot-and-Mouth, he had received a large compensation pay-out. It was enough to retire on, sell his farm, and move somewhere sunny. His kids were grown up with families of their own. Financially independent, he and his wife could have enjoyed a comfortable retirement, making the most of their newfound freedom. Instead, they had spent their compensation money restocking, buying more cows so that they could keep their dairy farm running. They'd chosen, like so many farmers, to go back to a life of financial insecurity, early mornings, never-ending work and elusive holidays. This was what they'd always done. Over a lifetime they'd built up a business and a community. It's not that they worked as farmers; they *were* farmers. Quitting wasn't an option. So, they had bought more milking cows from wherever they could get them and bought TB right along with them. It was unlikely their compensation would be so generous this time around. But I had no doubt how they would spend it.

Vets have a critical role to play, not just in animal health, but in public, human health. There are many zoonoses that can jump species, directly affecting the human population. There are many more that can devastate the animals we raise for food. In our increasingly globalised world, outbreaks that might have historically been localised, burning themselves out as they kill or infect the last remaining vulnerable creatures, can spread like wildfire from nation to nation. In the past, a local outbreak might have caused a local famine. Food could be brought from elsewhere, from unaffected areas. Our ability to travel has shrunk our world; now, even the furthest locations are less than a day apart. If we are not very careful, there will be no unaffected areas. However, it is not easy to do the right thing. There will be a cost. That cost will not be only financial. I'm glad I did the right thing, but it would have been only too human to turn a blind eye.

3

MYTHS AND LEGENDS

What can I tell you? Some things just cannot be explained by references to conventional wisdom.

Over many years I've experienced the very best or worst of country lore, depending on your perspective. Five years of veterinary school leaves you steeped in all that is science. Particularly in this day and age. I suppose I probably experienced the tail-end of the 'people of stature' phenomena. By this I mean the tendency to see senior staff as infallible fonts of knowledge. Looking back throughout scientific history, it is now apparent that, while replete with geniuses, it also had its fair share of seemingly credible and credulous chancers who wielded undue influence during their heyday. On closer examination, many of our undeniable geniuses were not without fault.

Isaac Newton, an intellectual giant on whose shoulders household names such as Einstein stood, was famously enamoured of alchemy and spent much of his time researching the possibility of 'transmuting' other substances into gold. If an individual of such undoubted genius can get it so wrong, we must all accept our fallibility, particularly outside our area of expertise. Humans are social animals and vulnerable to the cult of personality, particularly when it comes to charismatic individuals.

The certainty with which intelligent, popular individuals have expressed their ideas has led us down many a scientific rabbit hole. Medical history is full of now-defunct protocols, procedures, surgeries and drugs that were once believed to be highly effective treatments for no other reason than that they possessed a powerful advocate who firmly believed in their efficacy and would readily shout down any naysayer.

In the quite recent past, many communities were geographically, socially and, therefore, intellectually isolated. As a result, tales of witchcraft, wizardry and the supernatural have persisted longer there than in more cosmopolitan regions. It is easy for us relative youngsters to mock our elders' seemingly silly ideas. However, when I first graduated, some of my older clients had received their education in the 1940s and many left school young to help on the farm. As a result, much of their education came from their parents, grandparents and the community, some of whom had received their education in the late 1800s. For those of you keeping track, that's before the invention of flight, or for that matter, crayons. It is hardly any wonder that some of my clients held some interesting beliefs.

I had been warned. My boss took me aside and told me that I faced a difficult callout this morning. Not from a purely medical point of view, but from a partially sighted and somewhat superstitious farmer point of view. Being relatively new to the job I was optimistic in regard to my communication skills and thought that my boss was making an unnecessary fuss. So, woefully ignorant of the true nature of my predicament, off I went.

As I climbed out of the car, the farmer approached and seemed friendly enough. However, his eyes had a milky quality to them, and it was obvious that he could see very little. It was his farm; he'd worked there all his days and, despite his impairment, was able to negotiate the place with surprising ease. He would reach out with his hands and follow the system of gates, metalwork, fences, walls and doorways that made up his farmyard, with occasional touches to confirm his whereabouts. I followed him and marvelled at how he was running such an enterprise. He'd had some assistance from a neighbour earlier in the day to round up a young bullock with a suspicious lump on the back of its leg. Unfortunately, his kindly neighbour had left to get on with running his own business.

I was anticipating the usual hassle of retrieving some reluctant animal from a distant field, but was pleasantly surprised when I spotted a young bullock already in a holding pen immediately adjacent to the handling facilities. I could see a large swelling behind its right knee. Probably an abscess or haematoma in a young animal, or so I thought. So, with the farmer deftly operating the crush (the mechanical restraining facility) by touch and me shooing the bullock into it, we rapidly had the subject restrained and ready for examination. The creature was none too pleased to be put through his paces this time of the morning, but the situation was under control. Normally, I'd have placed a metal bar behind his back legs to prevent him from kicking me. However, when I placed the bar in position, it made access to the lump difficult. I would have to manage without. Situations like this are counterintuitive. Your first instinct is to put some distance between yourself and the agitated, deeply suspicious 300 kg animal. But all this provides is space in which a kick aimed at you can gather velocity, accelerating towards your soft, squidgy bits as it approaches. It's actually better to steel yourself and stand right up against the animal. Although it can now most definitely hit you, it's likely to be more of a shove than a strike and will probably be into your (hopefully steel-toe-capped) Wellingtons. Think jujitsu, but with a really big faeces-covered opponent.

And so, I was right up against my intended victim. An unfortunate side effect of this proximity is the heat given off by cattle. Within minutes you find yourself with rivulets of sweat pouring down your back. Anyway, enough about my discomfort. The mass was melon-sized and located directly behind the animal's knee (or stifle) joint. While I was already fairly certain of what I was facing, I got some further details from the farmer. It had recently appeared and had been getting bigger over the last couple of weeks. Haematomas are not uncommon in large animals, particularly if they are not used to handling. In their haste to get away from humans they will often collide with gates and handling facilities, causing bruising, or – should they burst a larger blood vessel – a haematoma: a large pocket of blood trapped in the tissues. This will usually clot over time and eventually fibrose into scar-like tissue. In that instance no treatment is warranted, and the lesion is merely unsightly. Abscesses are also common, and this felt like one. It was spongy and I could identify a thin spot in the wall of the mass. Abscesses are effectively balls of fibrous, scar tissue manufactured in the body's attempt to contain a seat of infection. The centre of the 'ball' is pus. This is usually a whitey/cream-coloured fluid that smells very unpleasant. With these two options at the forefront of my mind, I decided to carry out a simple test. I would insert a smallish needle into the mass using a syringe, then use the syringe to suck out a sample of any liquid inside. If I got back blood, it was a haematoma, if pus, an abscess. If nothing, I'd have to think again.

You might think that local anaesthetic is warranted in this scenario. But, in the first instance I would have to stab the animal with a needle to administer it, then carry out my sampling. Or I could just stab him once and do the sample. I opted for a 50 per cent reduction in overall stabbings and carried on. He was none too pleased, and I was not too happy to receive a stomp on the foot either. We agreed to disagree and once the needle was in place I drew back on the syringe and, *voilà*: pus. I informed the owner of the relatively good prognosis and the necessary treatment. I would lance the abscess at the lowest practicable point and allow it to drain. I would also give the animal a short course of injectable antibiotic in case my lancing the abscess introduced infection into the surrounding tissue.

Now, having reached a diagnosis and knowing that I would have to make a reasonably large incision in this poor animal's leg, some local anaesthetic was an essential. I clipped the area with my curved scissors. Having removed the bulk of the poo-contaminated hair, I cleaned the area as best I could. Achieving asepsis would be ideal, but not realistic. The application of local anaesthetic went fairly smoothly, but my patient was, ironically, losing his patience. I did my best to let the farmer know what was going on, but there's only so far a verbal narrative can go. As they say, a picture speaks a thousand words. Preparation complete, I got ready to make my incision. I identified the site where I would apply my scalpel. One hand on the cow, I advanced my right hand. My patient had other plans. He lashed out with his back leg, hit me in the shin and covered my face in poo from the floor of the crush. As I wiped clean my face and cursed his immortal soul, I heard an odd sound. Like someone running a sink. I looked down at my scalpel and realised that it was bloody. Suddenly realising what the likely problem was I glanced up to see blood spurting out of the bullock's leg and running on to the floor, rapidly forming a bright red puddle among the surrounding liquid poo. The combination of my advancing scalpel and my patient's rapidly approaching limb had caused me to miss my selected surgical site and simply stab the poor beast in an artery, likely his popliteal. I immediately sprang into action.

'Eh?' I said, followed by an, 'Um?'

But I quickly got a grip.

'Er, right, so …' I continued, quite unnecessarily. I mean, so … what?

'Um? Bloody hell!' I managed to blurt out. It's somewhat clouded in the mists of time, but I think this was the first time I had been the sole vet on the premises, witnessing a major haemorrhage and being clueless.

The farmer was partially sighted, but not deaf or stupid.

'What's going on?' he asked.

'Eh?' I replied.

'WHAT'S HAPPENING!' he asked, more forcefully.

'Er, well, there's a bit of bleeding,' I replied, engaging in what could be charitably called 'understatement'.

'A lot of bleeding?' the farmer enquired.

'Well,' I admitted, 'quite a lot.' By now I had actually got a grip. I informed the farmer that I was going to apply a pressure bandage. Unfortunately, the animal overheard the conversation and probably thought he was significantly better off without any more of my medical help. Instead of standing still and cooperating with my attempts at life-saving therapy he instead elected to attempt to kick me to death. A combination of adrenaline and grim determination led me to persist in my bandaging attempts. The combination of murderous animal, well-aimed kicks, airborne poo, sweat and a light refreshing rain was not an environment conducive to the application of a dressing. I was trying to hold his leg still with one hand and bandage with the other, and he was stronger than me despite my gym membership. Few, if any, universities opt to examine their students under such conditions. There may be money in some sort of 'level-seven nightmare bandaging scenario' capable virtual reality suite in the future, but not in the current academic climate.

My efforts had not gone unnoticed by the farmer.

'How're you getting on?' he asked.

As ever, I offered a brief, eloquent reply. 'Eh?'

'ARE … YOU … SUCCEEDING?' he asked, or something along those lines.

'Um?' I replied as I engaged in yet another round of 'restrain and bandage the mini-bull bleeding to death'.

'Right, I'm going to get help; I'll call someone,' he said, before making his way slowly but surely towards his house, using his normal reference points to navigate.

So, left alone, I struggled on. I would have handled the situation quite differently nowadays. I could have sedated the animal as soon as lancing the abscess became a necessity. But sedation costs money and I'd already had several farmers ask whether it was really necessary. The trouble is, you can often get away without it, but the only way to find out is the hard way, by which time you're battered, bruised and regretting your decision. Anyway, it was me and the steer, *mano e mano*, so to speak. The struggle continued, but only one of us was losing blood by the pint. Eventually a combination of blood loss and, perhaps, the acceptance that this foolish human was just not going to bugger off calmed my wrestling partner. Bandages started to go on and stay on. I had the bleeding under control. Taking the time to stand up straight, I noticed for the first time that the farmer had returned.

'Did you get help?' I asked.

'Yes,' he replied. I glanced around; there was no help. Perhaps they were coming.

'Eh, where are they?' I asked.

'Oh, I phoned them.'

'Ah, great. When are they getting here?' I enquired.

'Oh, they're not coming,' he added nonchalantly. Then, almost smugly: 'They've got the cure.'

'Right? Well, I mean, can they bring the cure here?' I asked. To be honest, I just wanted some extra hands to get the job finished.

'What do you mean, bring it here?' the farmer asked.

By this point I was probably losing my patience and getting a touch frustrated. I attempted to explain.

'Well, if they don't bring the cure here, how can we use it?' I said. The man was clearly a moron.

'No,' he explained, 'they've GOT the cure.'

'WELL … HADN'T THEY BETTER BRING IT HERE THEN?' I re-emphasised. What was wrong with this guy?

'You don't get it, do you?' he asked. Clearly there was only one moron present, and in his opinion, it was me.

'Eh? Not really?' I replied.

'I phoned this guy.'

'Yes,' I acknowledged.

'He's the seventh son of a seventh son,' he continued.

'Ah-ha,' I answered.

'And he's got the cure you see, because he's a seventh son of a seventh son.'

'Right,' I said. 'WELL, WHY DOESN'T HE BRING IT HERE THEN?'

'Oh, he doesn't do that. You just phone him; he's got the cure.'

'WHAT?! He doesn't come here?'

'No, no, you just phone him and tell him the problem, he's got the cure you see.'

'No offence, but how the flying fuck does that work?' I asked somewhat impetuously.

The farmer stared unseeing into space for a moment or two, then, with an almost imperceptible smile, asked: 'Has the bleeding stopped?'

'Yes, but …' I attempted to explain.

'Well, there you are then,' he summed up.

I was lost for words. Here was I, convinced that my titanic struggle with the bandaging session from hell had solved the immediate issue. I mean, the animal still had an abscess and it had now acquired a wound and lost some blood, but it was only slightly worse off than when I'd arrived on the scene. All in all, my efforts had been a qualified success. He wasn't having it. The cure had once again saved the day from afar without ever turning up or breaking sweat. We agreed that lancing the abscess would have to wait a day or two. In the meantime, some antibiotics and some anti-inflammatories would be allowed to do their work.

On return to the veterinary practice, I had a short debrief with my boss. I ran through a dramatic re-enactment of my morning, with probably slightly more gesticulating than was necessary. I think he was worried I'd ask him to play the cow during a re-enactment for the reception staff. However, as my description developed, he could see where my story was going.

'He phoned his cousin, didn't he? He's a seventh son of a seventh son, you know?'

'Yes …' I admitted.

'He's got the cure, you know?' my boss continued.

At that point I elected to go and get my own 'cure'; I excused myself and made my way to the breakroom for a cup of tea. Sadly, it was before lunch, so a couple of strong drinks would have to wait until later.

From afterbirths thrown in thorn bushes, covered in flies, to buckets of fresh cobwebs, I've seen some things in my time. Each presents a challenge of persuasion and communication. It would be unfair to pretend unfounded medical interventions are exclusively restricted to farmers or the countryside. There are plenty of city dwellers and even medical professionals indulging in practices with no evidence of effect. My own practices have changed over time. We practitioners of science must be careful we don't develop our own beliefs. Whenever a therapy, drug or vaccine is recommended or vilified, we are too inclined to say, 'this works' or 'that's nonsense'. Really, implicit in what we are saying, are the words, 'According to our current evidence and understanding …' I have found it helpful to be explicit in allowing for changing treatments or techniques. What I can say for now is that, according to our current evidence and understanding, a seventh son of a seventh son has six brothers and six uncles, and while between them they may be able to have a good game of seven-a-side football, that's the only special powers they have.

4

HAIL CAESAR!

No time was busier than spring, when most of our farm clients waited expectantly for the birth of lambs or calves that would be raised, fattened and, hopefully, sold for a profit. All beef cattle start out as cute little calves. One of three fates awaits them. If they are female, they might become a replacement for the herd, taking the place of older cows as those become less fertile or fall prey to illness. If they do not enter the herd, they are destined for the burger factory. Most males will accompany their female friends, fattened up prior to becoming sausages or the like. If they win the cow equivalent of the Lottery, they popped out as a male with good genetics. This gives them a shot at becoming a breeding bull. They will enjoy a life of relative luxury, occasionally being asked to mate as many cows as possible at the appropriate time. Alternatively, if used for artificial insemination, they will still be treated like royalty, but their semen will be harvested using an artificial vagina and a teaser cow, or electro-ejaculation which involves a rectal probe and electricity. Electro-ejaculation is now the most common method used for semen collection by vets working in bovine fertility. It is unclear to me if this is down to a preference expressed by the bulls or scientific progress.

Ideally, you want to mate your cows with the best bull possible. Quite a few of our farmers had one eye on the economics and tried to obtain the largest calves they could. Now, if you are raising an animal for meat, it makes perfect sense that the larger and, well, meatier they are, the better. However, there is a literal bottleneck in the process: the birth canal of the mother. If the calf is larger than the birth canal, it cannot be born in the normal fashion, *per vaginum*. Instead, a Caesarean section would have to be performed and the calf brought out through the 'side door'. Unfortunately, it is not easy to assess whether a Caesarean will be required ahead of time, although there are reasons why one may be more likely. Nowadays much of the professional breeding of cattle is done using Estimated Breeding Values (EBVs). These attempt to measure the value of an animal's genetics along various commercially relevant characteristics. Multiple factors are analysed, such as Ease of Calving, Birth Weight and Gestation Length. If a bull with a high score on Ease of Calving is used to inseminate a herd, fewer Caesareans can be expected. The opposite would be true of a high Birth Weight. Bigger calves are more likely to get stuck for obvious reasons. Production medicine is a whole speciality in of itself and something I'm no longer in close contact with.

All of this is lovely and interesting, and definitely something both our farmers, my colleagues and I should have taken more interest in. However, EBVs were not so well established when I first graduated. The ubiquity of technology was yet to come. Relatively small herds, a lack of analytical tools, and an absence of records, time and financial constraints meant that most of our farmers found out about the need for a Caesarean the old-fashioned way – when the mother got into difficulty. Many had calved plenty of cows themselves and were quite skilful at it. However, once they were at the limit, that's when the inevitable phone call would be made.

The mobile on my bedside cabinet went off. I'd been sleeping soundly, not because I wasn't worried about being called out, but because I'd been called out so often that I'd stopped showering after a callout unless I absolutely had to. Instead, I just undressed and climbed into bed, prioritising a few extra minutes of sleep. I'd wash the bedsheets after my weekend on call. I lived above the practice and used its washing machine, so my sheets would go in with the dog beds, but I suppose it was technically all bedding. My clothes I left on the floor in the order I'd be throwing them on again. I couldn't say why I didn't have a girl-friend.

I fumbled in the dark, the illuminated screen of my mobile lighting up my bedside cabinet while simultaneously making it difficult to focus on the phone itself. I knocked it on to the floor before eventually getting a firm grip of it, pressing the green answer button and holding it to my ear.

'Green Country Vet Group!' I said, perhaps a little too loudly.

'It's Seamus Flanagan here; I've got a heifer calving and I need a vet out.'

'Righto,' I answered. 'I don't think I've been out to you before; can you give me some directions?'

By now I had swivelled my legs out of bed, and I was holding a pen, poised to take down my navigational guidance. I had developed my own shorthand, as the locals tended to speak quickly and I'd found it impossible to get everything down fast enough. A roundabout became a circle with a number or a letter, according to which exit to take: OR meant take a right at the roundabout; ^5 denoted straight on for five miles, then a +L would take me left at a crossroads. I scribbled away as the directions came thick and fast, taking me past tractor dealerships and other agricultural landmarks. Once I had my instructions and a number to ring back on, I ended the call.

'I'm on my way; I'll be as quick as I can,' I lied, knowing that I fully intended to make a coffee in the hope it would help me keep the car out of the ditch.

It was 0100 on Sunday morning. I'd been at work since Friday at 0830 and on call since Friday at 1800; this call would be my twenty-third. I hadn't slept for more than 45 minutes at a time since taking over. Some calls were just an inconvenience, like a farmer who wanted to pick up some medication; the majority required me to attend their farm. We mostly did agricultural work, but I had the odd cat or dog to contend with as well. We had an unwritten rule that we didn't call the reserve, second-on-call vet unless we really had to. So far … I was having to swim hard, but my head was still above water; this was my problem for now.

I'd restocked my car as soon as I got back from my last visit, so, with coffee in insulated mug, I was good to go. I opened the door of the car and the smell immediately hit me. A combination of wet ropes, dirty wellies and bits of poo stuck to waterproofs, unseen at the last attempt to render them clean. No one is going to be bottling this scent any time soon unless we need something non-lethal to disperse crowds of social media influencers. Still, you get used to it after a while, so I climbed in, started up and set off. I had the directions taped to my steering wheel; they turned out to be pretty good and, before long, I was turning into Clay Farm road-end. The occasional ominous clunk indicated the collision of the underside of my long-suffering car with yet another unseen obstacle.

As I drew into the farmyard, my headlights illuminated Mr Flanagan and his son, stood waiting. I climbed out, quickly said hello and then donned my waterproofs and wellies.

'Hi, I'm Gareth,' I said.

'Seamus,' he replied succinctly, and we shook hands.

'Right, let's have a look at this girl. What do you reckon?' I asked.

'A Caesar for sure,' he said. 'She's too young to be in calf, but she got caught by the bull and I left it too long.'

This was all too common and classic mismanagement. A simple injection early enough would probably have ended the pregnancy and made this trip unnecessary, but we both knew that and there was no point in crying over spilled milk. The van in the yard marked Mr Flanagan out as one of our part-time farmers. When he wasn't here, he worked selling farm machinery.

Seamus led the way through an older building, out the other side and into a modern shed with a corrugated tin roof. As I closed the gate behind me, I could already hear my patient straining, mooing, as she tried to give birth to her calf. Another gate was opened and there she was, a little Limousin cross heifer. She was sat down, her neck cranked round as she stared towards her back end, perhaps wondering why her calf wasn't already out and struggling to its feet. Deciding on a Caesarean can be difficult. It's massive surgery; a lot can go wrong. The farm environment is far from sterile, so post-operative infection is common. It is better for everyone if the calf can be born in the normal way. We have a few tricks up our sleeves. However, none of them were likely to be of any use here.

'I'll take a look, but I'd say it's a C-section all right,' I said.

I put some lube on my hand and arm and approached the expectant mother. She got up and immediately tried to evade my examination.

'We'll have to get her in the crush,' I pointed out.

We used the nearby handling facilities to get a rope halter on her head; this would allow us to tie her to a corner of the pen for her C-section, if needed. With her properly restrained I continued my exam. I lifted her tail, accepting that I was about to get seriously dirty in the next few seconds. I used a nearby bucket of water to clean the worst of the faeces off her bum, then slid my lubricated hand inside her vulva. Even as I examined her, she was trying to push her calf out, squeezing my arm against her own pelvis, painfully grinding my appendage against her bone. Her pelvis was small due to her immaturity, her baby much larger than the available opening. The calf wasn't coming out, but was it alive? I pushed a finger inside its mouth and felt its tongue move immediately. It was alive; there was hope, but we had to be quick.

'Yep, Caesar.' I could be just as succinct when I needed to be.

Letting her out of the crush, we coaxed and pushed her until Seamus could get the end of the rope around a metal corner post. At the same time, I pushed from the back, my shoulder against her bottom. I sent Seamus and his son off to get me some more buckets of warm water, then made my way back to the car and grabbed what I needed. I already had a Caesar kit made up with all the paraphernalia I needed for two surgeries in case I didn't have time to return to the practice between calls.

Returning to the pen, I grabbed a nearby wheelbarrow used to distribute feed into troughs. This would have to serve as my instrument table. I started drawing up the drugs I would need, roughly in the order I'd need them. Antibiotics were vital. We try to avoid their routine use in animals, partly to preserve their effectiveness for humans. But, opening an animal's abdomen up in this environment, teeming with bacteria, meant that the cow's immune system needed a helping hand. Clenbuterol is a drug used to induce broncho-dilation in humans. In this case I'd be administering it intravenously to cause relaxation of the mother's uterus. It would stop her pushing so hard and make my surgery easier. I combined a local anaesthetic, Lidocaine, and a sedative, Xylazine, into one syringe. I'd administer this as an epidural. It would anaesthetise the area immediately around the vulva, hopefully reducing the heifer's impulse to shove her calf out.

If administered correctly, you can immediately feel the cow's tail go floppy as the local cuts off any conscious control along with any sensation of pain. A bonus was the fact that the cow would be unable to hit me in the face with her poo-covered appendage, a common defence mechanism. Anti-inflammatories would help with the pain and swelling. Perhaps most important of all, I drew up several syringes of local anaesthetic. I would use these to numb an area on the left-hand side of the patient's abdomen. That would allow me to carry out the operation, because, unlike in humans, Caesareans on cows are routinely carried out with the mother stood up throughout.

By the time Seamus and his son returned, I'd given most of the drugs needed. As soon as the buckets arrived, I added a surgical scrub to them; before long I'd be covering myself in it in an effort to keep the risk of infection to a minimum. I was almost ready. The next thing I had to do was prep the mother. I needed to shave the hair off an area on her left side, then administer my local block. The lack of a nearby power socket meant I had to use my scissors. I couldn't do as good a job as I would have liked, but I clipped a large patch on her side. Lastly, I used an old-fashioned razor blade to shave the central two centimetres or so, leaving a bald, pale line from the cow's spine vertically down towards her abdomen, stark against her ginger hair. Next, local; as I inserted the needle into her abdominal wall, she suddenly lashed out with a back leg and caught me on the front of my welly. There was a resounding 'Thwack!' as the blow landed home. I hadn't been expecting it.

'Son of a ...!' I exclaimed. 'Right in the goddamn shin!'

'You okay?' came Seamus's enquiry.

'Yeah, yeah. God, they're good at catching the right bit, aren't they?' I said through a half-smile, half-grimace. There was no point in being angry; I didn't blame her, and I had learned it is better to laugh than to cry.

I took a moment to recover. I gave it another go, standing slightly further forward. She lashed out again but missed. The needle was in. I slowly depressed the plunger as I manipulated the needle and syringe, spreading the anaesthetic throughout the area where I'd make my incision. I also moved the needle in and out, so that the skin and various layers of muscle were also numbed. The last drop in the syringe I spread out under the skin, exactly where my next injection was to go, hopefully stopping any messages making it back to the brain regarding stabbing and minimising the possibility of another 'Thwack!' to my shin. I worked logically down the line of my hair clip, from top to bottom. I would cut right through the area I'd numbed.

Before I started surgery, I made a quick call to the company who provided our answer service; they would have been picking up any calls, as I'd silenced my phone. Bad news, another calving had come in. I excused myself for a moment, walked outside, and gave the other client a ring. It sounded like the early stages of labour, but the farmer had already needed quite a bit of assistance in the last few weeks; he wanted backup. I told him I'd be on my way as soon as I'd finished surgery.

'Okay, we're ready,' I informed Seamus and his son, who I now knew was Sam.

Cutting a calf out is dramatic, but quite easy really; it's putting it all back together again that's difficult. Crucially, everyone needed to understand what they'd be doing. I started throwing water over my waterproofs, at the same time emptying surgical scrub on to them and soaping up as if I was having a shower in my slick protective outer clothing. I was also dishing out instructions.

'Right, Seamus, you're going to hold the uterus for me, so you need to scrub your arms. Sam, you get your hands clean mate; you'll be grabbing the calf when it's out. Happy?' Sam nodded with a little smile; he was excited, and perhaps a little apprehensive.

'Okay, here goes,' I said. Picking my position carefully, I made my first incision. The heifer shifted her feet, but there was no fuss, the local was working. I cut rapidly through the skin, exposing the deep maroon muscle underneath. Fine white lines within it gave away the direction of the muscle fibre's structure. Almost as quickly, I cut through the thick outer layers of muscle, the obliques. As it was cut, the muscle on both sides bulged and retreated from my incision as it contracted. Blood from the skin and muscle ran down the mother's flank, dripping on to my boots. It looked like a lot, but I knew from experience it was insignificant in an animal her size. Soon I was down to the thinnest and innermost muscle layer; stuck to its other side was the lining of the cow's abdominal cavity, the peritoneum. A careless cut at this stage could hit the cow's digestive system and flood her body with bacteria, sealing her fate. I slowed down, nicking away at the muscle until I had a glimpse of the thin silvery-white peritoneum. Very carefully, I made a digit-sized hole; on the other side I could see uterine tissue, my next objective. I used a finger to pull the peritoneum away from the abdominal contents. A sucking noise and an influx of air into the hole confirmed I was through the final layer. I swapped my scalpel for scissors. Using one hand to pull the tissue towards me and the other to cut vertically downwards, I opened up the mother's side. I dropped my scissors in the bucket of water. I needed both hands to grab the uterus.

I struggled to grip it and the baby cow inside. Imagine someone in a thick rubber sack, adhering to their body. Now imagine you've got to move them around inside the sack, until you can cut into it and leave them uninjured. That is not a training recommendation, just a metaphor. Finally, I had a grip of the right spot. My hands were cramping with the strain. I left one hand in place lest I lose my spot. Reaching blindly into my bucket of water with the other hand, I located my scalpel when I received a stab to the hand. I manipulated it the right way around, then pulled it out of the water.

'Right Sam,' I reiterated, 'I'm going to cut through the uterus and grab a leg. I'll pass it to you, then you grab it, yeah? Then I'll give you the other one. When I say pull, you pull the calf out, ready?'

Sam nodded; he was a quick learner. I started the cut with my scalpel. Once I had a little hole, I swapped it out for my scissors. I extended the cut and fluid poured out of the uterus. I nearly lost my grip on the calf; it was struggling to pull away from me. I dropped the scissors in my bucket, reached inside and grabbed a back leg belonging to my about-to-be-new-born patient. I pulled it out and passed it to Sam, he grabbed it, but just as fast, the calf pulled away and the leg shot back inside.

'Little bugger doesn't want to come out!' I said with a smile on my face – the calf was strong. Sam grinned back.

I reached inside and grabbed the same leg, once more pulling it out; this time Sam had a good grip. My hand dove inside the uterus again; I had the other leg. I passed that to Sam as well.

'Right mate, you just pull out and down; I'll catch the calf as it comes out. Seamus, you grab, the uterus.' Mr Flanagan approached and grabbed the womb, just above the incision I'd made. The legs stuck sideways out of the cow's abdomen, like some surreal painting.

'Ready?' I got two nods in return. 'Okay, pull.'

Sam was plenty strong enough and as he pulled the calf slowly emerged. I could see her hips, then her stomach. Things slowed as we got towards the shoulders, but I knew what was coming next. Suddenly Sam stumbled backwards and landed in the straw; I caught the calf as she flew out and also lost my footing. I found myself on one knee holding a new-born cow. I quickly set her on the straw and cleared any mucous from around her nose. She was struggling a bit, her chest moving in and out, but I couldn't hear any air movement. She'd been trying to be born for a while; perhaps she'd inhaled some fluid? I quickly grabbed her back legs and stuck them over a gate, with her head dangling towards the ground. A load of liquid drained out of her mouth. I gave her a few pats on her chest wall, then got her down and put her on the straw again. She looked as though she was struggling to get air in. I was just about to intervene again when: 'Mwaaahhhhh!' – she let out a deep cry, a sign she was getting plenty of air. She was doing okay for now.

'Cool! We're good.' I was relieved.

I turned round to face the next challenge: reassembling my patient. Seamus was holding the womb in place; he'd been watching earnestly as Sam and I dealt with the calf. I quickly gave myself another light scrub. Washed, I grabbed the large needle and thick cat-gut (actually sheep-gut) suture I would use to close our new mother up. A pair of needle holders would help me to control the needle, pushing it through whatever I needed to stitch. As I sewed the womb, the inverting technique would rotate the outer layer inwards, placing the two sides of my incision together and sealing up the calf's former home. I had done this a lot recently and I was fairly smooth. While I sutured, the uterus was contracting. This is quite natural, but it can make the job harder. It's like trying to sew two pieces of fabric together, while they are changing shape and pulling away from you. It also made the farmer's job harder. Strong though he was, Seamus was struggling to hold on to my project. He kept shifting his hands as they tired.

'Nearly there!' I said as I began a second layer of stitches, the gold standard of womb closure. I finished none too soon. As I tied off the last of my medical thread, Seamus dropped the uterus and it disappeared into the heifer's gaping abdomen. He turned away, shaking and massaging his exhausted hands. I quickly cleaned off my hands one more time. Next, I reached inside, ran my hand along the bottom of the cow's belly on the inside and scooped anything fluidy out. Clots of blood and amniotic fluid poured out of the wound and on to the ground. These could cause issues later, so I got rid of as much as I could. Now to close the abdomen. I started to stitch the peritoneum and first muscle layer together. Seamus had returned and was gently leaning on the cow's backside, pushing her against the barrier. I was about halfway down when the problem started. The mother was struggling to keep stood up.

'Woohah girl,' I said. She'd started to sink, then managed to get herself back on an even keel. As I started to suture again, she was slowly creeping closer to the ground. I moved towards her. I kept going, desperately trying to get the abdomen closed before she ended up on the ground. Much of her weight was now resting on me. In desperation, I gave her a dig with my right knee.

'Up now!' I shouted. She struggled to extend her legs properly, but her weight came off me. I felt slightly guilty prodding her, but if she lay down on her left side, her intestines would likely end up on the ground, not a good long-term strategy for life. We had to sort this.

'Right, she's going down,' I admitted, 'let's at least make sure she goes the right way.'

I held my suture in one hand. Seamus came round and untied her head. Between us we were able to walk her a few paces forward, then manipulate her on to her right side. She sank down the way we'd planned, her left side up; we were under control again. A few more needle passes and her abdomen was closed. I took a moment to relax slightly. The riskiest part for her was over. I glanced over at the calf. She was sat up, looking bright, but not yet on her feet.

I grabbed more thread and continued closing the rest of the muscles. Once they were done I had only the skin to get shut. Suturing cow skin is literally like working with leather. My hands were knackered by the time I'd finished, not to mention the stab wound. There was a chance I could catch something from her, my blood had mingled with hers, but I put it from my mind despite knowing that Brucellosis was rife in the local area. It could cause real issues and has been implicated in the high suicide rates of both vets and farmers. What the hell, I'd probably already got it. It was rare not to have little nicks or abrasions on my skin; it was just the nature of the job. I still had a youthful belief in my invincibility, however ill founded.

Skin closed; the job was done. Finishing off with a spray of blue, antibiotic-laden aerosol on to the wound, an extra layer of protection, I went through the aftercare with Seamus and Sam while they tried to get the calf to feed. By now it was able to stagger around. That the mother was down was actually useful at this point; it would allow us to easily get the calf feeding off mum. However, it did require an explanation.

'Why's she down?' asked Seamus. I explained that she'd been through a lot; trauma and blood loss could cause weakness. I think most of us would have wanted a sit-down in similar circumstances. There was another possibility. The epidural I'd given her might have diffused far enough through her cerebrospinal fluid to affect the nerves running to her back legs. I explained. Seamus's face started twisting and I could see he was about to have an outburst.

'So, she's fucking paralysed?!!' He had his head in his hands; clearly, he thought this was a disaster. I could see by his expression there was more coming my way.

'Look, most likely it's just exhaustion. I think I'd be pretty tired under the circumstances, wouldn't you?' He nodded. Rather than face more questions, I decided to get my explanation in first.

'If it is the epidural, it'll wear off over the next twenty-four hours. Just let the calf suck, make sure mum gets her antibiotics and anti-inflammatories. It's worth turning her every few hours as well; you don't want her on one side for too long. Keep plenty of grub and water nearby. She'll need all the calories she can get. It's pretty cold in here, find a horse rug or something and stick it on her, yeah?' Seamus nodded; he'd calmed down a bit.

I was pretty confident she'd be okay. The thing most likely to paralyse her was trying to pull the calf out through too small a birth canal, and we hadn't done that. I started to pack up. As soon as I'd got everything in the car, I gave the next client a ring. It looked like it was going to be a long night, but I was hopeful the next call would be simpler, though there was no guarantee. I currently had just that one more visit to do, but another could join the queue at any moment. The end was like a mirage; it could disappear at any moment. There's something particularly demoralising about working hard towards a goal, only for it to move further away due to forces beyond your control.

I wandered over to the tap and gave myself a hose-off. Clean, I made my way to the car, took a long draught of cold coffee, shut the car door and made for the next drama.

It proved to be a long weekend. By Monday morning I'd done 32 calls since my stint of on-call started on Friday night and I was knackered, having only managed to get a little sleep. Now all I had to do was get through the day and I'd be home free. Well, free to be unconscious in bed, but at least at rest. I was on TB testing all day, so at least there was limited intellectual strain. I made it back to the practice for lunch and as soon as I'd eaten, managed a 20-minute nap.

As the evening rolled round, I registered just how tired I was. I opted out of cooking and instead grabbed a burger and chips from the local carry-out. Munching through my burger in front of the TV, a few thoughts crossed my mind. I'd taken a job right out of university like most of my friend group. Vet school had been highly social; hardly a week went by without an event or cèilidh (a party with traditional Scottish dancing). Some weeks had several. However, as soon as we got jobs we were scattered across the UK. Many suffered from loneliness. A colleague in the year above me had got a job on the west coast of Scotland. The other two vets in the practice she joined were older gentlemen, nearing retirement and seemingly still working the way they had forty years earlier. A combination of lack of social life, difficult work relationships, a dearth of support, and frustration at how out of date things were, led her to quit after a month and return to an internship back at the vet school.

I was quite lucky, there were several young vets in my practice, and we offered each other a bit of mutual support. But they were all local; they had lives and friends there which I did not. I was still running regularly, getting to the gym some evenings, but apart from that, time off was mostly spent recovering. I was too busy to be truly lonely, but there was no doubt that I missed my friends.

I saw countless examples of poor management on the farms I visited and wondered sometimes if I was actually making things better. I estimated half the Caesareans I attended could have been avoided. I was pretty confident that short-term thinking was losing money for some of my clients. Pinching pennies was costing them pounds. My concern wasn't just for my clients' profits. It was animal welfare as well. Overstocking and poor ventilation were resulting in more pneumonia. The desire for big calves was swamping the on-call with C-sections. The fact that there had been no cases of a particular disease for a while led some to stop vaccinating, leading to an inevitable outbreak. However, I could do little about it. I was almost always the Fire Brigade. And, just like a firefighter operating a hose, I had little time to reflect over what had started the blaze. I just had to put it out quickly before moving to the next one. I had a lot to think about as I inevitably drifted off to sleep on the couch, still sat up, half a burger on my lap ... Tomorrow it would all start again.

5

FARMERS

I feel that on occasion farmers get a hard time, sometimes from me. That is rather unfair. They are individuals and I'm often deliberately trying to amuse. There are good and there are bad as in any profession. However, I have a huge amount of respect for farmers of all types. Why? Well, I'll tell you why ...

They actually 'make stuff'. Like, actual, real stuff; food, in fact. Something, without which, we cannot live for more than perhaps a few weeks. Pretty bad weeks at that. We live in an age in which vapid, seemingly brainless (I said 'seemingly') celebrities are paid thousands upon thousands of dollars or pounds for merely 'Tweeting' the brand of underpants they have chosen to wear today. Professional footballers are paid sums that are nausea inducing for chasing a ball around a field, while often dating aforementioned celebrities. In fairness, many of these instances are the result of market forces. It's the general public who buy match tickets, make-up and knickers. Our most base instincts are often concealed even from ourselves but are revealed in our economic realities. However, at the risk of sounding like a rather curmudgeonly old man: 'Are you fucking kidding me?'

We need to collectively get a grip. We really need food, and we really need to make it here in the UK. Something I rarely hear mentioned in any agricultural discussion is food security. Can we produce food at world prices? Probably not, not if we want environmentally sound practices, high animal welfare standards, living wages for farmers and so on.

Other countries frequently do not meet our standards in many respects. Yet we buy their produce at the expense of our own domestic suppliers, sometimes unknowingly. The fact that produce is often brought to the UK from abroad and then repackaged as UK produce is a travesty against our domestic food producers and wilful deceit of our well-intentioned public. How can we insist on our own farmers' adherence to ethical and environmental standards without being certain their competitors are doing the same?

What happens when 'bad stuff' happens? Disease, climate, war and international diplomatic spats can all affect our food supply. Would it not be advisable to retain the ability to feed ourselves? On top of which, we cannot send aid anywhere if we are starving ourselves.

Farmers make food; we should show them some respect. By we, I'm of course referring not just to us, but also to our political masters. Farmers are quitting at a tremendous rate across the UK, because their livelihood has been made untenable, particularly for smaller enterprises. If we allow such farms to go, before long the skills required to run them will cease to exist. You may not think that matters, but I've already mentioned food security. I think it's imperative that we can and do make much of our own food and retain the ability to make all of it *in extremis*. Nothing in this world is certain and we can only control or protect what we make within our borders. I don't wish to be isolationist or engage in protectionism. I want to take advantage of world markets but be prepared for the worst.

Second, we prize the countryside of our great nation. It is beautiful. I've been sometimes compensated for an early call by riding on the back of a quad, a four-wheeled motorbike utility vehicle much beloved by farmers, across dew-covered fields under an azure-blue sky to the aid of a sickly animal and have genuinely wondered if there is a limit to the beauty of our world. Moments like that are priceless. Suddenly everything seems as it should be; you feel a deep sense of connectedness and purpose. Admittedly, you then tend to end up with your arm inside some poor creature while you help it give birth. But when you're successful and that young calf or lamb takes its first few breaths, well, not even the mucous stuck to your nose can spoil the moment. It's alive! And you did it. Not pharmaceuticals, not a celebrity sing-along – you. Later, while drying your waterproofs over your car door, with the sun on your face, the sense of achievement and satisfaction is hard to convey. It feels good.

That world, in the UK, is largely man-made. Arguably, there are no wildernesses in the UK; the countryside we mostly experience is one of human creation. Hedgerows, ditches, fields, forests, rivers, canals; almost all have been created or influenced by humankind. For some thousands of years, those humans have largely been farmers. No one is quite sure exactly when, but at some point, humans transitioned from hunter-gathering to farming. This was probably an incremental change. People may argue over exactly where and when, but the point is that at some juncture we started to change our world in order to improve our lot.

Farmers built and maintain much of our countryside.

Gradually we transitioned from subsistence farming in which virtually everyone grew or reared something for food, to having individuals specialise and make an excess for trade. To this, we owe much of modern society. It was only with the production of extra food that some individuals could be freed from food production in order to pursue other ends. Agriculture permitted increased human population densities. More people engaged in more specialisation and more thinking permitted increased innovation. The precursor of science, natural philosophy was borne. When this started, we are not sure. In fact, not being sure is almost what science is, but we're working on it. I think what we can say is that Leonardo da Vinci was not tending his runner beans while he painted the *Mona Lisa*. But it wasn't just the chap with the idea for a helicopter and a keen eye for an enigmatic smile who required sustenance. Carpenters, blacksmiths, nurses, thatchers, soldiers, sheriffs, mothers, kings – all needed to eat, but only by being free from the need to generate their own food could they perform other jobs.

Farmers built, or helped build, our civilisation in a way that the cast of most soap operas most certainly did not.

Farmers are jolly important.

Third, most farmers I've met work bloody hard. In a way that many of us in the modern world do not. The consequences of inaction or poor husbandry are quite immediate. The bill is paid in sickly or dead animals, failed crops or lost milk. There's no putting it off until tomorrow or closing your laptop and pretending that your report is going to write itself. Bad stuff is going to happen, now! Often that means extremely hard work when you'd least like to do it. Like trying to dig an enormous bull out of a ditch it's fallen into in the dark, freezing rain running down the sleeves of your torn waterproofs to soak your clothing. That's work, usually on top of an already long, hard day. I know, I took turns digging. I can remember working on a dairy farm during the summer holidays. I needed to gain experience and managed to get a job as a labourer there to both earn some cash and satisfy the university that I knew something about dairy farming. I did care for and milk cows, but I was a general dogsbody and jobs such as knocking down walls with sledgehammers to build cow roads, and pressure-washing the outside of the house also fell within my purview. There's little possibility of overtime; most farmers work for themselves in some fashion.

Farmers work hard, so do vets.

That said, a lot of farmers spend a lot of time alone or with their sheep dog and have developed some interesting idiosyncrasies as a result. I've been treated with utter disdain by some farmers and like royalty by others. I remember calving a cow at about 3 o'clock in the morning, having been on the road all night, only to have the farmer insist on giving me a tour of his new sheds. They were nice sheds, but ultimately, I just wanted to drive home and go to bed. No number of polite noises could deter the tour. So, I wandered round, making appreciative sounds about architectural and agricultural terms that I found impenetrable. As we approached the end, I began to more actively wind things up. However, my client would have none of it; I simply had to see the house. With barely disguised frustration I followed him in, took off my wellies and washed my hands in the utility room. As we entered the kitchen, I steeled myself for a conversation on kitchen-cabinet technology. However, it was immediately apparent that I had worried unduly. In fact, his wife had been roused from her bed and extremely kindly prepared a full cooked breakfast for all of us. I was both grateful and a little ashamed of my earlier uncharitable thoughts! Time and again, I have received support and sustenance from many farmers for no other reason than their inherent kindness.

However, I'd also caution any young vet to cultivate their decision-making process regarding health and safety. The occasional individual will sometimes try to put the onus for a job unfairly on your shoulders. They don't, or at least didn't, offer much advice on this at vet school. I remember distinctly being once again called upon to assassinate a cow. At the time the country was much concerned about bovine spongiform encephalopathy (BSE), and as a result, no animal older than 30 months could enter the food chain. However, in compensation those animals over 30 months could be euthanised and the government would pay the farmer the going market rate. The animal would be cremated, but the farmer paid as if it had gone for meat. It was stipulated that these animals should be fit to enter the food chain. So, any overt sign of illness should have precluded the animal's entry into the scheme. However, it's fair to say that a liberal view was often taken. It was occasionally a rush to see if you could murder the animal before it died. If it died, it was almost certainly too ill to be in the scheme.

This animal was being culled (killed for being insufficiently productive, a harsh but necessary reality of farming). I didn't have a gun, so a lethal injection would have to do. The problem is that the lethal injection is an anaesthetic, so if you inject a standing animal, it may fall on you and crush you, possibly to death. Now if the injection is given with the animal in a crush (a metal crate designed to restrain and handle animals), the danger is largely removed. Perhaps you might just break a limb if you don't move fast enough? An open yard or pen is best; you've got space to make a girlish, high-pitched noise and dive out of the way. However, this particular farmer thought these were poor options. In either instance he'd have to get the carcass into his horse box. That would be difficult. Much better, he reasoned, to walk the cow into the horse box, then have me inject it. Thus, it would be dead and conveniently already inside. I mean, yeah; but if the animal dropped quickly, it would crush me against the wall of the box. It was not safe, and I said as much. He cited a female vet who had recently visited the farm and had no issues performing this task. I did not take the slight against my masculinity lightly. Nonetheless, I stuck to my guns and put the creature down in the yard. The farmer cursed my inconsiderate nature. Then he revealed that the lady in question had in fact broken her arm when the cow she'd injected had fallen on her. But it had saved him some hassle, so it was utterly worth it. I have no doubt he'd turned the screws on her as well.

Such situations are thankfully rare, but have the courage of your convictions. If someone is trying to save a few quid by risking your life or health, say no.

As L'Oreal would have it: 'You're worth it!'

Equally, don't let them have a go instead; you'll feel bad if they end up as a wet, red mush.

It occurred to me recently that in some ways the general public and farmers live in parallel worlds, adjacent, but separate. I was driving to a call, and as I glanced over the barrier on the side of the motorway, I realised I was passing a farm I had visited recently. So many of us drive past farms and farmers daily, unseen as the hedgerows, motorway embankments and woodland keep them from our view. Our modern transport systems mean that we cross agricultural land all the time without ever meeting its occupants or understanding their lives. At the same time, farmers are often part of their own community, helping one another, lending each other machinery, buying and selling animals, and engaging in the myriad of activities that make our agricultural system work. In the summers, near my home town, tractors and farmers will work from early in the morning into the early hours of the following day, sometimes 20-hour days, as they try to cut silage to feed their animals in winter. In the winter, dairy farmers will be out in the pre-dawn cold to gather cattle for milking, supplying our supermarkets and corner shops. All this activity is unseen and unconsidered by many of the general public.

Farmers deserve our collective and heartfelt thanks.

6

POLAR BEAR

I'm originally from a small town on the west coast of Scotland. It's a very rural area and farming is one of the major contributors to the local economy. I grew up with many kids from farms and it is still the case that if you want to blend into the conversation in the local rugby club, you had better know your kaie (cows) from your stirks (young weaned bovines, usually male). In the local dialect we still use a lot of words from Scots, the language of Robert Burns, Scotland's National Bard. Rabbie Burns was born near Ayr, about an hour's drive north of my hometown. Scots is an amazing language and some of the words are supremely evocative, conjuring a sensation of their meaning, even if you don't speak the language. I feel a short glossary is in order:

Fankle – Tangled or confused
Shoogle – Shake or wobble
Braw – Good, excellent
Keek – A quick, perhaps surreptitious look
Gey – Rather, considerably
Dreich – Dull, gloomy, grey and/or wet (in reference to weather)
Eejit – Idiot

Haver – Talk nonsense
Wheesht – Quiet

I'm convinced that no matter which language you speak, if I told you the weather outside was dreich, you'd grab a waterproof jacket.

I was fortunate that the area has an extensive coastline, beautiful hills and relatively quiet backroads. I can fondly remember trips to the beach as a kid. When I was younger, we shared a house with my maternal grandparents. My brother and I were close to them, and they were almost like a second set of parents. The six of us would pack the car and drive to the beach, often the only car there. We'd explore the coast and the rock pools, play rounders on the sand and swim in the sea. Even my grandfather, who'd lost a leg during the Second World War, would join in the games, sometimes going as far as taking off his prosthesis for a dip in the sea. For lunch or dinner, we'd start a fire with driftwood and cook a pot of potatoes. Even now these memories bring a smile to my face and I'm extremely lucky to have them.

We were also taken out in the hills hiking more or less as soon as we were able. A period when my extended household became fascinated with genealogy had us walking the local hills searching for abandoned crofts and landmarks linked to our family's past. As I grew older, I graduated from Boy's Brigade to Scouts and pursued my Duke of Edinburgh's Award. I must admit that, despite the fact these institutions offered a myriad of experiences, it was the outdoors and adventure that fascinated me. I was an avid reader. Some of the books I enjoyed the most described the exploits of Scott, Shackleton and, more recently, Fiennes. After the loss of his ship *Endurance*, Shackleton and his crew crossed the pack ice of the Antarctic before making their way, in the lifeboat they'd dragged with them, to Elephant Island. Having no contact with the outside world, and despairing of their prospect of rescue, Shackleton and a hand-picked few would sail 800 miles across the Southern Ocean in their reinforced lifeboat before conducting the first ever crossing of South Georgia, armed with only some knotted rope and a carpenter's adze. They were presumed dead prior to Shackleton turning up at the whaling station in Grytviken two years after they had disappeared. Eventually his entire crew was rescued, in no small part due to his leadership and determination. For me it is one of the greatest adventure stories ever told.

I was 16 when someone suggested to me that I might apply for a place on an expedition. Even the prospect of doing so seemed unbelievably exciting. I was too young, but after discussion with my parents I applied. The logic was that I would inevitably be declined, but I'd have made my interest clear, and it might help when I applied in future years.

My application eventually led to an interview in a tower, part of the imposing building of the University of Glasgow. The old university building at Gilmorehill, which houses the quadrangles, could have been transported straight out of a period drama or, indeed, Hogwarts. It was occupied by the university in 1870 and is an imposing gothic landmark. At 16 it was fair to say that I was well and truly intimidated. I took a seat on the solid wooden bench outside. I could hear voices inside. As I unconsciously eavesdropped, I could hear a man and a woman discussing my application. Unfortunately, I heard the woman snigger and make a few disparaging remarks due to my membership of my schools 'Young Inventors Club' – I was not one of the cool kids. This only added to my nervousness. The interview wasn't too bad, though the owner of the female voice seemed to have taken a dislike to me for no reason and chose to quiz me on the lifecycle of field mice on the Arctic

Archipelago of Svalbard, the intended destination of the expedition. I had to confess to being utterly clueless on the matter.

I left the interview somewhat despondent. I'd overheard one of the interviewers taking the piss out of me, so how well could it have gone? I was astonished when a few weeks later I learned that I'd been given a reserve place. I consoled myself that this was good news, and meant I would be sure to get a place in future years. However, only a few weeks later, I learned that enough people had dropped out to earn me an upgrade. I was going to the Arctic!

My family, friends and local community deserve a heartfelt thanks. There are too many individuals and companies who offered me money, equipment, discount or advice for me to thank them all here. It took months of fundraising, but in the end, I had enough cash and equipment to go on the trip. Above all I must thank my family, who contributed much of the money, ensured I had adequate equipment, and allowed me to go despite their misgivings.

On the build-up to the trip, I continued hillwalking and spending time outdoors. On one occasion my parents dropped a friend and I off and we walked up on to a local moor before descending through an estate and back along a long-distance footpath to home. As we strode through the woods, I spotted an object covered in flies on the path in front of me. I presumed it was animal dung of some kind – there had been plenty of cow, sheep and deer droppings on our walk as we traversed farmland, moors and woods – but as I went to step over it the flies suddenly dispersed in a cloud, and I realised that they'd been feasting on a dead cat. I bent down to examine it; the poor thing was caught in a snare fastened to a nearby tree. I was about to stand up and leave the flies to their business when something made me touch the cat; it let out a low moan. It was still alive!

Between us my friend and I were able to free it from the snare. Apart from extreme dehydration and a wound on its leg where the snare had trapped it, it seemed relatively uninjured. We quickly conferred and came up with a plan. I scooped it up and we hurried through the estate's woodland and into the nearest village, just off our route. From there we called my home from one of the ubiquitous red phone boxes and managed to get my parents to phone the local vet. The next phase of the plan called for them to come and pick us up, along with our critical patient. It was only a few minutes' drive from my house and in no time I recognised our family car approaching. We climbed inside and collectively made for town, pushing the speed limit. Gently stroking the cat, I tried to reassure it we had the best of intentions. Part way there, though, it lifted its head and gave a gentle meow … and then it was gone. The trip to the vet's became a formality, the cat was beyond rescue.

Perhaps the experience influenced my future; I couldn't say. I do remember the distress of realising just how much this poor creature must have suffered, and the frustration of lacking the skills or equipment to help. I remember the righteous anger that someone had left the snare but failed to check it regularly. The cat must have been there for a few days. Maybe we'd given it some tiny comfort at the end, just by offering kindness? I'd be no better equipped in such a situation now; I don't habitually carry around intravenous cannulas and bags of fluid. Without my veterinary degree, training, experience and the right drugs and equipment I'd be more or less useless in any animal emergency. I suppose what that incident highlights is that even the best of intentions is not enough. Veterinary medicine is a technical skill; it requires both the correct personnel and equipment to be of any use.

However, vet school was still a few years away. All too soon, it was summer, and expedition time! My family drove me to the airport before waving goodbye. They must have been concerned. I'd been a very homesick kid until recently. More than once I'd had to be picked up and taken home in floods of tears. However, in my last year of primary school, my headmistress had staunchly refused to facilitate my rescue from a week-long school trip. She'd made me stay and in doing so cured me of my homesickness forever.

The first few days went by in a blur of trains, planes and automobiles. When we landed at the airport outside Longyearbyen, we walked through arrivals and past a stuffed polar bear in a glass case. It was intimidatingly large. Initially, we lived in tents near the airport. We were told a female tourist had recently been killed by a polar bear, within sight of the passenger lounge. They were one of many hazards we would be exposed to in the coming weeks. I was the youngest on the trip, by quite a margin. On day one the Chief Leader, Chris, took me aside and admitted that there had been a bit of an error. I was too young, the next youngest kid was 18, the oldest in their mid-twenties. There'd been a bit of a mix-up with my birthday; really, I should be sent home. Since I was already there, I could stay if I wanted to. I opted to stay. I'm glad I did.

We were divided into 'Fires' of about twelve to sixteen kids. Each Fire had three leaders. Usually, two were senior and one junior, being developed for the future. As I lacked any formal qualification or speciality, I was put in the ornithology Fire, named simply 'Birds'. Our job was to explore the area, conducting ornithological research. However, the area we had to explore included frozen tundra, vast glaciers split by seemingly bottomless crevasses from which nunataks, ice-covered mountains, burst forth. There were also polar bears and the Arctic climate to contend with. We needed some training.

Once we had occupied our base camp, located on an ice-free beach, we were to strike out carrying heavy loads to our mountain training camp. Here we would learn how to use ice-axe and crampons, basic skiing and crevasse rescue. I still have a photo of me walking to the camp. I was probably five foot three and nine stone, my rucksack towered above me. But I was fit and strong, I'd recently won first junior in the local triathlon; I took my fitness seriously and was not a little competitive. However, I could not take the same length of stride as some of the taller team members. Whenever they weren't looking, I'd shuffle a little to keep up.

Even before we made for our mountain training camp, we had lessons in how to shoot a polar bear using a rifle. I'd never used a firearm before and most of us were pretty useless. There would only be one rifle in the Fire, so no doubt there would be a serious scramble if we ever had to use it in anger. We had lessons in chasing bears away using pots and pans and other seemingly optimistic strategies. Every 'night' we would lay trip-flares around our camp; if a bear stumbled in during our sleep and pulled on the wire, a rocket would shoot skyward and burst noisily, illuminating our camp and hopefully scaring it away. They were definitely about, and we saw footprints often, but they obviously didn't consider humans particularly delicious as we only ever saw them from a distance.

Once we'd practised at mountain training camp, our Fire was dropped off by boat at the front of a glacier; we were to ski up one glacier on to the ice-cap, spend a few weeks exploring, then return down another to get picked up. Our only means of communication with the outside world was a high-frequency (HF) radio set. These sets can transmit and receive globally, but they are notoriously fickle and there is a fair bit of skill involved in getting through to another station. The antennae can be arranged in a variety of ways to manipulate the propagation of its signal. Getting it the right length, the right shape and in the right place meant hours in the cold, working with thin wire, prone to tangling. Speaking with another operator often relied on the 'wave' of the radio signal bouncing off or bending through the ionosphere. All manner of atmospheric phenomena and even time of day could affect communications. It was possible to go days at a time without being able to contact the outside world. This was before the days of mobile phones, satellite phones and personal emergency beacons. I had been designated radio operator and had studiously learned all I could about HF. However, I was sacked almost immediately.

My first broadcast had gone something along the lines of: 'Well, I had a wee bit of trouble getting the set up and working. I got the wire in a fankle, but dinna worry, I gave it a wee shoogle and now we're just braw. I'd a wee keek oot the tent earlier and it's gey dreich up here.'

To which the reply had been: 'What?'

Clearly, they thought I was an eejit, havering and wished me to wheesht!

Other than family holidays I hadn't travelled all that much, so I wasn't used to making myself understood in a cosmopolitan environment with people from all over the UK, and certainly not from Norway, to which Svalbard belongs. I was also one of the very few kids from a comprehensive school and many of my public-school-educated colleagues struggled to understand me. I was rapidly dubbed 'Scotty' and demoted from my communications role. I still helped with the antennae and technical stuff, but I was no longer allowed near the microphone. Although I was crestfallen, it was the right decision. The transmissions were vital; static and interference made it hard enough to communicate and sometimes there would be only a few crucial moments to get a message understood.

If we had a casualty, there wasn't time for someone to decipher my dialect. However, I rapidly found another outlet. We carried our kit in large rucksacks. But not even the expedition-sized bags on our backs could house all our food and equipment. So, we also had pulks, a kind of sledge with a cover that you tow behind you. We had one rescue pulk in the Fire. It was bigger than all the others, designed to transport a casualty, and I rapidly claimed it as my own. Despite my size, I was determined to show I was as strong as anyone. It was a rare day when I didn't have the biggest, heaviest pulk and I took a lot of pride in it.

Over a few weeks we climbed mountains, fell in crevasses, skied through storms, waded freezing rivers, slept in igloos and became a tight-knit team. Cooking was done on paraffin stoves with old army rations, and we lived in three-person tents. It was a mixed group and I probably spoke to girls more in that few weeks than I ever had before. Throughout the day we were tied together with climbing rope lest one of us fall into a hidden crevasse. Unroped, such a fall would likely be fatal. Each of us was utterly reliant on the others for our survival.

By the end of the trip I had utterly fallen in love with expedition life, and was almost tearful at the thought of going home. That's no reflection on my home life, but on how much I'd enjoyed the trip. Adventure is a funny thing. There was a time when I thought it was a thirst that could be quenched. I have come to learn that, for some, it is a permanent state of affairs. One successful challenge or adventure only provides temporary satisfaction. With each trip, more experience means that the next must be further, higher or harder to provide the same thrill.

I'd met someone from the local mountain rescue when I'd been fundraising for the trip. They were there to ask the same organisation for money towards a new Land Rover. We'd got into conversation, and he'd suggested I join the team when I got back. That winter I started training with them, though I wasn't allowed on callouts until I turned 18. I'd learned basic rope work in Svalbard, and I took to cycling to local cliffs and teaching myself to climb. Soon I was climbing the mountains of the UK in summer and winter.

A couple of years or so after we got back, I was offered a place on another trip with the same organisation, which is now called the British Exploring Society, this time to South Georgia. I felt the same yearning to go as previously. South Georgia! The very place Shackleton's journey had culminated. It was almost too good to be true. However, I'd also earned a place at vet school. South Georgia would have to take a back seat for now; I was off on a different path.

That trip all those years ago taught me some vital lessons for the future. Working in a small team required everyone to pull their weight. It's not always about you; the team comes first, even if your feelings are hurt, or pride dented. It's worth persevering for something you really want, there's no telling what might transpire to help you.

In one of Ranulph Fiennes' books I once read a quote from Goethe that I've always found inspiring: 'Whatever you can do or dream you can, begin it. Boldness has genius, power and magic in it!' It applies equally whether your ambition is physical or intellectual. Vet school fell under the intellectual heading, but I've never lost my appetite for a practical challenge. I've also learned that the best endeavours have aspects of both.

I'd been in the job now for a few years. I'd sampled life in different practices and locations. Vet school had already delayed my pursuit of other passions. I enjoyed my work, but I was so busy I was missing out on other activities that I found deeply satisfying. I needed more time off, with more flexibility than any potential employer could offer. I decided I would take a leap of faith. I would continue to work as a vet, but I would become a locum. Instead of permanent employment I would work in temporary posts, travelling from practice to practice as required. I'd have to manage my own taxes, book my own work, pay my own insurance, professional memberships, ongoing education and any other expenses I incurred. In return, I could decide on my own days if not my own hours. My life had been out of balance for a while; I needed another outlet. With some regret, I resigned. I decided I'd rather become a good locum, than a bad employee.

7

BEN

Orthopaedics, the treatment of disorders of the bones, is an area of veterinary medicine that is uniquely attractive to the average male vet. It's replete with long words that make you sound smarter than you really are, a large selection of expensive toys is necessary for its practice, confidence bordering on arrogance is practically compulsory, and, critically, it's actually quite simple. No advanced intelligence is required, but a practical knack and good spatial awareness are of paramount importance. There is also no question that it's enormously satisfying. Try to picture, if you will, a young dog that's run out in the road in its youthful excitement. It's been unlucky enough to get hit by a vehicle and it's been brought to you by the owner. Unfortunately, it's immediately obvious that the dog has broken its right, front leg, straight through the radius and ulna. The dog is in a lot of pain and its future is far from certain. There are three options in principle:

1. Fracture repair – this may take the form of internal or external support of the bone in order to allow it to heal. It must be 'reconstructed' into an approximation of its original shape in order to heal without significant deformity.

2. Amputation – in some instances, even in human medicine, a limb is too badly damaged to repair. In these cases, the limb may be amputated. This tends to have less impact on an animal's quality of life compared to how a human might be affected. Self-image is less of an issue in our furry friends. Most species we routinely treat have four legs, so an amputation causes only a 25 per cent reduction in available legs. For a human, one leg is a bit more of an issue, being 50 per cent of the average total leg-age. About 65 per cent of a quadruped's weight is borne on the front limbs, as the head and vital organs are located towards the front, so the loss of a hind limb is much less of an issue for a dog or cat than you might assume. I've seen many amputee dogs running, and, at full pace, it's hard to even make out a limp. It's only at walking pace, when there is less momentum, that a limp or a hop is apparent. A foreleg is more of a problem, especially in larger dogs. Nonetheless, amputation is a legitimate and valuable weapon in the vet's arsenal. One distressing consideration that contributes to the choice of treatment is money. On occasion, amputation is necessary even though reconstruction is technically possible. For example, the animal may have another condition that would complicate healing. But, by far and away the most likely scenario is lack of money. It's awful to have to take off a limb that might be saved. But vets have to make a living just like everyone else. Most will push things as far as they can. Charities may help, some economies might be made, some vets will even do it at cost in order to develop their skills. However, occasionally, we cannot manage it, and we must submit to the inevitable. One thing to perhaps consider is that

many pets in the First World receive healthcare that the average citizen of Liberia or Afghanistan could only dream of.

3. Euthanasia – the worst possible outcome.

Occasionally this is the only answer. In older animals or those where recovery is unlikely, it may be the only humane decision. The severity of a fracture is directly linked to the energy dumped into the body during the initial injury. A puppy that tumbles off the couch can expect a less severe injury than one run over by a car. I've seen animals where more or less every major bone in half of their body is broken. Even with every effort, these animals are going to endure a lot of pain during recovery. Surgeries will be painful in themselves, and a few may be needed. The animal cannot rationalise the need for the pain, knowing only that it hurts. And, at the end of it all, their quality of life may be unacceptably poor. Then, euthanasia becomes mandatory, but you've already put them through a lot and to no end. These are hard choices requiring intelligent guesses.

Already we can see that even the initial decision making is complex. I do mean complex, not complicated. To clarify, a watch is complicated. It's going to be tough to whittle one out of wood. But the outcome of its operation is entirely predictable; in fact, that's the point. The Swiss would have it no other way. Now the weather, that's complex: tiny local differences can mean the difference between a storm naturally dissipating and it forming a devastating hurricane.

The decision making in these cases is complex. There are a huge number of variables, and we don't even have a useful way of measuring many of them. In an older dog, its health may be insufficient to allow it to heal. Depleted physiological reserves may mean vulnerability to infection or failure of a fracture to heal. Subsequent interventions may seem to help, but, after weeks of effort, treatment fails.

How old is too old? If we could measure this type of variable with exact accuracy, we would know that on Monday healing seems assured, but, come Tuesday, things will have just tipped ever so slightly the wrong way and we are in the realms of the unfortunate. To be honest, that's not even the hardest variable to measure. How is the owner going to cope? Will they adhere to the post-op conditions? Will they give the right tablets at the right time? Will they do the physio? Or will they allow the dog to chase a tennis ball 24 hours after surgery, breaking its surgical implant? It's happened, I can assure you. The decisions around treatment choice are fraught with hard choices and 'best guess' assumptions.

Once we have decided that surgery and reconstruction is the appropriate treatment, then we have to decide on the treatment itself. There are multiple ways of repairing fractures. At the most basic level, a broken digit may require only minimal intervention. If the fracture is not displaced (so the bone is broken, but the fractured ends are sat in the correct anatomical position) then only light support might be needed.

I've been treated in this way myself. I foolishly agreed to box a friend in a charity bout. I'd just come back from an extended period working abroad. I was fit, but probably a little run-down and malnourished. By malnourished, I mean I had a newly found and soon-to-be-lost six pack. I managed to break my hand on the other chap's face and was left with a fractured metacarpal, the bone on the back of the hand. I knew as soon as it happened; it was sore, and I still had to fight another two and a half rounds. It's amazing what adrenaline and a sense of pride will do for you. I had it x-rayed by the local hospital and they assured me both that it was broken and that it required no treatment. I wasn't to use it too much, but that was about it. Within days I could carefully use the gym. It healed without major incident. My hand looks slightly different to the other one now and my pinky is a bit shorter than it used to be, but it's perfectly functional. This is the ideal case.

At the opposite end of the spectrum, a gunshot wound to a femur might cause a section of the bone to be reduced to multiple fragments. The energy dumped into such a wound might effectively destroy the bone in the immediate vicinity of the injury. That section may die, necessitating its removal and the joining of the two, newly adjacent, ends of bone. This will shorten the bone but save the limb. I once worked with a friend who had suffered this exact wound and complication. If the bone isn't dead, it will almost certainly be fragmented. The result is that the two unbroken ends must be fixed in location and prevented from moving while the multiple fragments in the middle gradually knit together. This can be achieved using an external frame fixed to pins that penetrate and secure the bone. The external frame allows force to bypass the broken section of bone while it heals.

Sometimes a joint is involved and, rather than a fractured bone, a ligament is torn. The most common example is probably the cruciate ligament. Footballers and rugby players often rupture theirs. So do dogs. It's a real risk if you go running around enjoying yourself, whether you are chasing a ball or just out on your walkies. The cruciate ligament secures and stabilises the knee joint. Without it the joint is unstable and painful to use. Replacing the ligament, or at least its function, is necessary for many animals to achieve an acceptable outcome. There are multiple ways of achieving stability in the joint and considerable skill is involved in any chosen technique.

So, now we have a broad awareness of the issues involved, we can move on. I have done quite a bit of orthopaedics over the years. I'm largely self-taught. That term should be alarming to anyone who understands the way medical qualifications work. 'Self-taught' is often interchangeable with 'incompetent lunatic'. Now, this term does not apply to me. But then, of course, I would say that; what self-respecting lunatic wouldn't? But it really doesn't. I became self-taught initially through necessity.

Ben was a four-year-old Border Collie. He'd leapt over a fence in pursuit of a rabbit, hooked his back paw up on the barbed wire and dislocated his hip joint. The symptoms were initially fairly obvious, especially since I'd seen a few similar cases. We x-rayed Ben and the dislocation was immediately visible, confirming my presumptive diagnosis. The x-ray process was an ordeal in itself. I was working in rural Wales at the time, for a chap only a few weeks away from retirement. Digital x-ray was not a luxury the practice had access to; even an automatic development machine had proven to be too expensive an indulgence for Alun, the owner and principal vet. We also lacked a dedicated development room, central heating or a waterproof building. These things had been invented, but not introduced at the practice.

Developing an x-ray worked thus:

1. One vet gets in the under-stair's cupboard with three cat litter trays. One with developer, one with water and one with fixer. No cat litter should be used at any stage. The cupboard is shut, rendering the inside completely dark. Everything must be done by touch and familiarity.

2. Another vet sits in the corridor outside. Their job is to hold the door shut with their feet, placing their back against the opposite wall for purchase. This keeps out the light, which would ruin the delicate x-ray film. A secondary task is to man the stopwatch and shout to

the vet in the cupboard when it's time to dip the x-ray in each fluid.

3. On command from the timer vet, the cupboard vet dips the x-ray film in each fluid in turn, rinsing it in water as appropriate.

Once the film is developed and fixed, it may be examined. The combination of antiquated equipment and rudimentary techniques meant poor quality x-rays in many cases. That usually meant examining your picture, realising it was what we call 'fucking useless', then going through the whole rigmarole again ... and again. However, we managed to get a useful picture after two attempts, and it told us what we needed to know.

A bit of manipulation and the hip popped right back in. It felt pretty good, and the joint could be smoothly manipulated. Sometimes this is enough. If the hip stays in, problem solved. Unfortunately, in many instances dislocation has stretched or destroyed ligaments and structures that stabilise the joint. As a result, it often re-dislocates easily and a permanent, surgical fix is necessary. Ben was one of the unlucky ones. There were a few options available, all were specialist procedures and expensive as a result. Ben's owner was a local farmer, and he took a practical view of the situation. Ben was an asset if he could work, not a pet. If he could not work, the game was up. Ben's owner was willing to pay for treatment, but nothing like the cost of specialist surgery at a referral centre. Ben would never be able to work again without treatment, and he'd be left barely able to walk. He could get around on the other three limbs, but the pain from his injured leg would cause him permanent discomfort. We could amputate, but his owner was clear: either we could return him to full four-legged function, or he would have to be put down. Foolishly, and with reckless disregard for said foolishness, I volunteered to perform an operation called a femoral head and neck osteotomy. I sounded intelligent when I said it. I'd look up its meaning later.

The hip joint is a 'ball and socket' joint. The ball is the end of the femur, and the socket is called the 'acetabulum', formed by part of the pelvis. In a dislocation, the ball is no longer in the socket and grinds against adjacent bone; it's very painful. The operation would remove the ball from the head of the femur, then smooth it down. The joint would be permanently destroyed, but the surrounding muscles can form a pseudo-arthrosis or false joint, which permits reasonable function and, critically, removes the pain involved in the grinding of bone on bone. It's what's called a 'salvage procedure' done as a last resort to facilitate quality of life and minimise pain. It's also often performed by someone who knows what they are doing. We didn't have one of those, so I started brushing up. The owner of the practice, Alun, assured me all the necessary equipment was available. He wasn't up for doing the procedure, but the stuff was there.

I scheduled the surgery for two days hence and spent the evenings swatting up. I had to learn and memorise the surgical approach; how to get through the surrounding soft tissue structures without causing irreparable damage. Meanwhile the nurses prepared and sterilised the kit. I can only presume Ben sat at home, seriously mulling over his choice of surgeon. On the day, Ben arrived, cheery and with his tail wagging. Our preparation went smoothly and in no time at all he was on the operating table. I made my approach, apprehensively dissecting soft tissue around the joint until I reached the joint capsule itself. Once through the capsule, there is a short ligament, joining the head of the femur to the acetabulum. In Ben's case this was ruptured, broken during the traumatic dislocation. To a degree, this simplified things as I would not have to fiddle around cutting it. Most soft tissue out of the way, I could move the head of the femur sufficiently to begin amputating it. I'd have to cut through the neck using an osteotome, which is effectively an expensive chisel. The head and neck are a bit like a squat mushroom. The neck is like the stalk, if that makes visualisation easier. So, bones in the right spot, I could begin the traumatic bit. Having gained confidence from the approach procedure, I used my best 'surgeon voice' and piped up: 'Osteotome.'

There was an awkward pause, then the nurse, Sarah, spoke up.

'What?'

'Osteotome?' I said, semi-hopefully.

Sarah looked at me blankly, mouth agape.

'Erm?' I said.

'Eh, we don't have one,' said Sarah.

'What do you mean, we don't have an osteotome?' I said. This was seriously messing with my ch'i.

I was initially indignant, but quickly slipped into hopeful negotiation and, eventually, acceptance. We didn't have an osteotome. Alun had assured me we did. Sarah was quite clear that he was prone to occasional exaggeration and that I had fallen victim to it. All interesting, but I had an unconscious dog needing an operation and I lacked the tool to perform it. My mind was racing. I could phone the owner, explain, and be putting Ben down in minutes. The owner would accept it; he and Alun had known each other for a long time. I could legitimately say I'd encountered a problem that I didn't have the specialist tool to deal with. He wouldn't ask for more explanation; he'd accept my word – he was from that generation.

No! There had to be a way. Faced with this kind of problem today, I'd deal better with it. In fact, I'd never be caught out like that now. But me now wasn't there then, more's the pity. Okay, what did I need? A chisel, basically, if only I could get something like that. Only I couldn't. Unfortunately, unlike the late-model Terminators, I couldn't forge surgical instruments out of my limbs.

Unless?

There was a hardware store in town. They would sell chisels. I mean, chisels, not orthopaedic instruments, but beggars cannot be choosers. I quickly covered up the wound with damp swabs, got my gloves off and left the nurses with Ben. I headed out the door, half jogging down to the hardware store. The guys at the store knew Alun and kindly allowed me to put two chisels on account. I needed a spare in case I dropped or broke one. Choosing the size was a bit of guesswork. I opted for wooden handles. They wouldn't sterilise so well, but neither would they melt in the autoclave (an autoclave is a device used to heat and sterilise instruments for surgery). The autoclave would go up to about 130 °C, with steam, so fire wouldn't be likely. I rushed back to the practice. We got the chisels straight in the autoclave and set it to the fastest cycle available. They might not be perfectly sterile, but Ben had received antibiotics already and we'd probably achieve the desired effect; at least, that's what I told myself. I had an anxious cup of tea while I monitored the autoclave for signs of fire or explosion, uncertain as to what I would do about either. The cycle completed without incident. I scrubbed again, gloved up and, newly equipped, got on with the surgery. The first chisel served admirably. It cut through the neck of the femoral head like a blunt butter knife being hammered with a mallet through hardwood. But it got through. It's very important to rasp the remainder of the femur smooth to avoid the grinding of bone on bone, which can cause severe pain. I spent quite a while making sure it was done to the best of my ability. Bony bit complete, I allowed myself a small sigh of relief. I closed the soft tissue, then the skin. I'd done what I could. It would now be a case of awaiting the outcome. It would be six to eight weeks at least before best results would be seen. However, I'd likely know in days if I'd cocked up. I'd be furious with myself, but Ben would be the one picking up the ultimate bill.

Ben's owner came and picked him up. He carried him gently to his Land Rover and laid him in the boot on top of some straw covered with dirty sheets. Great, perfect start if you're looking to ensure a wound infection. I warned Ben's owner against anything other than walking outside to the toilet for at least 10 days. Then it would be very slow physio and rehab for weeks. I wanted to see Ben in two days to check for any signs of infection, and his owner had a long list of things to look out for as well as my personal mobile number.

Four days later, Ben and his owner arrived without announcement or apology. Ben had obviously been outside, as he was filthy. Clearly, his owner hadn't listened to a word I'd said. In addition, he was disappointed. Apparently, Ben was limping quite a bit. I had a tough job biting my tongue. Of course the bloody dog was limping. I'd just cut off the end of one of his major bones with a wood chisel. Would the owner care to experience something similar and see just how well he could get around afterwards? No, you're bloody right he wouldn't. I admonished his carelessness and explained, yet again, the necessary aftercare. I wanted to see Ben again in another two days. For now, he was doing quite well. He would allow me to move his limb around and it moved smoothly. He was a tough bugger, like most Collies. Four days later he was back. Yet again he was filthy; worse, if anything. His owner was no happier and explained that Ben was not able to work at full capacity. Despite my lack of religious faith, I fantasised about a righteous thunderbolt hitting this clown in the face, saving me the bother of choking him to death with my bare hands. However, Ben was looking happier and his leg even better. He was bearing weight on it, and as I called him over, he walked towards me, jumped up, stood on both hind legs and planted his front paws on my waist. As I rubbed his head, I knew he was going to be okay. Despite my errors and his owner's pig-headedness, he was going to be fine.

I never saw Ben again; I was a locum at the practice and my final day was the last of its existence. Alun was retiring and selling the practice to another local vet. It was an odd few weeks. I'd really enjoyed my time, but I'd watched Alun struggle with retirement. He'd been the local vet for over forty years. It was as much his identity as his job. More than once I'd seen him get a bit tearful when he thought no one was looking.

It's amazing: half a career later, and despite myself, I remember Ben fondly. Hopefully, he went on to do many more seasons' work. There is little a farm Collie loves more than to herd sheep; we've bred that into them. I'm glad I was able to buy Ben a few more years to indulge his passion.

I've subsequently done many more orthopaedic operations. These days I'm happy and confident plating a cat's leg, applying tiny pins to a dog's broken metacarpals or using an external fixator for complex fractures. I even paid £1,600 for a course once, but found I'd already learned far more by treating the cases I could. I also benefit enormously from the innovations in technology that have revolutionised what we can offer. Digital radiography (x-ray) allows me to measure the size of bones virtually. I can then order the right implants and parts and expect them to be delivered the next day. Smaller systems allow me to treat even our tiniest patients, and idiot-proof kits make me look better than I really am.

More recently, I turned up to cover a shift in a practice I regularly work with. There was a cat booked in for an amputation. I had a look at the x-rays and realised it was fixable, but no one at the practice had the skills. The fracture was a few days old; I wouldn't be back for a while, it was today or never. I approached one of the nurses to ask her if we might try to repair it instead. She grinned. 'I knew you'd say that!' We rifled through the available bits and bobs in the practice. There were spares I'd ordered for previous ops and, in the end, we were able to save the leg.

A few months later at the same practice I was walking across the car park when a bloke waiting in his car shouted, 'You Gareth?' I cautiously replied in the affirmative.

'You saved my daughter's cat's leg!'

We had a quick chat and it certainly perked up my day. The downside was I'd never met the guy before, so he must have recognised me from a description. I realised the words short, Scottish and chimp-like must have been in close proximity at some point, so I couldn't get too big-headed.

To date, I've been fairly lucky. I'd still send my own dog to a specialist if I had the money. I recommend that owners do the same. But, occasionally, the money isn't available and I get to indulge a satisfying passion. To summarise the satisfaction of this kind of surgery:

Dog broke, dog fixed.

If you're a vet, it doesn't get much better than that.

8

SAMSON

There are few words that strike fear into the heart of the average general practitioner more than Horse.

I was working in mid-Wales at the time. On arrival at my new job, the practice owner, Dave, made it quite clear that he did not care for horses or their owners. Fortunately, he did not have to routinely deal with them. In all likelihood that was because the horses and their owners felt the same about him. There was a local one-man-band horse practice that took care of the various equine residents of the beautiful Welsh hills. However, the vet in question rather selfishly insisted on the occasional holiday. That's where we came in. Or at least, where *I* would be coming in. Dave was polite, but it was clear I'd be dealing with the cavalry division of the practice whenever it was required. In his defence, I semi-volunteered because I actually quite liked horses and was looking forward to getting reacquainted with some equine medicine. I should add to this that the one-man-band elected for a system of simply going on holiday, rather than alerting anyone to the possibility. So, horse calls generally popped up out of the blue.

I received an early-morning call to a horse with 'choke'. In humans, we associate the idea of choking with interruption to our ability to breath. In horses, choke is a lay term (i.e., used in common parlance, rather than being a specific medical term) that refers to a blockage of the oesophagus; the pipe that connects the mouth to the stomach. It can lead to breathing difficulties, but it is not the trachea (windpipe) that is blocked.

In my experience, one of the most common reasons for horses to develop choke is the ingestion of un-soaked sugar beet pulp, especially in uncontrolled quantities. In this case the canny equine had managed to get out of his enclosure and knew exactly where the munchables were stored. The owner had left the cupboard containing the beet open, and it had proven irresistible.

Although usually not an emergency in the sense that the animal will rapidly die, choke is distressing and more likely to have a negative outcome the longer it persists. The beet pulp swells as it absorbs water. Saliva is mostly water and is rapidly absorbed by the beet, making the blockage worse. Not only does it become sticky, but it also swells, increasing its grip on the sides of the oesophagus. At the same time, the oesophagus may spasm, again increasing the severity of the choke. The horse can be very uncomfortable and is often coughing as it tries to dislodge the blockage. Added to this, saliva, which would normally be swallowed, is often regurgitated along with bits of beet. In its distress the horse can inhale this mixture of saliva and vegetable matter. This can lead to inhalation pneumonia, infection in the animal's lungs, which can be life threatening.

I already had all the horse stuff in my car, since it was my night on call. Our selection of kit was pretty limited; any self-respecting equine vet would probably have laughed derisively at my stock of equipment. But it was too late to worry about that now; I had what I had, and it would have to do.

On arrival I met with the owner, who was understandably cursing herself. She had known this horse could open his own enclosure. Some horses are very bright and can figure out latches and bolts quite quickly. They are often adept enough with their lips, tongues and teeth to be able to manipulate fastening systems surprisingly well. In this case, the cupboard for the beet did not have a lock, as it was not expected the horses would have direct access. The recriminations would have to wait. Samson was coughing up food, sweating and clearly distressed.

He was a big horse and quite intimidating. Horses can be quite the characters. They are also capable of being extremely dangerous. For starters, they can bite. I have been bitten by a cow, but it's fairly unusual and it's not their speciality. Horses, as discussed above, can be quite adept and sometimes vicious. A horse bite can leave you with a nasty wound coupled with a lot of ancillary bruising. Generally speaking, horses are going to be taller than you, at least full-sized adult ones. They have four legs, and, unlike cows, they can kick effectively with all four of them, though not simultaneously. No one will forget a decent kick from a horse wearing shoes. The metal shoes are highly efficient at transferring force. Even a playful kick can result in severe bruising or even broken bones. A kick intended to cause damage might be fatal. Cattle tend to be a bit slower and clumsier. Horses are much more athletic and can rear up in order to strike higher with either their front or rear feet. Then there are the techniques of just crushing you against walls, head butting and so forth. Over a normal career an equine vet can expect seven or eight injuries. One-third of those will require hospital admission and about 10 per cent will result in the vet losing consciousness. Being an equine vet is one of the most dangerous peacetime occupations in the UK. It may even be riskier than the traditionally action-packed role of firefighting, and with far fewer opportunities for napping, weight training or photoshoots for titillating calendars.

Fortunately, Samson was a fairly gentle soul. The first step was to give him some pain relief and moderate sedation. Sedating him would offer two advantages. First, he would relax, hopefully allowing any spasm in his oesophagus to subside and helping the choke to ease. Second, this relaxation would allow me to examine him more safely and ensure his cooperation in any intervention. His owner fitted a head collar and lead rope so that she could assert some control over his head. While she was doing that, I drew up some acepromazine (ACP) and butorphanol. The ACP is a tranquilliser and the butorphanol is an opioid. The two combined would provide me with a decent level of sedation, while still keeping the horse on his feet. I drew up the required amounts and gave Samson an intravenous injection into his jugular vein. It was a bit harder to find than average as he was a muscular individual and clearly no stranger to the munchables, but I found the spot and blocked the vein at the base of the neck using my left hand. The right I used to wield the needle and syringe. I pinched the skin over the injection site with my right hand, held for a few seconds, then gently slid the needle into his vein. I drew back on the syringe and got the dark red blood I expected from entering a vein, then I depressed the syringe and emptied the drugs into his system. I left the owner with him while I went and got some supplies. I'd need my gag to secure Samson's mouth in an open position so that I could inspect it. I'd also need a decent supply of water, my stomach tube and a funnel.

I trotted off to the car and got my various bits and bobs. By the time I'd returned Samson's head was drooping towards the floor, indicating that his sedation had kicked in. The gag I had looked like something the Spanish inquisition might have used during their more inquisitive moments. It fitted on Samson's head and had two bits, which would engage his upper and lower incisor teeth. This would allow me to open his mouth and a ratchet system would keep it open, enabling me to inspect his oral cavity without getting bitten. I wanted to check there wasn't any food stuck in his mouth or in danger of obstructing his airway. I fitted the gag with a bit of fiddling. Then the owner got under his head, rested Samson's chin on her shoulder and stood up, making it easier for me to examine his oral cavity. With my head-torch on I had a good look and feel around in his mouth. I pulled out some sugar beet and saliva he had coughed up, to give me a better view. A quick inspection of his teeth revealed no problems. Horse's teeth continually erupt (or grow), and overgrown teeth can cause issues. Any dental issue might stop Samson adequately chewing his food and contribute to his choke. In this case his teeth were fine. I removed the gag and moved to stage two.

My next step was to insert a nasogastric tube. This involves passing a rubber or plastic tube up the horse's nose, over the back of the throat and into his oesophagus. It's important to select the right size and make sure it's well lubricated, as there are delicate bony structures in the nose called turbinates. Trauma to these is painful and can result in fairly spectacular bleeding. Some trauma is unavoidable, but care must be taken. I roughly measured off the stomach tube for diameter and length, then marked it with tape. I made sure it was well lubricated and started to pass the tube gently up Samson's nostril. A firm but gentle pressure will usually propel the tube where it needs to go. Once it's passed over the back of the hard palate (the roof of the horse's mouth; the tube is passing above this structure) the tube should start to descend towards the elaborate structure that is the larynx. The larynx is where the respiratory and alimentary (eating) systems meet. It has an important role in protecting the airway. When we eat or drink, the epiglottis covers the entrance to the trachea and guides food into the oesophagus. The fact that these two systems, which must remain separate for safety reasons, are interconnected in this way suggests to me that no god designed it. Or at least, if they did, they were in a rush and presumably in the midst of the office Christmas party. Why not separate breathing and eating holes? Would that have been so hard? It would certainly have made my job easier. Anyway, as the stomach tube reaches the end of the soft palate it's important to slow the insertion rate and allow the horse time to 'swallow' the tube. As it advances further it can often be felt in the oesophagus, which lies behind the trachea in the horse's neck. If you have a horse to hand, you can easily feel the ringed tube, like the tube of a vacuum cleaner right at the front of the neck. Immediately behind this is the muscular tube of the oesophagus. This cannot normally be felt, as in between meals it collapses flat. But the semi-rigid nasogastric tube can often be felt as it enters and expands the oesophagus. It's imperative that this tube is inserted in the correct place. If it's in the trachea, you're about to introduce fluid directly into the animal's lungs. Too much and you'll drown it on the spot.

I passed the tube gently forward, paused as the horse swallowed, gently advanced it again, then allowed the owner to hold it in place. Once more, Samson's muscular neck made my job difficult, but after getting the owner to wiggle the tube I could feel it in the right place. I advanced it until it hit a stop. I'd reached the choke with the end of the tube. Now the plan was to introduce a bit of water, then drain it out again. I'd keep repeating this process to soften the blockage. I'd also intermittently apply pressure to the choke in order to push the blockage in to the stomach, hopefully. This required a lot of patience and care. Too much water and the horse breathes it in. Too much pressure on the nasogastric tube and you could perforate the oesophagus, giving its contents direct access to the chest cavity and sealing the horse's fate. I'm sure equine kit has improved, but, at the time, this involved a delicate ballet (read clumsy ruck) of holding head collars, lead ropes, supporting Samson's head, keeping the stomach tube in place, holding the funnel on the end of the tube and pouring water into it before draining it out again. Needless to say, in no time at all both the owner and I were drenched in water and covered in bits of sugar beet. However, after thirty minutes or so, I gently pushed on the stomach tube, and it suddenly moved forwards easily. I looked at the tape I'd marked it with earlier and knew the end must be in the stomach. Samson was un-choked!

Another trip to the car and I returned with antibiotic and anti-inflammatory injections for Samson. The antibiotic was in case he had inhaled any fluid (almost inevitable) in order to prevent a pneumonia from developing. The anti-inflammatory would reduce any excess inflammation that might contribute to him suffering another choke. At the same time, it would provide some pain relief. I gave the injections. Samson was starting to come round a bit. It was time to remove the tube. This was not my first rodeo. It was common to see some bleeding when removing the nasogastric tube. Due to the size of the horse and the tendency their breathing has to create a 'mist' of blood, this can look quite spectacular and can often induce panic in owners. Therefore, I pre-empted any panic and warned Sally of the possibility. There would be bleeding, I said. It would look quite spectacular, but it's nothing to worry about and it will stop. Well, there was, and it didn't. As soon as I removed the tube, Samson's nose started to bleed. Like, really bleed. I repeated my previous caveats. It'll be fine, nothing to worry about. It's only a wee bleed, I've had worse at the rugby. At the same time the voice inside my head was saying the exact opposite. It was screaming: 'Emergency! Emergency! Fuck, that's a lot of blood, fuck, fuck, fuckity fuck fuuuuckkkkk!'

My internal voice took a brief moment to calm down, gather itself together, then said: 'That's not a mist, it's a jet! Did you feed the tube directly into Samson's heart? Did you??!!! How is that even possible?! You're a moron and you've murdered this horse with a unique combination of stupidity and overconfidence!'

Sometimes my inner voice can be hurtful.

While this was going on in my head, I tried to appear outwardly calm. I resisted the urge to race to the car and get … well, I didn't even know what I would get, but I'd be able to escape from the situation for five minutes and think. I held Samson's head level and asked the owner to go get some bales. On top of everything else we were both now covered in blood, mingled with the saliva and sugar beet from our earlier struggles. It looked like we'd been involved in a failed daytime TV show based around crossing the *Texas Chainsaw Massacre* with *Celebrity MasterChef*. I stuck Samson's head on my shoulder to rest my arms and thought.

What had I done wrong? Nothing, so far as I could tell. I'd seen this kind of thing dozens of times, but never so severe. The owner returned with some bales; I started stacking them under Samson's chin. I reckoned that about four square bales one on top of the other should hold his head fairly level. Hopefully, by raising his head, we'd reduce the bleeding by dropping blood pressure at the site of blood loss. At the same time, I didn't want to elevate his head too much and have blood running backwards towards his lungs and getting inhaled. Between shifting bales, holding horses and moderate to severe panic, I was now sweating intensely. However, as I manoeuvred his head on to the bales, I could see the blood was starting to slow down.

Fortunately, although he was coming around somewhat, Samson remained quiet enough that he'd stand still with his head resting on the bales. I could finally take a moment to look around. With my realisation that the situation at least appeared to be under control, I could now make eye contact with the owner again. Her eyes were like saucers, and she obviously had just as much adrenaline running rampant through her system as I did. I admitted I'd never seen a bleed as bad when removing a stomach tube. The plan was just to monitor Samson for now. I said I'd do that if she had other stuff to do. Fortunately, she took the hint and offered to make a cup of tea. Having been there for about two hours at this stage, I gladly accepted. On her return, it was clear things were going to be okay. Samson was brighter, and while there was still a trickle of blood at his nostrils, it was certainly non-lethal. We drank our tea in companionable silence. As we finished up, I started to regain my wits and went through the aftercare. Food mixed with water to form a gruel for the next 72 hours, anti-inflammatories and antibiotic.

Tidying up back at the car, it occurred to me I'd forgotten to include the most important medical intervention I could make on Samson's behalf. I wandered back through the stable and across the yard to the farmhouse. It was a beautiful home, worth a fortune no doubt. I knocked on the door and Samson's owner appeared. She had the phone to her ear and was obviously in the middle of telling a friend about that morning's events. Looking slightly embarrassed at what I'd overheard, she made her excuses and hung up so that we could talk.

'Hi,' I said. 'I just realised I forgot something.'

She raised a quizzical eyebrow, no doubt wondering what crucial medical detail this dunce of a vet had left out.

'Any chance you could get a lock fitted to the cupboard with the beet in it? Just, you know, it could save you a lot of money in the long term and they're only around fifteen quid? I don't want to do myself out of a job, but …' I trailed off as there wasn't much more to say. Sometimes it's too easy to focus on the medicine after the event. But, as the saying goes, prevention is better than cure.

*   *   *

I packed up and set off for the practice as morning consults were officially starting soon; a change of clothes and a shower would have to wait. It was about 0820 and I usually got to the practice around 0830. It was a good drive back to the surgery and I thought I'd ring and let them know I'd be late. I dialled the number for the surgery one-handed in between glances at the road (it was legal then, if bad practice). No sooner had I dialled out than I had an incoming call. I tried to answer it but was immediately cut off. No doubt some poor farmer in the corner of a field somewhere was trying to get through, signal one minute, none the next. I checked the signal bars on my Nokia phone; it wasn't me, I had full coverage.

I waited a minute or two, then rang the practice again. Incoming call! I tried answering it and was again cut off. No doubt they'd be as frustrated as me, trying to get the vet out first thing in the morning and receiving no answer. I pictured some farmer, hand in cow, trying to get hold of me for a calving.

I dialled out a third time. Whoever was trying to get through had some serious bad luck with timing. They were trying to get through again.

'Hello, hello, helllooooo?' I said as I placed the phone to my ear.

There was nothing but silence in reply.

I was starting to get annoyed. Here I was, desperately trying to get through to the practice to tell them I'm going to be late, and some idiot keeps ringing every five minutes. I began to mutter to myself in the car.

'Bloody idiot, how hard is it to walk up the hill and get proper reception?' I asked my Land Rover dashboard.

I stewed for a bit.

'I mean, really, you'd think by this stage you'd just walk back to the house and use the landline!' The dashboard, I felt, concurred.

I drove on for five minutes or so. Nothing. I decided to risk dialling out; maybe they were on their way to the land-line after all? I pressed the button with the green phone symbol on it. Another incoming call!

'Jesus! Who is this idiot ...'? I began. Then it hit me. The phones in the practice were diverted to my mobile overnight and hadn't yet been un-diverted. The moron who kept phoning me was ... me! After the success of Samson's treatment, I'd been on a bit of a high. I'd been bathing in endorphins on the return drive until some eejit phoned me. Turns out that eejit was me and I was having humble pie for breakfast!

9

CAT-ASTROPHE?

Sometimes, just sometimes, you have one of those days. One of those days when you can barely drag your exhausted body into bed. Because you done good, as they say.

Often, in veterinary medicine, animals that are suddenly ill or injured are either dead or going to recover well before they get to you. Your job is to clean up the mess or speed their recovery. However, now and again someone gets an animal to you quickly enough for your skills to save them when nothing else could.

Kitty was a young cat with a litter of new-born kittens when she was suddenly extremely unwell. She was having severe difficulty breathing and her owner rushed her straight in to see one of my colleagues. Jade could see that the situation was critical but could not immediately identify the problem. An examination of Kitty's upper, visible airway showed no obstruction. However, when listening to Kitty's chest, Jade could hear very little air movement. Kitty was suffocating, we just didn't know why and there wasn't long to find out; she was dying in front of us. Technically, she was in 'Respiratory Distress', which is extremely unpleasant. If you've ever been to extreme altitude, you may have experienced something similar. It's exhausting. Instead of breathing evenly, using your diaphragm with little effort, many other accessory muscles are used. Limbs will be pushed away from the body to allow maximal lung inflation; the neck is straightened to provide minimal resistance to air movement. The effort in breathing results in elevated body temperature and sweating. It's exhausting and eventually the effort becomes too much. The lack of oxygen means these compensatory processes are unsustainable, rapidly burning through the oxygen available. It's a vicious circle. Extreme effort to breath requires oxygen, which you don't have. Eventually, you die, exhausted.

This was going to be Kitty's fate if we couldn't identify and fix the problem, quickly.

Jade immediately rushed Kitty through and took a chest x-ray with the assistance of one of the nurses. Anaesthetic was not necessary or wise. Kitty could barely lift her head, let alone escape. She was immediately put on supplementary oxygen using a mask held near her face. It would help while the x-ray was developed. This was still in the days before digital radiography, which provides an image almost immediately. A few minutes were required to develop the radiograph. As soon as it was ready Jade stuck the film to an x-ray viewer – basically, a flat, white panel with a backlight that allows the x-ray image to be viewed clearly.

The problem was immediately apparent. Kitty had something stuck in her trachea, right down where it splits into the two main bronchi. She was dead unless the obstruction could be removed. Trouble is that thoracic surgery is fraught with difficulties. While the chest is open, the animal cannot breathe for itself. Kitty would need an 'artificial lung' or ventilator to forcibly inflate and deflate her lungs, keeping her alive. We didn't have one. She was a small cat, the same weight as a new-born baby; getting into her chest would be incredibly fiddly and the space available to operate through would be tiny. Then, there's the important stuff issue. The chest cavity is crammed with really, really important stuff.

Stuff you just can't do without, like the heart and lungs, the aorta (huge artery), vena cava (huge vein). None of these things react well to being poked or indeed stabbed with a clumsily wielded scalpel. What's more, any such stabbing would probably kill Kitty quicker than any surgeon could react to it; all in all, not a great situation. Essentially, such surgery is best carried out by a practice specialised and equipped for the operation.

Added to this was the kitten issue. In the entirely likely situation that Kitty didn't survive, her kittens might rapidly follow suit. They were a few days old. They could be hand reared, but that's often unsuccessful. No pressure then.

Jade had another problem. Specialised surgery was the answer, but the owner didn't have the money; and Kitty didn't have the time – she'd certainly die en route to it.

Jade did the only thing she could think to do. She got someone who she described as 'surgically braver' – at least that's the version of events she sold to me. I imagine what went through her head was 'some idiot who'll try anything because he doesn't know what he's getting in to'. Long story short, Kitty's surgery fell to me, and I didn't know what I was doing, certainly not in detail. There wasn't long to plan or discuss the options with the owner. I made the situation clear. Surgery or euthanasia. Euthanasia would involve us using drugs to deliberately end Kitty's life in a humane manner to avoid further suffering. I emphasised I wasn't an expert. I stressed likewise that I'd be 'giving it a go', and offered an optimistic 50/50 chance for Kitty. The owner readily agreed; I guess he hadn't a lot of choice.

While we got everything prepared, the unfortunate cat remained on oxygen; she couldn't cope without it. Meanwhile the nurses got everything ready. I couldn't help; I was busy reading a textbook, brushing up on the surgical anatomy and making sure I was as familiar with the operation as I could be, given that I'd never attempted it before. A big thank-you to Theresa Welch Fossum for writing and editing a book that veterinary medicine cannot do without. I took the textbook into surgery and laid it on an adjacent table, where I could ask one of the nurses to turn the pages if I needed to refer to it. In the meantime, the nurses had prepped Kitty.

It was time. I injected propofol through Kitty's drip line, inducing her anaesthesia. As soon as she was under, we shaved her chest wall. The plan was to approach through the side of her chest. After a surgical scrub, she was moved to theatre. With a last glance at the book, I was as ready as I could be. Gently, I incised through the cat's chest wall, between two ribs. I cut through the skin, muscle and, lastly, the pleura, the smooth membrane lining the chest. As soon as I did, Kitty lost her ability to breathe. From this point on, Poppy, one of the nurses, would have to manually breath for her, gently squeezing a bag about every five seconds or so until the operation was over. I enlarged my incision and used a tiny retractor (a device for pulling things apart) to hold Kitty's ribs in position, allowing me slightly more space to operate. Immediately I could see the heart and lungs. The heart was beating away, pumping blood through the aorta at high pressure, supplying the body with oxygenated blood. Simultaneously, the lungs were inflating and deflating in concert with Poppy's gentle artificial respiration.

Having examined the x-ray, I knew roughly where the object was. In the image it appeared to fill the inside of Kitty's trachea. I had imagined that I'd be able to easily identify its location, cut over it and remove it with some forceps (imagine giant tweezers). I couldn't, despite Poppy expertly timing her 'breaths' to facilitate my search. I fumbled around, gently feeling the trachea, but to no avail: I couldn't find the problem. I was starting to sweat. I had imagined this would be easy, though high risk. Now it was looking like I'd be forced to admit defeat and put Kitty to sleep on the table.

It would be preferable to waking her up and allowing her suffering to continue with inevitable results. I had a decision to make. There was no doubt people were watching; we didn't do this sort of thing every day. Probably six or so had stopped what they were doing to help or observe. That wasn't helping me though!

I decided it was all or nothing. Very carefully, I started to cut into Kitty's trachea. It wasn't simple. It's a flexible tube, and I couldn't grip it firmly without cutting off her oxygen supply, so I had to gently make repeat scalpel strokes over the same area until I got through the tissue. The trachea is also reinforced with cartilage rings, which stop it collapsing. Fortunately, these are not hugely thick in a cat, and I was able to get through after a few goes. I could now see into the tube where the obstruction was located. I could see ... nothing.

There was some foam and blood from my incision, but no obstruction. I sweated some more. We'd been at this for about an hour and a half. I was beginning to look foolish for even trying, or at least that's what was running through my adrenaline-addled brain. As she continued to breath for Kitty, Poppy had a brainwave.

'What if I tried moving the oesophageal?'

This was the oesophageal stethoscope that had been placed in Kitty. It was in the tube running from her mouth to her stomach, with the end positioned adjacent to the heart. The oesophagus is adjacent to the trachea at this point. It might just move things around a little, worth a try.

Poppy gently moved it up and down Kitty's oesophagus. Nothing ... then, suddenly, it was there! I grabbed the small stone with my forceps and threw it over my shoulder. Eureka! I couldn't help but let a huge grin break out on my face. Poppy was wearing a mask, but I could see she was grinning underneath it. I took 10 seconds to compose myself and then began the hard part; putting everything back together. The trachea was perhaps the most important part. I couldn't afford to make my sutures too big, or I'd narrow Kitty's airway, causing her permanent breathing difficulties. Equally, if I stitched it badly, it might reopen, filing her chest with air, and probably ending in her having to be put to sleep. I used tiny sutures and great care to close it up. Then I used larger sutures to pull her ribs into the normal position and take any strain off the tissue between Kitty's ribs. Finally, I stitched the pleura and muscle together, closing the chest cavity. At this point, Kitty still had a pneumothorax, air outside her lungs but in the chest cavity, collapsing her lungs. The next step was to push a needle through her chest wall and suck out this air, reinflating her lungs. As soon as this was done, Poppy stopped breathing for her. There were a few anxious seconds, then Kitty breathed. We were monitoring her oxygen saturation; it would probably drop if things were bad. I closed the skin with sutures. The anaesthetic was turned off, and we waited, monitoring all the while.

My clothes were damp from sweat and I would have given a month's wages for a pint. But alas, afternoon consults were about to start, and I had to leave Kitty in the capable hands of the nursing staff. I could take a mental breather knowing she would enjoy the best possible care. I quickly rang the owner and let him know; so far, so good.

It was hard to keep my mind in the moment as I dealt with the afternoon's caseload. All the while I was waiting for someone to burst through the door and tell me Kitty had crashed. It never happened. By the time I'd completed consults, Kitty was up and around, feeding her kittens. Cats are tough! She'd need antibiotics and some pain relief for a while, but unless her wound broke down or an infection developed, she was going to make it.

Another vet was on call that night, but I lived close by and couldn't help but pop in to check on Kitty later in the evening. She was a good mother and purred as soon as she was offered attention. I stroked her chin, sipped my tea and basked in the sense of deep satisfaction that comes from a hard job well done. I guess I'd forgotten that we'd only barely saved her.

We kept Kitty in for a day or so, her owner visiting daily. He was a nice chap and seemed genuinely impressed and grateful. When it came time for Kitty to go home, he came and picked her and the kittens up. I wasn't there. Having got them in the carrier and made his way to the front desk he surprised us …

'I'm not paying.'

'Oh.'

'I mean, not £600, that's ridiculous. I guess something like £150 would be reasonable?'

Moments like this can just spoil your day, and, if you let them, your life. Ultimately, the surgery Kitty had would have cost a couple of thousand pounds at any referral practice anywhere, minimum. But try explaining that to an owner who can't get their head around it. I'm sure whoever was there tried. It was a while ago and I can't remember whether he paid the full amount in the end; most likely not. It's hard not to feel unappreciated in those moments. However, I've chosen to look at it a different way. I got to perform a surgery I was barely competent to perform, Kitty lived, and I learned a lot. I'm proud that I managed it, proud the cat lived and confident I'd be able to perform a good deal better next time. That said, no practice can sustain many of such cases. Ultimately, it's a business, and if it doesn't at least break even, it ceases to exist. Who's saving Kitty then?

10

SKYWALKER

I have come to dislike the term Gold Standard Care (GSC). In theory, at least, it should have only good connotations. I mean, what kind of care would you rather have? Silver? Bronze? I think if I had to choose as I booked into a private hospital I'd probably opt for 'Gold' and worry about the credit card bill later. However, I think the impact GSC has had in general, everyday practice has been mixed. We should all strive for the very best medicine we can provide to our pets or clients. But what does that mean? I mean, really mean? The answer is obvious, you might say. But try expressing it in one succinct sentence. Not so easy, is it?

I'll give an example of what I consider to be GSC gone mad. I was working for a practice in a small seaside town. As a locum, I was relatively immune from the directives pushed downwards by the management staff, though I couldn't entirely ignore them. The practice couldn't meet their workload without me; I was a necessary evil. My job would only exist until a new, full-time vet was found. I was also experienced and not without my own ethos and methods of doing things. As a result, I was granted some latitude. Not so the other staff: they had targets to meet and were actively encouraged to sell whatever they could.

For a variety of reasons, I think sales targets are a big mistake in any medical profession. The minute someone thinks they're hearing a sales pitch; they aren't looking at a trusted medical advisor any more. They are looking at a salesperson. In my opinion, you've lost their trust. Once that happens, you're going to have a hell of a job winning it back. Every time you advise a procedure, drug or supplement they are going to wonder what it really is. Is it what their pet needs? Is it proven to be effective? Or is it another £50 a month for the practice for what is an elaborate placebo? I would urge any vet to really ask themselves what their motivation is in each case. Sometimes it's tough to be honest with yourself. Even just verbal praise from a senior person in the practice can easily skew someone's thinking. That praise can become addictive and suddenly you're actively working to increase those fees, knowing there's more flattery where that came from. You might not even know you're doing it. But the client will; they're not daft.

I'm a terrible salesman. I find it impossible to recommend something I don't really believe to be necessary or effective. I get uncomfortable, my mannerisms and language shift. Other humans are pretty effective in picking up on both your phraseology and what are now called 'non-verbal cues'. Your body will betray you. Your vocal tract might be saying, 'Trust me, this stuff is good,' but your body language is saying, 'I'm really uncomfortable, because I wouldn't buy it myself.' Now you're on the naughty step from an owner's point of view and you're going to have to work to get off it.

I was scheduled to do the consultations, so my job was to see a new client every 10 to 15 minutes and solve whatever medical conundrum they had chosen to bring to the practice that day. The other vet on duty was a bit younger and had trained overseas. She'd only recently moved to the UK. Despite having pretty good English, she was having a hard time. Drugs often have different names in different territories; vaccines may be licensed to cover different periods of time; local dialects and slang can be hard to decipher in a new area. I've worked in practices where the clientele of two local branches are remarkably different, requiring quite dissimilar approaches. It must have been much harder to adapt to an entirely new country. The other vet, Tina, would frequently ask for my advice. I enjoyed our clinical chats and tried to be the kind of mentor I would have liked to have had. I always listened and tried to give the impression that nothing was too much bother. I'd finished my consultations for the morning and made my way out back to help Tina with any operations still waiting to be performed. The routine stuff had been completed and she was left with one case that she was personally managing.

Skywalker was a large tom (i.e., male) cat. He was knocking on a bit at 10 years old, and a dental problem had been picked up at his last annual vaccination. One of his lower canines had some tartar and purulent (pus-like) material around its base. The gum tissue surrounding it was inflamed and the tooth itself was a little loose. The cat had shown no symptoms and the owner had been unaware that there was any problem. Skywalker was eating well; his weight was stable (he was a little bit chubby) and he was living a full life. Tina had booked the cat in for treatment after making the recommendation to his owner. The plan was to take blood for full biochemistry and haematology, get some urine for urinalysis, and put the cat on intravenous fluids. Then we'd x-ray his skull and mandible to assess his teeth; and x-ray his chest and abdomen to look for metastatic spread from potentially cancerous tissue near his tooth. The gum near his tooth would also be sampled and a portion sent to a pathologist for histology to identify any primary tumour. All in all, the owners, or rather their insurance company, were looking at an £800 to £1,000 bill.

If that sounds like a comprehensive plan, it is. So, we proceeded. Blood was taken with only the minimum of cat wrangling. It revealed that Skywalker's organs were present and correct, no problems there; his biochemistry and haematology were completely normal. Taking these parameters, pre-anaesthesia is undoubtedly best practice, especially in older cats. If any organ is not functioning optimally, then the effects of anaesthesia may worsen the situation. Renal impairment is extremely common in older cats and may be occult (i.e., hidden). An animal or human can lose about 75 per cent of kidney function without any clinical or biochemical change; that's why we can donate a kidney. With further loss of function, the filtration effect at the kidney is reduced and biochemical markers such as urea and creatinine will start to rise. Anaesthesia usually lowers blood pressure, reducing renal filtration even in a healthy animal. In one with early-stage renal impairment, it will experience a further drop in function. To preserve renal function certain drugs, such as anti-inflammatories, can be avoided. The animal can be given intravenous fluid therapy (IVFT), which helps maintain blood flow to the kidneys and other organs. This was the next indignity that Skywalker had to endure. He would have to tolerate an intravenous cannula being inserted into his cephalic vein (front-leg vein). He did it with a quiet dignity, choosing not to bite anyone for the moment. As it was, some deep growls and spitting conveyed his message, which by now I knew to be the feline equivalent of, 'Bastards, you're all bastards.'

With his organs all functioning and fluids already running for a while, Skywalker's cannula allowed the injection of an anaesthetic induction agent and he slipped off to sleep. Once he was under and stable, we examined his mouth in detail. I had a good look. He had a bad tooth, no question. The gum was slightly erythematous (red) and a little swollen, but essentially normal. The gums are technically called the gingiva and inflammation of them is known as gingivitis. There was thin, watery pus emerging from between the swollen gum and his tooth. In my opinion this probably indicated a tooth root abscess oozing away at the base of his canine. From my point of view, we had a 99 per cent diagnosis and the best thing to do was remove the tooth; not an easy job in a cat.

Cats' teeth have long roots, longer than the visible part of the tooth, and they are embedded in a socket within the bone of the skull or mandible. They can't simply be pulled out. Coupled to that, their jaws are fragile compared to the force needed to remove a tooth. The tools used to perform dentistry have changed only a little from medieval times. 'Dental Elevator' sounds like it might be some complex instrument designed to achieve an extraction with only the minimum of trauma. In reality, it looks much like a screwdriver. The practitioner removing any tooth must exercise care. That may sound like an obvious statement, but there is a dichotomy here. Canine and feline teeth are strong and well attached to the adjacent bone. A fair bit of force is required to make progress. It is all too easy to slip and cause unnecessary trauma, and there are plenty of horror stories. Given the infection present at the base of the tooth, the surrounding bone may not be healthy. In severe cases the infection may have spread, causing osteomyelitis, an infection of the bone that can significantly weaken it. Many a vet has broken a cat's jaw by accident.

However, any extractions were in the future. Tina wanted to x-ray Skywalker's skull and mandible. Ideally, he'd have dental x-rays, but we lacked the specialist kit. Personally, I wouldn't have taken the x-rays, but it was arguably 'best practice' as we could confirm the problem and potentially spot any other issues not picked up by the dental examination. The x-ray of the skull was unremarkable. That of the mandible showed a loss of density, known as a lucency, around the root of the dodgy canine. The surrounding bone looked normal and did not have the 'moth eaten' irregular pattern associated with osteosarcoma, which is a type of bone tumour. The lucency was very focal, so a spreading, severe osteomyelitis was also unlikely. Time to remove the tooth. The gum and bone were normal; the issue was a bad tooth, not cancer.

However, Tina wasn't done yet. She wanted to sample the gum. I was resistant; the gum looked inflamed but normal. It wasn't cancerous. Of course, I could not be 100 per cent sure, as cancer in the beginning is a single aberrant cell, but I'd have put a month's wages on it. I took a deep breath and guided Tina through taking a sample of the gum tissue. The cat could spare it and it would confirm what we knew already. The results would take a few days, so any information would be of no help to us now. Okay, tooth time ...

Nope, Tina also wanted to take x-rays of the chest and abdomen in case any cancer had spread. Now, okay, cancer does commonly metastasise to the lungs, liver and spleen. Imaginary cancer does not. Also, whilst many tumours do spread to those sites, others metastasise elsewhere first, such as in local lymph nodes or adjacent tissue. Depending on what you're looking for, you might look in different places. Since the cat didn't have oral cancer, it was all moot. However, Tina wanted to proceed, it was her case, and I didn't want to be overbearing. So, we took the x-rays of the chest and abdomen. They were normal. Of course, rather inconveniently, that doesn't rule out metastasis. Remember I said cancer can start out as a single aberrant cell? Same goes for its spread. Procedures all done; we'd have to send the sample of gum off to get the pathologist's opinion. The results for that would take a few days.

So ... finally we'd get that tooth out.

I was wrong. Tina was on the phone talking to the owner. I could overhear her, but I didn't want to interrupt. She was explaining the situation to the owner and emphasising the risk of removing the cat's tooth. By the time she hung up it was obvious the tooth wouldn't be coming out. I was really struggling by this stage. From my perspective the whole thing could be summed up as follows.

An older cat comes in for vaccination. As far as the owner is concerned he is well. He *is*, in fact, well. Okay, he has a slightly dodgy tooth that requires removal. A cursory examination told us that. Admittedly, it's a bad idea to go firm on a diagnosis without a good exam of the oral cavity and that, in any cat, means an anaesthetic or at least a deep sedation. The pre-anaesthetic tests were justified, but I would have been willing to proceed without them. The fluids? Yeah, even if I'd skipped the blood tests, I would have given him the fluids. The x-rays of the jaw were a nice touch, confirming our diagnosis via a different modality. Once Skywalker was under, I'd have examined his whole mouth thoroughly, then I'd have removed his tooth surgically and left it at that.

I'll be honest, I felt an excess of tests had been done. So many tests and precautions against misdiagnosis or complication, and yet, despite a firm, actual diagnosis, no treatment. To not remove the tooth? Crazy. However, it's completely consistent with defensive medicine: the practice of anticipating likely errors or complaints, and guarding against them. This is where a practitioner carries out, or avoids, a procedure or drug; not to help the patient, but to avoid an accusation of malpractice if a problem occurs. I was glad none of my elderly relatives were using the practice. I could only imagine what they'd end up paying in unnecessary bills.

Eventually, any clinician must make a decision based on the evidence at hand. You always want more, of course you do, it's perfectly natural. But in the real world you will always have to make decisions based on imperfect data. Buying a house? Are you going to have it taken apart brick by brick and inspected? If you don't the survey might miss something. Buying a horse? Perhaps you could have it cut into thin slices, checked by the world's leading equine specialist and then reassembled, presumably by the same specialist.

The problem with GSC is that it's open-ended. The more money you've got, the more tests and precautions you can afford. Your vet can just keep adding more and more until all resources are expended. When is a precaution reasonable and when is it excessive? There is no definitive answer to that. Even if you perform a test, occasionally a laboratory will make a mistake. It's not common, but it happens. Do you take two samples and send them to separate labs? What if they disagree? Best of three? Diagnosis is nothing more than the performance of a series of tests in order to prove or disapprove a theory. The same as any scientific theorem, our diagnosis is subject to revision as new evidence is presented.

If you visit your GP for a cut on your leg you got falling over, they are unlikely to book you in for a whole-body scan. Maybe a brain tumour affected your balance, causing you to trip and cut your leg? It's possible, but not likely given your presentation. That's how it works. You establish a working theory, in some cases after your initial tests because clinical signs are not always enough to give you a best guess. As you eliminate possibilities, you refine your tests more and more until you reach an answer with sufficient certainty to say you have a diagnosis. Then you act on that diagnosis. Otherwise, what value are you adding?

For each patient-and-owner combination, GSC means different things. It's not just about their financial where-withal. It might be they have all the money in the world, but the answer is to take the animal home and monitor it for a day or two. It may be that they are penniless but need thousands of pounds' worth of treatment they cannot afford. Then, it's the vet's job to figure out what can be done within budget. I think this is more challenging for any practitioner.

Another aspect of the GSC mantra that irks me is the attitude adopted by some of those who would seek to practise it. In certain instances, I've heard colleagues admit that if a client balks at the cost of GSC treatment, it might be suggested to them that: 'This practice engages in Gold Standard Care; there are other practices in the area that do not. Perhaps you'd be more comfortable taking Barney there?'

Times have changed; local vets were, and are, quite good at quiet wealth redistribution. The insured pets and the folk for whom money is no object are those who largely make the business work. The reality is that there are some other people at the opposite end of the scale. Treatment of their animals is often not profitable for any practice. I've had more than one older client who would come in as much for a chat as anything else. You can't run a business on them. But you can give them the time of day. I see that as part of any local vet's duty to the community. If one practice decides it wants all the Range Rover driving, insured-to-the-hilt Labrador owners, that's fine as long as they'll put up with the mad little old ladies as well. When they start turning them away because they're not profitable? Now you've annoyed me. Veterinary medicine has always been about more than profit, though it must be profitable. If every small practice has its fair share of the good ones, then we can work together to provide a good service all round. When we start cornering only the good ones, who is going to provide for the marginal cases? The charities cannot do it all and some people still value the personal service of their local vet.

I'd like to introduce the term 'Copper Standard' into the veterinary lexicon. The first few pennies, or coppers, that we spend on the care of our animals should be the most effective. The Pareto principle, in this context, postulates that 80 per cent of the effect comes from 20 per cent of the interventions. For example, cat's that have suffered a blockage of their urethra are true emergency cases; they are also in severe pain. Without rapid intervention their bladder may rupture as it fills with urine they cannot pass. The back pressure on their kidneys means filtration ceases and the accumulation of toxins and electrolytes results in all manner of derangements and ultimately death. The GSC approach described in seminars recommends a battery of tests, fluid therapy, urethral catheterisation, hospitalisation for multiple days and regular monitoring of renal function. A tube attached to their urethral catheter allows for the monitoring of urine output. Despite all this, some cats are still euthanised, as their urethra constantly re-blocks and a life spent being poked, prodded, drained and manhandled is not a life to speak of. I've nursed these cats in hospital and their owners are often left with a huge bill, occasionally accompanied by a deceased pet.

In recent years I've increasingly worked for practices that no longer provide 24-hour cover in house. Instead, patients and phones are transferred to an emergency service overnight. I occasionally work in these services myself. Out-of-hours (OOH) cover has become very expensive; many clients cannot afford it. Patients must also be shuttled between regular and OOH services. Stress itself is a factor in cats getting urethral blockages; the catheter, a foreign object sitting in their urethra, causes inflammation and predisposes to infection. Reading a 2020 review of recent research, one thing is clear: there's a lot we don't know. Increasingly, I'm faced with clients who simply cannot afford the gold standard approach. Truthfully, we vets aren't 100 per cent sure what that is in any case.

Rather than putting these cats to sleep, I have had a lot of success by sedating or anaesthetising the cat, draining their bladder, passing a urinary catheter, flushing their bladder out thoroughly and administering a cheap steroid. A muscle relaxant, dantrolene, is given in tablet form and ongoing fluids administered via subcutaneous injection and adding water to food. If there is evidence of infection, I add an antibiotic. Then they go home and are managed as an outpatient. According to the available literature, a similar regime is less effective than the traditional, interventionist one, 30 per cent recurrence vs 10 per cent. However, I can offer the outpatient regime for hundreds instead of thousands of pounds; I can offer it to more people and patients. I can also offer it more than once, still at a fraction of the cost. For each condition we should seek to identify the key 20 per cent of interventions and these are the ones we vets should strive to make as accessible as possible.

For conditions like arthritis, there are now a plethora of available treatments. I'd like to see us as a profession look at cost effectiveness. We could rate the severity of an animal's disease from nought to five. In terms of lameness, a normal dog scores nought, a dog that is just perceptibly lame scores one, and a dog that cannot walk scores five. We'd have to adapt the scale for each disease process. Then, we could rate a drug or intervention's efficacy, or how well it works, according to how many units of improvement it provides. If we know its cost as a monthly average, we could then express its effectiveness as pounds (or pennies) per unit of improvement. A very cost-effective drug or intervention would be £5/unit/month and a less effective one £20/unit/month. In the case of arthritic patients, we now have an almost mind-boggling array of potential treatments available to us. Just to list a few, we have pentosan sulphate injections, nutraceuticals like glucosamine and chondroitin, omega oils, green-lipped muscle extract, physiotherapy, hydrotherapy, intra-articular injections, regenerative techniques, monoclonal antibodies, arthrotomy, joint replacement, and even amputation. I used to routinely recommend glucosamine and chondroitin, but it seems the evidence for their use is weak at best and I no longer do so.

I haven't mentioned two key interventions, the ones I think are most cost effective. Weight optimisation and non-steroidal anti-inflammatory drugs (NSAIDs), like meloxicam. One is nearly free, maybe even money saving in some circumstances; the other is relatively cheap compared to many others. There are notable exceptions, but if your dog is stiff, overweight and only receiving glucosamine and chondroitin, I'd have to recommend a change in strategy.

There are other factors such as side effects, intolerances, lack of response and so on. Surgeries might be very effective but have a high upfront cost. However, if we had this information about cost effectiveness available, vets could ensure that we are spending our clients' money wisely. It would ensure funds are not squandered on expensive drugs that are no more effective than a cheaper alternative. It would even inform GSC, ensuring money is not wasted on ineffective therapies. The reverse is also true. Gold Standard Care drives research forward, new treatments may be more effective, and their cost usually drops with time. As the equation shifts, new treatments may migrate up the affordability/ effectiveness hierarchy. The important thing is that clients and patients with limited resources would get the most bang for their buck. I think we could call this the Copper Standard, though for some the information might feel like gold dust.

Gold Standard Care? Well, if we take a holistic approach to achieve optimal care, I'm sold. If you're just talking in abstract, clinical terms, you've lost me I'm afraid.

11

PIP, THUMPER AND LULA

First, two words of advice for pet owners: Get Insurance.

The very best care, well, it's very, very expensive. A fair percentage of clients cannot afford it even with insurance. Medicine that is 80 per cent effective may cost £100. You might reasonably suppose that medicine that is 90 per cent effective might cost £112.50 (90 per cent being 12.5 per cent more than 80 per cent). But you'd be wrong; the law of diminishing returns means that it's much more likely it'll cost £1,000. Ninety-five per cent effectiveness? I hope you brought a wheelbarrow full of cash. When I first graduated, pet insurance was either in its infancy, or a twinkle in its father's eye. Since then, it has changed the face of veterinary practice in a very significant fashion. Like any other science, veterinary medicine is driven forward by research and experimentation. Such things cost money. There is no incentive for commercial companies to develop drugs or equipment that they cannot sell.

The pace of improvement in veterinary medicine, much like in other fields of medicine and technology, has accelerated in recent years. New diseases have been discovered. Some didn't exist before and have recently emerged. Others were always present but had gone unidentified and untreated. When I was at vet school a new drug called trilostane was on trial. This was developed for the treatment of Cushing's disease or hyperadrenocorticism, the overproduction of a naturally occurring hormone, cortisol. High levels of cortisol in the blood have a myriad of effects, including changes to skin and hair coat, polydipsia (increased drinking), polyuria (increased urination), hyperglycaemia, skin thinning, fat redistribution, weight gain, liver pathology and immunosuppression. It was treated at the time with Lysodren, also known as o,p'-DDD, a derivative of the pesticide DDT, and fairly nasty stuff. Trilostane turned out to be effective in treating the two different variants of hyperadrenocorticism with fewer side effects. It's now the mainstay for treating Cushing's disease in the veterinary world. However, it isn't cheap; shopping around, you might be able to supply your medium-sized dog with it for about £50 a month.

The problem with veterinary medicine is that pets are worth – prepare for a shock – what we think they are.

I've been confronted with both extremes. I've been faced with the reality of having to consider putting an animal to sleep over the price of a night in a cheap hotel and two beers. There were some extenuating circumstances. Nonetheless, to me £70 seems paltry. It isn't, though, if you're a single parent struggling to make ends meet and when it isn't likely to be the end of the matter.

The chap that brought Pip in was a genuinely lovely guy. His intentions were utterly laudable. One of his work colleagues had bought Pip, a Border Collie puppy a few weeks ago. Unfortunately, Pip had become severely ill. Being a practical man, his colleague had resigned himself to putting the dog out of its misery with a shovel. I can only hope he was supremely skilled in such matters. However, this fellow had intervened, bought the dog for £30 and was now placing him in my tender care.

The problem was anaemia, the lack of red blood cells. Blood is what makes your mucous membranes pink. Your lips, tongue and conjunctiva are pink because bits of them are red. Bits of them are red because they contain blood and blood is red; blood is red because erythrocytes, red blood cells, are red. They are red because haemoglobin is red, and they contain that in order to transfer oxygen around your body and allow you to remain conscious throughout this mind-numbingly boring explanation regarding redness.

This dog's mucous membranes were not pink. They were white; not white-ish, magnolia or off-white.

WHITE! The same way a sheet of A4 paper is white.

He was severely anaemic. In fact, I suspect that he had but one red blood cell flying around his body at only just sub-light speed trying to keep things going. He also gently wagged his tail when he got some affection. I was working in a rural practice in Ireland at the time. I had limited equipment, but I drew an extremely small amount of blood and ascertained that his PCV (packed cell volume – a measure of what percentage of circulating blood is red blood cells; normally 35–45 per cent or so) was 4 per cent … theoretically impossible; certainly, impossible in acute, rapid blood loss.

There are numerous reasons why a dog might be anaemic, but they fit in three broad categories. Maybe they are not making enough to begin with; perhaps red blood cells are being destroyed in circulation somewhere, or possibly red bloods cells are leaking out of circulation (bleeding). Pip was not going to survive very long without a blood transfusion. There are now pet blood banks, but one unit of whole blood is around £400. Geography and cost ruled out that option. However, one of the nurses had a large and cooperative dog who would do anything for a ham sandwich. You can transfuse any dog to any dog, once, without risking too high a chance of a transfusion reaction. So that just left the kit to perform the procedure. This was not highly specialised, but the practice charged £70 for a transfusion to cover its cost and disposal. In medical terms, cheap.

However, it was beyond the resources of our otherwise heroic animal welfare enthusiast. He'd paid £30 for the dog and that was it. Added to that, £70 was hardly the ceiling of expected costs. That was just to give Pip a few red blood cells to keep the other one company. We'd next have to figure out why he was so anaemic in the first place and then do something about it. I was genuinely tempted to offer to pay for it myself, but that way madness lies. Before long you're living in a tent surrounded by anaemic dogs and working just to pay for dog treats and poo-bags.

So, reluctantly and with a heavy heart, I drew up the necessary lethal injection. The chap was entirely in agreement, but seriously tearful. While he retired to the waiting room, one of the nurses gave me a hand. She gently restrained Pip, though he hadn't really the energy to fight. She would apply a light pressure to the blood vessels near his elbow, making it easier for me to see the ones nearer his paw. I would insert my needle into one of them, then depress the syringe plunger with my thumb, taking my anaemic patient's life. We carried on and, like many dogs, he had only a quizzical look on his face as he allowed me to advance a needle into his vein without protest. I gave him a little rub on the head, saying, 'I'm sorry mate.' He responded with a cute, mischievous look and even wagged his tail. Then I pushed the plunger and he gently fell asleep ...

Or rather, he didn't. He just looked at me; he wasn't even sleepy. I hadn't given him a huge dose, but he was a seven-kilogram anaemic puppy. A stiff breeze should have finished him off. I'd definitely hit the vein. There was no swelling at the site of the injection, a sign that I'd missed. The lethal injection stung like hell if incorrectly injected; he'd have let me know. We waited a bit, fussing over him.

Then I incredulously drew up twice that amount and tried again ...

It took a third dose and a total of 30 millilitres to render him unconscious and slow, then stop, his breathing. Then a minute or so for his little heart to fibrillate and stop. My veterinary colleagues, will, I hope, agree that that is rather a lot for a small dog in his condition. After the second dose I did wonder if I was, in fact, doing the right thing. Maybe he was some new type of uber-hound with genes from the planet Krypton. But I continued, because, well, that was the plan, the equation hadn't changed, and I had a waiting room full of people to see after dispatching him.

On the other hand, I was once presented with a rabbit. It was ill, really ill. Like, practically dead. Rabbits, no matter how they initially become ill, often then have issues with their guts. Compared to us their intestines form a much larger percentage of their mass and any disturbance is serious. Thumper was moribund, he was laid flat out on his side, practically immobile and unresponsive. He was extremely hypothermic, probably part of the problem and common in sick rabbits. His abdomen felt as if someone had opened him up, inserted a scrunched-up piece of cardboard, then sewed him up again. His gut should have felt soft and pliable. His chances of survival were minuscule, and then only with aggressive, expensive therapy.

I explained that he'd need intravenous fluids, warming, gut stimulants, pain relief and intensive nursing. All of that before we could really try to work out what was wrong in the first place. Any delay in treatment was a death sentence. I had outlined the treatment programme and come up with a rough idea of what it might cost ... £300 to £500. Too much; he was, after all, a rabbit.

'Treatment is going to cost £300 to £500; he is severely ill and I think it's unlikely he will survive the hour, let alone the night. The other option is that we put him to sleep ...'

The look on my face, I hoped, conveyed my firm belief that putting him to sleep was the only sensible option.

'Okay, I want you to do everything you can.'

'I see. Well, I think it's for the best, poor little ... I'm sorry? What?'

'I'd like you to do what you said: drip, warming, thing-ey-me-what-not, etc.,' said one of the owners.

Thinking that I couldn't possibly have explained properly, I reiterated treatment plans and costs.

'So, as you can see ... (thinking – death) ...'

'Yes, exactly, do everything.'

'What now? He's a rabbit ...'

'Exactly, we'll have to hurry to save him.'

'Eh?'

I'd never encountered anyone willing to consider paying that much to treat an almost certainly mortally ill rabbit. The inevitability of putting him to sleep was obvious ... to me.

So, we treated him, fruitlessly, or so I thought. Unbelievably, in the hours of the morning I came into the exotic (rabbits are 'exotic' to many vets of my generation) ward and Thumper was hopping around and nibbling on some hay. I had to marvel at both the rabbit's will to live and my own, clearly exceptional skills. The nurse, Madelaine, came down and I informed her of my excellence. She rolled her eyes and let me have my moment. A short victory dance ensued. I'd gone from would-be assassin to rabbit-saviour in only a few short hours.

I took the time to make a coffee and bask in the glory of my newfound rabbit-saving-ness. I then phoned the owner with a status update, feeling quite smug. As I finished my preamble and got on to just how marvellous I was and how miraculous her bunny's recovery was, Madelaine appeared from the exotic ward urgently shaking her head and waving her arms. Once she'd caught my eye, she made the universal sign for all things associated with death. She drew her index finger across her neck as if trying to sever her head from her body. The bunny had died suddenly. I wound up the call quickly, but left things at 'amazing recovery'.

I needed to check for myself. I don't know why; Madelaine wasn't prone to practical jokes of this nature. Once I had conducted a thoroughly unnecessary and detailed examination of the rabbit and concluded that it was, indeed, kaput, I had a dilemma. How long should I wait prior to phoning the owner? To do it now would make me look foolish, to say the least. But there was hardly much point in denying reality for long. Not unless I planned on trying to source another, similarly coloured rabbit once the pet shops opened …

No, I would have to confess. I gave it a few minutes, phoned back and revealed Thumper's untimely demise. I expressed my great surprise both at the rabbit's recovery and at his sudden death. The owner was extremely understanding and thanked me for my help. I couldn't fault her given the hour and the emotional rollercoaster she must have been through. The next day she came in, paid her bill without complaint, thanked me, and then paid another couple of hundred pounds to have Thumper privately cremated and his ashes returned to her for scattering.

I was once nursing a Staffordshire bull terrier or 'Staffy' called Lula; she had developed peritonitis after abdominal surgery. Peritonitis refers to inflammation within the abdominal cavity. Not in the intestines, but within the cavity that contains them. The peritoneal or abdominal cavity; the 'belly', if you will.

The abdominal cavity is a sealed chamber and if antibiotics are insufficient to kill off the infection, fluid often fills the cavity, spreading the bacteria responsible and inhibiting any treatment's effectiveness. We have learned that treating these cases 'open' using a drain is preferable in some instances. It allows the drainage of infected fluid and the insertion of antibiotics and flush. However, the body produces something called fibrin in peritonitis and attempts to wall off and isolate the source of infection. In doing so it uses large amounts of protein. This must be replaced if levels drop too low. Lula was having hers topped up with units of plasma from a pet blood bank. She was fortunate that her owner could afford it. I called the owner to update him on cost for the umpteenth time in a few days. We try to keep people informed of costs. Better they faint several times daily than have a massive stroke just the once. I passed on how the dog was (fair to middling), what we were doing for her, and what costs we had and were likely to incur. He was extremely unhappy.

'Stop phoning me. I don't care. My wife and I have no children, Lula is my child. I don't care what it costs, I don't care what you've spent, and I don't care what you're going to spend. Save that dog!'

I thanked him for his time and quietly added the cost of my fancy coffee to his bill …

Perhaps not, but I did receive an object lesson. I thought that the costs were escalating to an alarming degree, now just into five figures. The prognosis, the likely outcome, was guarded; there was no guarantee that the dog would survive. To my mind we were very much at the point where euthanasia had to be considered, but I didn't have this chap's means. I was after all a lowly vet. The equation was simply different for him. We continued to treat Lula and, ultimately, she did survive. We were lucky, she was a model patient. Staffies are notoriously tough, though often fantastic with people. She must have been in considerable pain despite the drugs, but she stoically put up with countless injections, being manhandled, having her abdominal dressing changed, being woken up at all sorts of times for monitoring and treatment. Yet, she would almost invariably wag her tail if you whispered her name. She'd even roll over so that her poorly belly could receive an extremely careful rub, bringing a smile to even the most hardened and exhausted of night staff's faces. I sometimes wondered who was comforting whom; she was a joy to treat in many ways. Had she been a large, aggressive German Shepherd, we simply could not have performed the same clinical interventions; practical constraints would have rendered treatment impossible.

I don't know if any of this surprises you, but some of it surprised me at the time. Our pets are worth what we feel they are worth, monetarily speaking. Their value is not in the material, but the intangible. The joy we have in their companionship; the love they display towards us and our children; the comfort they can offer when seemingly no one else gets it; the hope they give us when they pull through the impossible, survive the improbable or endure the seemingly unendurable. Several charities have begun bringing particularly well-mannered dogs into hospitals to visit patients. This has real value. The unconditional love that animals display and their joy in human company is truly uplifting. The psychological aspects of healing are not yet entirely understood, but I'd be surprised if a visit from a Labrador with the waggiest of tails didn't improve your odds. Of course, the Labrador would have to be fully vaccinated and preferably insured.

What we can do in veterinary medicine has come on leaps and bounds. MRI scans, joint replacements, spinal surgery, shunt closure, heart and brain surgery. Novel medications, blood transfusions, even prosthetic limbs in large animals. The scope of possibility in veterinary medicine has changed apace. However, this all costs money in research, materials, time and education. I've heard people long for the old days, when vets 'just knew what was wrong' or 'you could get all you needed for £50'. These thoughts are an illusion. Going back in time, treatments were more limited, misdiagnosis was more common, diseases were unrecognised or untreatable. None of this reflects badly on the vets of the time. We just know more now, because we have stood on their shoulders, pushing our horizon ever further away. Our successors will look back on us in the same way, marvelling that we could ever have known so little.

Many years ago you probably could get all you need for £50. You would have explored the outer boundaries of our medical knowledge, particularly in rabbits. All possibilities explored, you could opt to put an animal to sleep knowing that you had tried everything. Not so now. So much more can be done. If you want to be able to offer that to your beloved pet on the worst of days, get insurance, get good insurance; you won't regret it. There are alternatives. You could save up some money every month against the day a big vet bill arrives, but few of us have the discipline to stick to such self-control. Added to that is the problem of an early illness, before you have accumulated sufficient funds. You could get a credit card, which you leave with a zero balance against the day you must hand it over to settle Fido's surgery bill. But again, will you have the discipline?

The cat that's currently staring at me is the most expensive, most useless moggy I've ever come across. He's allergic to human skin. He's had two knee surgeries and requires high-dose steroids constantly in order to stop him from itching himself bloody. He once ruptured his own cornea and we had to refer him to an eye specialist for surgery. He arrived as a stray and my then-girlfriend and now-wife took pity on him. He was free initially, but today he has a street value of about £12,000. They say time is money, but actually it's the reverse. Money is time, that's what it buys. You may think you paid for a car, but you didn't. You paid for people to mine copper and produce steel, and the engineering skills to turn those into a vehicle. You've paid thousands of people for work you'll never see them do. In a veterinary context this means drug development, learning complex techniques that take years to perfect, and purchasing everything from lasers to textbooks. My pets are insured. Sure, I treat them myself, but when I reach the limit of my expertise, I want to be able to hire a specialist. Without insurance, I wouldn't have the money.

When you are shopping around for that insurance, read the small print. There are different types of insurance schemes. Some are limited by the total they will pay out in any one year. For example, they might stop paying at £1,000. Some are similarly limited, but by disease. They may pay out £1,000 per condition per year. Clearly, if these two different schemes are charging you the same, the second is the better deal. Providers may well also limit your cover by time. For example, they may stop covering any given disease after a year, clearly undesirable if your pet has developed a chronic disease such as diabetes. Something that is inevitable is that any provider may decide to revise their fees at renewal time. That revision is unlikely to be in a downwards direction. Any hike in premiums is likely to be increased if you have claimed a large amount in the last financial year. I've listened to many clients complain about their insurance provider. It's easy to forget that they are ultimately profit-making enterprises. The hope is that over the lifetime of the policy you will pay in more than you claim. This will not be the case for all clients, but all told, their customers will pay in more than they claim; otherwise, the company won't be around for long.

Get the best and most expensive policy you can afford. You generally get what you pay for.

Insurance has both simplified and complicated a vet's decision making. The money is there, but spending the money wisely is another matter. I saw an animal once that, in my eyes, was killed by its vet, yet you'd have struggled to accuse her of negligence. The animal had been involved in a car accident and it arrived at the emergency vet for treatment. As a rule, first-line emergency vets don't do orthopaedic surgery; the repair of bones is very rarely imperative in the first few hours of treatment. Instead, resuscitation, pain relief, stabilisation, damage control and infection control are the priorities. Then the animal may be sent to where its injuries are more definitively treated. In this instance the dog had a badly broken hind limb that would require advanced techniques to mend.

We worked on a basis that we received 10 per cent of our gross earnings as a bonus, and this could have applied some extra, subtle nudging towards generating larger bills. I found that it had the opposite effect for me. It made me feel that I had to be able to defend every penny of bill I generated for fear of someone accusing me of money being my prime motivator. In the case of our accident victim, the vet took extremely good care of the animal; by morning she had spent about £1,500. The animal was insured up to £3,000. Once we were able to contact the orthopaedic specialists, they simply could not perform the operation for £1,500. They were prepared to knock some off, but not that much. The operation would cost at least £2,500, probably more like £3,000.

Ultimately, the dog was put to sleep as the owners couldn't cover the gap in finances and did not want amputation. Now, that happens sometimes, and maybe no one is to blame. On examining the procedures conducted the night before, I had some questions. Lots of monitoring tests had been performed. Fine, as long as they are relevant. But why measure a dog's electrolytes every hour or so? Thoroughness? Well, perhaps for some diseases like Addisonian crisis (a hormonal deficiency that deranges electrolytes), but in a trauma patient they are not very relevant after the initial screening test and not even then if you're on a tight budget. I think it would be fair to say that I thought the bill had been padded. I brought it up under the guise of general inquisitiveness and was not satisfied with the answers. To me, 'I was just being thorough, it's insured', isn't good enough.

Our job as veterinary practitioners is to get as much appropriate healthcare as possible for our patients with the funds available to us. That includes insurance money. Insurance does alter our behaviour, we're only human. In those borderline cases when you're wondering whether to run routine bloods or not, it's easier for both you and the client to say yes if a third party is paying; it just is. If spending on one thing now means denying a more important intervention later, then it's our job to consider what is the greater need and advise our patient's carer accordingly. What's more, unnecessary procedures will inevitably bump everyone's premiums up in the long run; then we risk dealing with more uninsured animals. So, a balance must be struck. These days I always stress that the owner or farmer and myself are a healthcare team, working together to get the most for the patient.

There is another point to be made. It's one of ethics. The resources and ability to do something do not mean it should be done. This is a hard one. The owner wants it, the animal would perhaps benefit in some respects, but a vet may have to advise against it. Sometimes the right thing to do is to say no to more and accept that the end of the road has been reached. I've refused to put an animal through more in the past. Not because it was beyond my skill, but because it was no longer best for the animal. Sometimes, this takes considerable self-control on the part of the vet. If they own the practice, they may stand to make several hundred or even thousands of pounds. They're not even going to have to ask for the money; it's the insurance companies' problem. Fortunately, I've never owned a practice and never had to test my self-control in this way. A bit of financial security for the family? Or doing the right thing? Especially when the decision is right on the line. Who might not be nudged, just a little, towards the money?

We have to balance what, if any, overall benefit there is to the animal against the pain and recovery that it must go through. Then weigh that against the animal's likely remaining life span and make a judgement call. A procedure and the necessary recovery time are key decision makers. A painful operation with a four-month recovery time is one thing in a two-year-old dog with a decade to live. The same operation in an eleven-year-old with a year to live is quite different. Suddenly the operation and recovery represent a third of their remaining life. This example is oversimplified. No one can say exactly how long the remaining life span is, only guess. Thus, your vet must advise you based on their SWAG, short for Scientific Wild Arse Guess. Wrong or right, they are almost certainly doing their best. As an owner, it may be hard to hear some of what your vet has to say. It may be upsetting, initiating emotions of guilt or anger. It's easy to forget that the vet will be enjoying the conversation no more than you. They will no doubt be choosing their words carefully, but miscommunication is only a syllable, a raised eyebrow or intonation away.

The important thing is that both parties maintain the correct focus, which is the welfare of the patient. That is much, much easier if we have some insurance money to play with.

12

PRINCE

One of the receptionists approached me to apologise. Mrs Pretentiös had phoned and made an appointment for later today. She would be accompanying her friend and her friend's Miniature Dachshund, Prince. Mrs P was a self-declared 'lovely person'. She was also a healer and a white witch. She had been very explicit on the phone: she did not want to see a male vet, and she definitely didn't want to see me. I try not to take this kind of thing personally. If a woman would prefer not to see a male vet, I have to wonder why. Perhaps a man would remind her of an abusive ex-partner, or a son lost to an accident? Maybe the case involves lady-bits and it's all a bit embarrassing. I'll always politely offer to see clients if I can spare them a wait. If they reject the offer, that's fine, I just let it go; it's none of my business.

However, in Mrs P's case she had proven herself to be such a pain in the arse that no other vet of any sex was prepared to see her. I have a firm policy on seeing clients: I see them. I'm Scottish; even if you walk through the door dressed as Edward Longshanks, Hammer of the Scots, holding a voodoo doll of Mel Gibson's Braveheart with some miniature arrows and a longsword sticking out of it, I'll see you. I don't have to like you to be your vet, though it helps. And so, Mrs P would be mine to deal with this evening.

Mrs P was an avowed activist and quite the bohemian and artist, evidenced by the purple beret she sported everywhere. We had fallen out previously after I treated her cat. She had initially brought in the long-suffering Berty because he'd lost a lot of weight and was eating loads. A quick examination led me to believe that Berty was probably suffering from an overactive thyroid: hyperthyroidism. I recommended some lab tests and that is what caused the initial falling out. We were profiteers, parasites in fact, according to my client. Our practice offered some care through the RSPCA or PDSA. We were permitted to offer some subsidised or free care via their schemes. The truth was that both were a financial drain on the practice, but the owner continued to offer them because it was a rural area, clients were also members of the local community, and we ran a service as well as a business. After some phone calls and form filling, we were able to offer subsidised care. Tests confirmed that Berty was indeed hyperthyroid, but otherwise okay. Fortunately, tablets could address the issue, though they would be lifelong. I dispatched Mrs P with a request to re-examine Berty in ten to fourteen days.

A few days later, Mrs P lodged a complaint. Why, she asked, did she have to give tablets twice daily? She had been on the World Wide Web and a once-daily treatment was available. We had to explain that the once-daily tablets were not approved by our charity partners at that particular moment. This, we were told, was an outrage. Mrs P was an animal lover and a lovely person; we were charlatans and fools to boot. After some negotiation and the filling in of special forms explaining that Mrs P was struggling to give tablets twice daily due to her artistic and witchcraft commitments, one of the charities agreed to supplying cheap, if not free, once-daily tablets.

In the next appointment the real reason for Mrs P's issues came to light.

'I brought this cat in thinking he'd be put to sleep,' she said.

'Right?' I wondered where this was going.

'Then you tell me he's got hypothermia …'

'Hyperthyroidism,' I corrected.

'Whatever, you know what I mean. Next thing he's having tablets, putting on weight. Look at him, he's practically fat.'

I explained that gaining weight was a good thing; it meant we were controlling his overactive thyroid gland adequately.

'Well, yes, but I thought you'd put him down. It's just I'm going on holiday for the first time in a few years, and you know …'

'So, to be clear, your complaint is that we successfully treated your cat?' I asked, eyebrow raised and twitching.

The bottom line was that Mrs P wanted to go on holiday, Berty was a bit of an inconvenience and if we could just see our way to murdering him that would be terribly convenient. I refused, and thus Mrs P and I had a lasting enmity. As the latter part of the morning rolled around, I was conflicted. The part of me that enjoys an easy life was dreading the arrival of Prince. The part of me that loves mischief and a good argument was quietly licking its lips. Soon enough, I found myself calling in Mrs Brown with Prince. Mrs P also made her way in.

'Right,' began Mrs P, 'the first thing is we don't want to hear anything about his weight.'

That was going to be difficult, Prince was at least twice the dog he should have been. If nothing else, they were going to hear about his weight via the groaning sound the consultation table was making under the strain. I let it go for now.

'Okay, what seems to be the issue?' I asked.

Prince had a bad ear and wounds under his armpits and on his belly, I was told.

'We've tried everything for his ear,' explained Mrs P. Clearly, Mrs Brown was not going to be allowed to speak for herself.

I conducted a full clinical exam, struggling to hear Prince's heart through his considerable girth. He was quite a sweet little fellow and seemed to appreciate the attention. The only time he got a bit 'bitey' was when I went near his bad ear; it was obviously very painful and covered in the stinky goo of bacteria and failed treatments. I clicked on Prince's notes. The screen was blank; either we had an IT glitch, or we'd never seen Prince before.

'Has he been here before?' I asked.

'No, first time,' Mrs P placed a comforting hand on Mrs Brown's shoulder, silencing her. The fact that Mrs Brown's mouth was open and mid-answer did not deter her one jot. I asked if he'd been anywhere else. It wasn't a problem, I explained; we could just get the medical notes sent over from any previous vet. Prince had not seen another vet recently.

'Okay, but you said you'd tried everything. What have you tried?' I enquired.

'Everything,' I was told. 'Coconut oil, olive oil, turmeric, homeopathic belladonna, garlic ...' the list went on. Prince also had horrible, infected skin ulcers in both his axillae (armpits) and on his abdomen. Coconut and turmeric had been applied to them. From what I could see, the wound on his abdomen was caused by the dog's tummy being so large it was dragging on the ground. He had so much subcutaneous fat on his torso that the movement of his legs was abrading his skin, literally rubbing it away and leaving him with painful ulcers under his legs. I had a lot of things I needed to talk about, but I had to be sensitive. The poor dog was in quite a state, and a lot of that was owner or owner's friend inflicted. I couldn't lead with that though; I might alienate my client and lose my ability to help the dog. I decided to simply list out his problems, then offer a remedy to each one.

I opened my mouth to speak, but before I could get a word out, I was interrupted.

'Remember, we don't want to hear about his weight,' cut in Mrs P.

'Okay, well ...' I started again.

I explained that Prince had a nasty ear infection. Often allergy is an initiating factor, but sometimes it is just chance. He certainly had some nasty wounds both on his tummy and in his armpits; they were infected and that was playing a large role in their failure to heal. Prince would need his ears cleaned and a proper examination done; we'd swab his wounds and send a sample off to the laboratory to find out if it was a resistant bacterium. Once we had some results, I could be more specific about what should be done and which drugs we should use. However, I had to address the miniature elephant in the room.

'I would be remiss, though, if I didn't mention Prince's weight ...'

'I thought I said we didn't want to hear it?' said Mrs P.

'Well, that's as may be, Mrs Pretentiös, but I absolutely guarantee that his wounds will not heal without weight loss.'

'What should I do?' interrupted Mrs Brown. She had plucked up the courage to speak for herself.

Mrs P glared at Mrs Brown as if she had just defecated in Mrs P's cornflakes. I explained that there are reasons why Prince might be prone to weight gain. He might have hypo-thyroidism, an under-active thyroid. He might have hyperadrenocorticism, Cushing's disease, a disorder of the pituitary or adrenal gland. There could be genetic factors. Unfortunately, neutering, carried out routinely by vets, is also a large contributing factor, as it reduces the animal's metabolic rate, whilst increasing appetite. However, the usual cause of obesity in dogs is overfeeding.

'It's not because of what he eats,' stated Mrs P.

'Mrs Pretentiös, in my experience, in over 90 per cent of cases, it's because of what they eat.' I shut her down.

I wanted to speak to Mrs Brown. Mrs P seethed under her purple beret, her face increasingly resembling its colour. I had no doubt a hex, curse or something similar was coming my way later. I offered to take some bloods for the two most common endocrine disorders, but I suggested that it would be more efficient for us to look at Prince's diet and assess it first. If he was obviously eating too much, we should try a dietary change. A quick conversation revealed that Prince was being fed like royalty. Breakfast was a slice of toast with pâté. I weighed him and he was 12 kg. It's not possible to give an on-the-spot 'perfect weight' but by my estimation he should have been nearer 6 kg. I explained that since Prince's normal weight was perhaps a twelfth of mine, his breakfast was equivalent to me eating 12 slices of pâté-laden toast for breakfast. I think we can all agree that is a bit much.

'Okay, look, I don't know what to do for the best. He's in a right state, I just want him better. What do you advise?' Mrs Brown was into her stride now. It was clear she wasn't too concerned about the money side of things, so I didn't need to worry about economising. I suggested we book Prince in, clean up his ear under sedation, examine it properly, and take whatever samples we required.

'Let's do that,' agreed Mrs Brown.

Mrs P just glared at me, but I honestly didn't care.

We cleaned up Prince's ear; the various concoctions that had been applied had combined with bacterial infection to leave his ear a yellow-brown, sticky, ulcerated and bleeding mess of swollen tissue. Eventually I was able to see inside properly. We swabbed his skin, irrigated the wounds and applied a barrier cream. For his abdomen we fitted him with a stretchy cotton superhero-like costume that would stop his tummy rubbing on the ground. I started him on broad-spectrum antibiotics for his skin wounds, anti-inflammatories for the swelling and pain, and ear drops containing steroid, antibiotic and anti-fungal agents. When the time came to discharge him, Mrs Brown arrived alone.

I asked Mrs Brown to stop using all other treatments apart from what I'd given her. Viscous, thick fluid-like olive oil will tend to go into a dog's ears and not come out. Unlike our short ear canals, theirs have a 90-degree bend in them. Using coconut oil alongside his medicated drops could inactivate them, which wastes both time and money. There's no evidence that homeopathy has any effect at all, and garlic is toxic to dogs, potentially damaging red bloods cells. Similarly with his wounds, I wanted to be able to understand what was going on and why.

A couple of days later I received the laboratory results from Prince's skin. The bacteria isolated was *Staphylococcus aureus*. It is present on normal skin and was probably only able to cause a problem due to Prince's damaged epithelium. It wasn't a resistant bug and his current antibiotic would be suitable. I'd assess Prince at his next visit. If things were going well, we'd maintain our regime. If they were going badly, we would have to reappraise the situation. I rang Mrs Brown: Prince was doing well, his ear was more comfortable, and she thought he might even have lost some weight.

I didn't see Prince for another week or so. I was talking to another client across the reception desk when I saw Mrs Brown come in with her four-legged companion. I finished my conversation and, on my way back to my consult room, took a quick detour to give Prince a pat on the head and ask how he was doing. Mrs Brown was upbeat, and Prince looked both happier and even a little slimmer.

'See you soon little fella,' I said as I made my way back to my consult room/cell.

I worked my way through a puppy vaccination and a cat with vomiting and diarrhoea before Prince's turn came. He walked into the consult with his distinctive gait, half down to his breed's short-leggedness and half to his culinary excess. He was definitely happier, and his little tail wagged rapidly, confirming his changed demeanour. Before I could even get a word out, Mrs Brown gave me a status update.

'He's lost 600 grams! Haven't you, you little twister!' she exclaimed, glancing at Prince, who barked in either puzzlement or confirmation, it was hard to tell.

I lifted him on to the table. As I started to examine his ear the most telling improvement was that he didn't require a muzzle. Previously, he wouldn't allow me to put my otoscope, a special optical device for examining ears, anywhere near his left ear. Now, I could have a good look with relative ease. It still wasn't normal, but it was improving. His wounds appeared smaller, some of that due to reduced inflammation, and some because they had started to heal. Distinctive red, rough-looking tissue was forming. It was granulation tissue, the first step in making new skin. Prince was on the mend.

Over the next six months, things continued to get better for Prince. He had a couple of relapses early on when his wounds went backwards a bit. We discovered that he was allergic to some pollens and dust mites. Dust mites live on just what you'd expect. Household dust is about 50 per cent human dander, which is a polite way of saying the bits of skin that we continuously shed as our skin cells replace themselves. You're living with arachnids that are eating bits of you; do say hi. Prince never got down to 6 kg, but he settled at 7.5. Although he was still a little heavier than ideal, he was a different dog. He was now energetic, able to jump on the sofa, climb the stairs, and leap on to Mrs Brown's bed, which she was now sharing with His Highness. He seemed to look forward to his walks and barked at the sight of his lead. Before, he'd sullenly suffered through a brief plod around the block; now he was enjoying trips to the beach. Mrs Brown was embarrassingly grateful. Ironically, we received a hamper of chocolates and some whisky as thanks, but I wasn't complaining.

Prince had been a challenge in many respects, chiefly communication. His case also raised some interesting points. We are often confronted with animals that have had alternative therapies prior to seeing us. We're often seeing them because those therapies have failed. Sometimes, it's the opposite and owners have sought alternatives because of our failures. I want to flesh out a few of the things I think are worth talking about.

Prince had been having both coconut oil and turmeric applied to his ear. They perhaps represent what I'll call herbal medicine here. It's worth understanding that herbal medicine isn't really an alternative model of what we call pharmacology, the study of drugs and their actions. In the case of coconut oil, would you prefer to have it, or 1-monolaurin applied to your pet's wound? What about 2,3-dihydroxyproponyl dodecanoate, which sounds a bit chemical and unpleasant? Well, 1-monolaurin is an alternative name for 2,3-dihydroxyproponyl dodecanoate; it is present in coconut oil and there is some evidence it may be anti-bacterial among other things, but no one to my knowledge has tested it in dogs' ears. Turmeric is related to ginger and its root or rhizome is harvested and dried, then used in everything from food preparation to Ayurvedic medicine, an ancient practice originating in India. Curcumin is the 'active' part of turmeric and chemicals related to it are called curcuminoids, or linear diarylheptanoids. Despite quite a bit of research, there seems to be little evidence that curcumin has any use as a medicine. According to a 2017 article in *Nature*, there is no evidence that it has any specific therapeutic benefit despite over a hundred clinical trials and thousands of research papers. Another slightly later article in the same magazine urges us not to discount it entirely.

Contrast that with digoxin. This is derived from plants of the genus *Digitalis*, or foxgloves. William Withering first described its use for treating heart disease in 1785. The muscle cells of your heart are complex, with many proteins in or on their surface, or cell membrane. Some of these proteins are receptors, channels and exchange mechanisms that allow the cells to perform their function. They metabolise adenosine triphosphate (ATP), the molecule used as energy currency inside cells, to pump ions in and out of the cells. Digoxin interferes with their function, causing more calcium to be pumped in. Calcium is intimately involved in muscle fibre contraction and more of it inside the cell increases the force of muscle contraction and the heart beats more vigorously.

Digoxin is used to treat congestive heart failure and atrial fibrillation in both human and veterinary patients. The mechanisms of its actions are well, if not completely, understood. I'm simplifying things hugely here; feel free to do your own research later. In some instances, the protein mechanisms I'm referring to have been visualised using electron microscopy. The point I'm making is that herbal medicine, where it is effective, is really just the use of unrefined drugs. Digoxin is still derived from farmed plants, then purified. Many modern medicines were originally derived from plants but are now artificially synthesised. If the original plant is simply crushed up and ingested, the drug is accompanied by many other substances, whose effects may be unknown or harmful. Researching, purifying or synthesising, then trialling drugs is a protracted and expensive business, but it allows us to keep the baby and avoid the bathwater altogether.

Homeopathy was brought into the world by Samuel Hahnemann about 1796. He became interested in the effectiveness of cinchona for treating malaria (originally thought to be caused by bad air, hence the name). He decided to try it for himself and in doing so experienced fever, shivering and joint pain. He concluded that since the effects of cinchona were similar to that of malaria, like might treat like. He began to develop texts that detailed a variety of substances and their effect on the body; these were known as provings. As he developed his work, Hahnemann formulated several hypotheses. These have been expanded and adapted by later practitioners.

In order to analyse homeopathy reasonably fairly we must break it down into its key claims. I'll concentrate on two.

1) Like cures like

This could be the most fundamental 'rule' in homeopathy. However, we encounter problems from the very outset. It is safe to say that this is at odds with almost all modern therapeutics. Morphine does not cause pain, but it will numb it. Antibiotics do not cause bacterial infections, but they will kill susceptible bacteria. Dexamethasone, a steroid, does not cause inflammation, it reduces it. Immediately, homeopathy sets itself at odds with everything we know about pharmacology.

Most of the provings were done in adult humans. They recorded the effects of various substances on them in journals and interviews, which were then collated. We know that environmental, genetic and physical factors will influence an individual's vulnerability to a disease or toxin. And that's before we look at confounding factors such as ingestion of other substances, concurrent disease, psychology and so on. Had a sore head? Was that caused by the substance under trial? Or the stress of debt?

Genetics play a huge role in the vulnerability of an individual to toxicity from a substance. Dogs, for example, can tolerate paracetamol quite well and it is a useful analgesic in that species. However, it is lethally toxic to cats in small quantities, as they lack the glucuronyl transferase enzyme that would allow them to metabolise it in quantity. Immediately we can see that provings are unlikely to be transferable between species.

Many substances are used in homeopathy, from table salt to snake venom. It is not implausible that these substances may treat disease. Our knowledge of the effect medications have within the body has exceeded the wildest dreams of someone from Hahnemann's era. Ultrasound scanners can let us see the effect of drugs on the heart in real time. Tests can detect not only changes in the make-up of blood itself but the amount of oxygen it is carrying, levels of hormones secreted by glands, concentrations of drugs in circulation and even damage to organs via biochemical markers. Functional MRI can now detect changes to blood flow in the brain as subjects engage in conversation or manual tasks, further elucidating the complex working of our little grey cells.

2) Preparation – dilution and succussion

This includes two key ideas in homeopathy. Hahnemann realised that the use of pure substances in the provings often caused significant side effects. He hit upon the idea of dilution in order to reduce these undesirable reactions, but noticed that this reduced the potency of his preparations. Supposedly, he also noticed that potions agitated in transit, whilst being carried on horseback, retained more of their effectiveness. As a result, he hit on the idea of 'succussion' (violently shaking the potion, these days carried out by machine). Dilution and succussion are paired processes.

Together they are dynamisation or potentiation. The extent to which a homeopathic product has been diluted is indicated by a number paired with a letter. More dilute preparations are said to be more 'potent'. The letter X denotes dilutions whereby one part of the original preparation is diluted with nine parts diluent (diluting stuff). Water is the most common diluent, but other substances such as alcohol are also used. This is then succussed. One part of this mixture is taken and diluted again with nine parts diluent, and succussed. This process is repeated to a specification and recorded as a number. A 24X solution would have undergone 24 sequential dilutions and succussions. The letter C denotes dilutions that have one part of the original diluted with 99 parts diluent. So, a 30C homeopathic remedy would have undergone this process 30 times.

Homeopathy predates the discovery of molecules, the atom and its structure. We now know that dilution must have its limits, as atoms and molecules are discreet entities and cannot be infinitely diluted. Imagine, if you will, a children's ball pit. Let's say you took out 99 per cent of the balls and added water, then took out 99 per cent of that mixture and added more water. Keep repeating the exercise and eventually you will have a pool of water and no balls. A dilution routinely prescribed by homeopathists is 30C. Let's try producing some homeopathic beer. The problem is excessive sobriety, so something that causes soberness should be an effective treatment. I've always used caffeine-rich coffee when trying to sober someone up. Let's be sparing and use a single molecule of caffeine. We will need a very small spoon. An initial 1C dilution gives us one molecule of caffeine and ninety-nine of water, one part in a hundred. A 2C gives one part in ten thousand. When we get to 12C that's one in 1,00 0,000,000,000,000,000,000,000.

For there to be even a single molecule of caffeine in a 30C dilution, you would require: 1,000,000,000,000,000,000,000,0 00,000,000,000,000,000,000,000,000,000,000,000,000,000,0 00 molecules of water.

Using a scientific calculator and some high-school physics, that comes to: 2.989×10^{22} cubic kilometres of H_2O. Or a ball of the wet stuff approximately 27.6 billion times the volume of the planet Earth.

There would be an enormous number of lawsuits as people are crushed to death in homeopathic bars throughout the country. I'm being facetious, but dilutions of this nature rapidly become farcical. The odds that there is any of the original substance in the preparation you've been offered are astronomically small and it would be swamped by contaminants. In fact, many homeopathists do not claim that there is any of the original substance in a 30C dilution. Instead, the dynamised dilution contains some 'memory' of the original agent selected. Water can and does form complex structures under certain conditions. In fact, it can form a beautiful crystal structure that has some incredible properties. It is transparent if manufactured without air bubbles; you can make a pane of glass-like quality with it. It floats on water and much of the world's fresh water is locked up in its sub-zero grasp. It's called ice.

Tiny differences in the electrical field surrounding water molecules cause them to move into a lattice structure as they freeze. It is this lattice structure that causes water to expand and lose density as it freezes, and why ice floats on water. Unfortunately for homeopathy, this lattice contains virtually no information, as it is repetitive – one section looks much like another. Water has not been found to preserve any information from substances it has encountered. In many instances what is administered to people or animals is not actually a 30C dilution anyway. It's often sugar tablets that have had drops of the dilution applied to them. So, once the tablets dry out, what then? The water had the memory, right? What did it do? Nudge the sugar gently and whisper to it before disappearing in a cloud of vapour?

Homeopathy's implausibility, whilst amusing, is irrelevant. Many seemingly implausible things have turned out to be true. What is important, is that no scientist has been able to prove homeopathy is superior to placebo. To bring us full circle, Hahnemann was right about cinchona. It is useful in the treatment of malaria. It contains quinine, which is now synthesised artificially and is on the World Health Organization (WHO) list of essential medicines. The adult dose used to treat falciparum malaria is 600 mg three times daily. No dilution or succussion is required. I'll give Hahnemann his due: I think if he were alive today, he'd follow the evidence. I don't think he would be a homeopathist, and I don't think he'd tolerate anyone using it on his pets.

There are many alternative and complementary therapies out there. It can be hard to tell them apart. Some have validity, some are elaborate placebos, and some are downright harmful. Our intuitions about what might work are almost entirely faulty. Humans tend towards believing that what is natural is good; this is called the naturalistic fallacy. Digoxin, covered earlier, is derived from a plant. What could be more natural? However, it has a very narrow therapeutic range. The right amount is helpful; too much is fatal, and both humans and animals receiving it require careful monitoring.

Few of us worry about the salt on our dinner table. What could be more benign than good old sodium chloride? It is made up of the elements sodium and chlorine, chemically bonded together. Sodium is an alkali metal and in its pure form explodes when dropped into water. Chlorine is a halogen, and a yellow-green gas at room temperature. Its harmful effects are probably most infamous in its use as a chemical weapon in the First World War. Its colourful tendrils meant death to those who breathed it in. Yet, in combination, the two are a vital part of our diet. If I were to expose most people to a sodium explosion, then give them a light chlorine gassing, I think it's unlikely they would suggest that the two combined might be a useful addition to the dinner table. I suppose I would also have to investigate non-extradition countries.

We are easily deceived. I think many alternative therapies enjoy success in areas where conventional medicine is itself lacking. In some instances, like aromatherapy, they give an adult a chance to have an hour in a dark room, away from the kids, warm, dry, comfortable and probably having a nap. Who wouldn't feel better? Many diseases are self-limiting. There's a concept called 'return to the mean'. In other words, if you are ill, most likely you'll get better. Your own body is an exquisite mechanism, constantly adapting and self-medicating to achieve a healthy equilibrium. This is homeostasis.

The very idea that you're receiving a medical intervention can make you feel better: the placebo effect. Well-known brands of pain-relieving tablets are more effective than generic tablets. Injections of saline and sugar pills are equally pharmaceutically inactive when it comes to blocking the pathways involved in pain, yet the injection provides better pain relief. Why? Well, we don't know, but we think it's that the injection is perceived by the patient as a more powerful medical intervention. You feel better because you expected to feel better; the mind is a powerful tool. How does this work in animals, you ask? Well, it doesn't have to; it has to work on their owner or the vet. I've had some tricky conversations.

'Is Billy any better, any less lame?' I asked.

The client did some facial gymnastics, then managed, 'Well, maybe a little? Yes, a little bit.'

I had spotted the strain that this white lie imposed on my kindly client. I smiled and told her that I wouldn't be insulted if she answered no. After all, I wanted Billy better as well, even from the entirely selfish viewpoint of professional reputation. I explained that we had many treatment options available and that she should just be honest. There was no need for embarrassment, certainly not on her part.

She looked relieved. 'No, he's no better to be truthful,' she admitted.

How often have I been fooled? I don't know, but I try not to be. There are countless other ways in which we may either be tricked or, perhaps even more commonly, trick ourselves.

I like to think I'm fairly open-minded on the medical front. In fact, I think I've become more so as I've seen things I was taught at vet school proven wrong. I've seen treatment protocols that were considered gold standard superseded by new drugs or regimens. In some cases, highly interventionist treatments have been replaced by more modest but more effective treatments as evidence-based medicine has revealed that more isn't always more.

I've been using Manuka honey in wound management for several years. Very useful for infected, traumatic wounds, it has anti-bacterial effects and encourages granulation tissue, mentioned above. So, honey good, yeah? Well, unfortunately it is not quite that simple. Honey applied to surgical wounds makes them more likely to break down and fail.

Hemp and cannabis-derived products are increasingly popular in human health. There have been some recent studies that suggest they might also be of use in veterinary medicine. Products with cannabidiol (CBD) and cannabidiolic acid CBD(A), have anti-inflammatory and anti-anxiety effects, among others. However, it is important that any product we use in veterinary medicine is free of tetrahydrocannabinol (THC), the psychoactive component of cannabis that results in a 'high', which might be distressing to animals, who cannot rationalise the effects.

Something most of the public are unaware of is the 'cascade'. This restricts and guides what vets may prescribe.

I'll offer an abbreviated explanation. In the first instance a vet must use a veterinary product licensed in the UK for the species under treatment and licensed for the condition being treated. If that is not possible, the vet may use a product licensed in the UK for a different species or different condition. Step 3 allows the use of human drugs licensed in the UK or veterinary drugs licensed in the EU. Step 4 allows drugs to be specially prepared by qualified vets or pharmacists. Lastly, an exception allows for other measures, such as the special import of a human drug from another country, but a Special Import Certificate is required.

What that means for a drug like CBD is that I cannot recommend it as a first-line treatment as it is not yet licensed. What this discussion is getting to is that the best person to advise you on which drugs to use and why is your vet. There are no 'good' or 'bad' drugs. There are only appropriate or inappropriate drugs, and what might be appropriate today, may not be tomorrow. For me, I'm willing to listen to anyone's suggestions, but listening must be a two-way street. The most important thing is using treatments that are likely to work. When it comes to 'alternative' medicine, I'm not sure there's such a thing; there's what works and what doesn't work. If there's good evidence that something is effective, I don't know many vets who won't be willing to give it a try.

There is one treatment we have not covered, but happily it doesn't involve tablets, liquids, creams or bandages. The number of overweight pets we are seeing increases daily. In the vast majority of cases, they are being overfed. I understand why people do it. Who can resist the puppy-dog eyes or the distressed meowing of an apparently hungry pet? I think many people substitute treats for the ever-precious commodity of time. Instead of a walk, the pet gets a treat. That pets will happily keep eating more than they need is a product of evolution, just like the same phenomenon in humans. In times of scarcity, gorging on rich foods while they were available made good survival sense. However, in much of the developed world we now live in times of permanent plenty. Our ancient instincts are backfiring badly.

I have seen pets who are so overweight it would be hard not to define their condition as abuse. It's not that their owners are cruel, just nice. But nice and good are not the same. Sometimes a hard truth is kinder than a comfortable lie. Excess body fat in both humans and animals is a major health issue. We used to think of fat as a benign, inert substance whose main crime was just weighing the body down. However, we now know that this excess tissue is metabolically active. In humans it is a common cause of type 2 diabetes; the same is true in cats. In both species, losing the weight can reverse the disease. Obesity leads to chronic inflammation in the body, which has many negative effects; it has been implicated in premature ageing and cancer to name but two.

It is true that staying slim is harder for some humans and animals for a variety of reasons. However, the first law of thermodynamics is clear: energy may be converted from one form to another, but not created or destroyed. If you, or your pet, are burning more calories than you are ingesting, you will lose weight. I will happily accept a challenge from anyone or anyone's pet, but you have to come and stay with me, and I get the keys to the food cupboard. In the vast majority of animals and people, less food, particularly of certain types, combined with more exercise will produce healthy, sustainable weight loss until an ideal is reached. I encourage those struggling with their pet's waistline to weigh out their companion's food. Too often we humans look at pet food through our own eyes and think, 'that's not much', forgetting that our furry friend is a fraction of our weight. Pets may still enjoy treats, but any extra snacks must be factored into the dietary equation.

For most of us and many of our pets, two simple interventions will lead to much healthier lives across many parameters:

More exercise

Less food.

Happily, these interventions are very nearly free, natural, carbon-neutral, vegan-friendly and may even be endorsed by most if not all white witches.

13

SENTIENCE AND SENSIBILITY

Experiments carried out on humans and animals have revealed startling results. Results that suggest we are not alone. We share our earth with other sentient beings; not little green men, but *other* animals. They are capable of suffering, and in many instances, we are making that suffering worse. We can't be blamed for it all. Nature is red in tooth and claw. Life in the wild often means a grim death at the hands of a predator, disease or the environment.

But we must not shirk our responsibility. We are animals, but ones with extraordinary powers. The difficulty often arises in our own psychology. Very few people are deliberately and wilfully cruel to an animal in their midst. Those that are, in my opinion, need swift and severe punishment. Partly because they deserve it and partly because there is some worrying evidence about where such behaviour might lead. For those who engage in the most deplorable acts of cruelty, I would happily advocate a policy of 'an eye for an eye', and I do not mean that figuratively.

However, cases of extreme and wanton cruelty do not form a majority of the cases seen by vets and bystanders throughout the world. No, most cruelty comes down to two or three factors.

Ignorance is a huge one, and we can broadly speak of two different types. Ignorance in the first instance can be a lack of scientific knowledge. Not that long ago, it was postulated by theologians that in order to suffer, one must have an immortal soul. Due to some bafflingly arrogant thinking, it was thought that only humans had this remarkable property. Only we, *Homo sapiens*, possessed this ethereal quality. All other life was thought to be a kind of facsimile or imitation of true, human life. Animals lacked souls, and as a result, the ability to suffer. This led vivisectionists to literally nail animals down and then operate on the poor things. I very much doubt these people were oblivious to the pitiful barks, meows or screams of their victims. But they just didn't think it reflected true distress. What you believe, regardless of its validity, affects your behaviour ... a lot.

We know now that *Homo sapiens* is remarkably unremarkable. We are one of many hominins. Neanderthals, Denisovans, *Homo erectus*, Australopithecus, to mention but a few that I can immediately recall. Neanderthals had larger brain cavities than us and interbred with us. Some of us have Neanderthal DNA. We are genetically so similar to chimps that I'm weekly surprised one does not feature on some reality TV show. Although last week ... well, maybe it was just that the guy hadn't shaved, but ...

Only recently yet another supposedly unique human trait was struck off an increasingly small list. In Indonesia a shell was found with a geometrical pattern painstakingly scratched into its surface. As far as we can reasonably assume, it had no other purpose than adornment. It was done only for the pleasure that the intricate pattern gave its owner. Perhaps it was to be a gift, or maybe it had some ceremonial value. The important thing is that it was over three hundred thousand years old. It was probably not decorated by a modern human, but likely by the previous dominant hominin, *Homo erectus*.

What I'm ineloquently trying to get at is that we have, at times, assumed that animals are not sentient, that their consciousness is somehow different from our own. The evidence is now unequivocal: our historical, default position was wrong. I don't think any truly right-thinking person can now doubt that this is the case. Where suffering begins, and what suffering is, may still be up for debate. Insects' nervous systems will fire when damage is caused; they will move away from undesirable environmental stimuli. Even bacteria will move in response to noxious chemicals or nutrients. However, it could be debated as to whether these responses are true suffering or intelligence. Whatever the answer, we can now be sure beyond any reasonable doubt that 'higher' animals do indeed suffer just as humans do, and not just pain. No. Hunger, thirst, fear, anguish, jealousy, remorse – almost all our emotions – are recorded in the animal kingdom somewhere. We need to treat our neighbours better.

A second type of ignorance is simply created by distance and the number of hours in the day. Many of us unwittingly contribute to animal suffering despite our genuine horror of it. Trawlers drown aquatic mammals constantly. Whales and other marine animals are injured or killed by nets and lines. Deforestation, industrial meat production, habitat loss, pollution, plastic micro beads and outdated cultural practices – all impact on our world and its inhabitants. In many cases we unwittingly engage in behaviour that directly results in damage. Only recently has palm oil hit the headlines. Seemingly it's in everything. Most of us buy it. I don't think you'd find many moisturiser purchasers willing to cut down some virgin tropical forest and replace it with the biodiversity disaster that is monoculture. But, they saw that advert for Beautex-5000 that tackles all 37 signs of ageing, they spotted some crow's feet on Sunday morning, and something must be done. It is unreasonable to expect that each one of us engage in permanent global surveillance in order to keep our purchases ethically clean. However, I think we should be able to trust that huge corporations are not allowed to simply cut down, dig up, harvest or destroy whatever they like in the name of profit. That whole industries cynically grind out a litany of nonsense in order to persuade us to buy the latest evidence-free cosmetic or muscle-building supplement is one of the greatest ironies going. Never have people had access to so much information yet struggled so badly to differentiate fact from fiction.

I've treated several cats for permethrin toxicity, rarely with success. They've all come in with horrendous, uncontrollable seizures, so hot that they are literally slow-cooking their own brain tissue. Most have died despite every effort. Readers are perhaps wondering what kind of monster would poison a cat in such a way.

Well, almost invariably, it was the owner. The horrified owner, crying and sobbing in empathy with their pet. Their emotional state very rarely improves when they find out that it's all their fault.

You see, permethrin is quite an effective insecticide. It kills fleas. It's harmless(ish) to humans and dogs, lethal to cats. Sadly, it's a component in some cheap flea products sold in supermarkets and pet shops. In fairness, the products usually say NOT FOR CATS on them, although I must admit, not in big enough, red enough letters for my liking. Every few months, someone will come in with their beloved moggy, whom they have unwittingly assassinated. It would be nice if retailers stopped selling this stuff. It would be nice if the manufacturers stopped making it for sale to the general public. In the meantime, read the label and if in doubt, ASK A VET. Yes, they will cynically try to sell you a product from their own shelves because they can guarantee its contents. Yes, they will check the dosage, and ask to weigh your animal if necessary. They'll probably do all that in between emergencies and surgeries. Then, when a client says they'll just order it from a dodgy website, they'll just sigh, wish them good day, and quietly go about their day.

Check! And check somewhere reputable. If you live in London, perhaps don't look on the 'Louisiana Moon-sceptics, Alien Abductees and Chihuahua Breeders' home site. Where it's appropriate, object or protest, but get your facts right first.

From traditional dolphin slaughter to dog meat festivals, these things go on partly because of our almost wilful ignorance. Proximity is one of the greatest drivers of ethics and distance one of their greatest detractors. Those who argue that we should simply 'put illegal immigrants back on the boat they came in on' are not typically found pushing rafts of foreigners out into the English Channel. Indeed, once they look into their eyes and see another human, they're more likely to be found helping to feed, clothe or house them. We cannot all be expected to engage in global surveillance, but we can support those who do. Join a club, give to a cause, write a letter, speak to a friend.

Do not underestimate the power of the apparent few. Do not ask, 'What difference will it make?'

For the youngsters in the audience, John F. Kennedy (JFK), was the US president famously assassinated by ... well, let's not get into that. Needless to say, there's a whole internet of speculation out there for you to explore. Let's just say he had some inspirational qualities, some dodgy habits and a sticky end.

Watch the clip of JFK's celebrated speech: 'Ask not what your country can do for you, ask what you can do for your country.'

I challenge you not to feel the hairs on the back of your neck rise, your heartbeat increase and your will to act stir. Years back, someone was the first to question slavery, someone wondered if perhaps 50 per cent of society shouldn't have the vote as well, despite their delicate gender. Your legacy is not going to be what you preach, but what you tolerate.

Last, but certainly not least on our list: poverty. Now, sat here in the Western world, in only a moderately economically deprived area, it's easy to be the critic.

We've all seen the adverts, forcing us to stare into the deep, soulful eyes of an overworked donkey as it stumbles under the excess weight of its burden of bricks. Its owner beats it in a combination of ignorance, indifference and frustration. It's tear-jerking stuff, it really is. I hear too often veterinary staff say: 'Well, you shouldn't have a pet if you can't afford it.' This when we've had to put down an animal suffering from some preventable, but painful or fatal disease.

They have a point. But it's hopeless idealism, and a little patronising. What do I tell the little old lady who comes in with the stray cat she's been feeding for four years, only to find out that its dying of a preventable viral disease? Maybe I should lecture her on the unnecessary death, the economic sense of vaccination and the cruelty of her inadequate vaccination, flea and worm regimen? Or maybe I must accept that we live in a non-ideal world, and that she has probably done her best given constraints of finance and practicality?

I grew up in a house with, at one point, 13 cats. Vet bills were considerable. The cats got vaccinated, wormed and treated for fleas when we could afford it; simple. We bought none of them, rather they were strays and attracted by the cat food my mother insisted on putting out in the garage to save them from starvation. The garage was basically an elaborate cat trap. Many turned up in a dire state, no longer able to live independently. Looking back, I'm glad we were able to give them a loving if imperfect home.

It's all too easy to point out that healthy animals can work harder, for longer, than those that are neglected. I once witnessed a Nepalese woman sell a bracelet and a necklace made from tiny seeds to a friend of mine. She didn't have the jewellery on her, oh no. She showed him a sample and said she could have them ready in a couple of days. She would take no money in advance. Alas, we were moving on the next day and the day after to a mountaineering base camp thousands of metres higher and several tens of degrees cooler. No problem, she'd make them and bring them up. These accoutrements were made of tiny seeds, maybe 3 to 4 mm across. She would have to gather a couple of hundred, take off the flesh of the fruit, flatten the edges with a knife, drill a hole in each one and then thread them together. This woman lived in a wooden shack with her partner at about 3,500 metres up in the Himalayas, reared yaks and grew a few hardy vegetables. But she smiled constantly, despite having never been treated to so much as a tube of lip gloss. Two days later and perhaps 1,500 metres higher, she arrived in base camp smiling and gave my mate his gifts for home. I forget exactly, but I think they cost him the equivalent of £7. I doubt you could get the average UK citizen out of bed half an hour early for that. People are a product of their environment to some extent, and we must not judge prematurely. Where life is hard, hard things happen.

My experience of less developed (in our eyes) countries is that most people treat their animals well. Their welfare is intimately linked with those of their animals in a way most Westerners find hard to appreciate. But everyone and everything must pull their weight. Diseases that we would routinely treat in the UK or the US, thinking nothing of it, may simply be an intolerable economic burden in other, less fortunate areas of the world. The best thing in these circumstances may be to humanely end the animal's life.

There is also another issue that we should consider here. Fitness; not in the Yoga, Pilates or Cross-fit sense, but in the

Darwinian one. For most of us, our relationship with our domestic pets is skewed by their primary role as pets and dependants; not so in many areas. Animals are providers and workers. If they are particularly vulnerable to disease or infirmity, they may have no place. Their removal from the gene pool makes that infirmity less likely in the next generation. Harsh, realistic, and perhaps even something that will prevent greater total suffering in future generations. Before we judge, balance that with our Western practices. We breed dogs that cannot breathe properly or give birth naturally: British Bulldogs. We breed dogs that are condemned to skin problems and ocular discomfort: Shar Peis. We breed dogs that can barely walk because of their poor conformation and luxating patellas: Miniature Yorkshire Terriers. You could well argue that our refusal to tackle undesirable traits leads to ill health and causes greater total suffering than the seemingly harsh utilitarian approach taken elsewhere. We must look at total, not just individual welfare.

In many of the cases where I have witnessed significant welfare issues, exotic animals are involved. I am quite willing to treat exotic animals and continue to do so. There are an increasing number of exotic specialists, and they are usually very generous with their time. I also make some effort to keep abreast of all things exotic. It probably takes up a disproportionate amount of my ongoing study time, given how many cases I actually see. However, I have a firm position when it comes to exotic animals. They are exotic for a reason. They live in exotic places; i.e., not Wolverhampton, Swansea or Glasgow.

Leave them where they belong. The appetite for exotic pets such as snakes, lizards, spiders, birds, terrapins and so on seems to be increasing. I really wish it would not. It drives an illegal trade in these animals, which are often captured from the wild, farmed and transported in terrible conditions. All to appease us humans, because we want one. Humans who are often clueless in regard to the complex needs of their new companion.

There are many amazing wildlife documentaries, but I must confess to a weakness for David Attenborough. Chances are that any kid seeing one of his films is going to understand that the re-creation of the rainforest in their bedroom is not a viable prospect. We have no right to these animals. The parallel with dogs and cats is incorrect. We have lived alongside dogs and cats for thousands of years. For the most part they are comfortable around us. We have arguably co-evolved with dogs, selectively breeding them as assistants in everything from hunting to watching Netflix.

Raising exotic species in captivity to save them from extinction, to research disease, or in anticipation of restocking the wild population, yes. Stealing them from their habitat, trafficking them across the world in order to have a talking point when you have the neighbours round, no, just no. The same goes for zoos; conservation, yes, amusement, no.

Animal testing is another blight on our collective conscience. It is a genuine ethical conundrum. I think it remains the case that we will sometimes have to test vital drugs on animals in order to preserve human life and welfare. However, I think the cases where this can be justified are growing increasingly small in number. If you want to test make-up on animals, no. We have reached a stage in make-up technology where it is possible to paint over your own face with someone else's face with about 90 per cent effectiveness; further research is not warranted.

If we look at medicine, animal testing is more justifiable, but it has significant issues. Many drugs get through initial testing in mice, rats and even primates, only to be proven useless or dangerous in humans. We have no proof, but the opposite is also likely the case. Drugs that have been eliminated early in the trial process due to lack of effect or dangerous side effects may in fact be both efficacious and safe in humans. As we understand more and more about molecular biology, hopefully the necessity of animal testing will become a rarity or, better yet, a thing of the past. *In extremis*, patient-advocate groups are now playing a vital role in allowing terminally ill people to opt into trials of potentially useful drugs. These individuals have little to lose and everything to gain. Such measures are not enough on their own, as they are highly likely to skew the trial negatively. But they are only one innovative measure; I'm sure we can come up with more.

When we talk about human rights, I think we often fail to grasp an important point. There is no such thing. Nature grants you no rights. The universe will hit you in the face with an asteroid and wipe you and the rest of the species out without so much as a warning or an apology. Human rights are entirely a human invention, something we have carved out of an unforgiving world. Really, human rights are one side of a coin; the other is human responsibilities. Our right to go about our day free from physical assault only means something if others have a responsibility not to attack us. The question is, where do our responsibilities stop? Dostoevsky, author of *Crime and Punishment*, wrote that a society could be judged by how it treated its prisoners, the individuals over whom it has complete control. I think it is high time we extended that thought to the sentient animals around us.

The recent decision by the UK government to enshrine animal sentience in law is a welcome move. It is yet to be seen how that will look as policy and implementation, but I'm hopeful. The road to improved animal welfare world-wide and particularly in underdeveloped regions is paved with education, economic growth and redistribution of wealth. Such things take time. So, we must fight little battles, play the margins and count every small victory. Some effort will be wasted. Some feelings will be hurt. But I think our victory is inevitable.

14

MURDER!

When working in the beautiful countryside of Wales, I was involved in an incident that turned out to be profoundly weird. Someone was attacking swans. One at a time, but with increasing frequency, swans were being found with horrific injuries. They were turning up badly injured or drowned and no one could figure out who was doing it or why. Swans are protected and technically owned by the Queen (or, at least, all the unmarked mute swans in open water are). I can only imagine Her Majesty's consternation at the death of these beautiful animals and the failure of police, vets or the RSPCA to identify and prosecute the perpetrator.

Examination of the victims yielded little information. Poisoning certainly wasn't the problem. It appeared to be trauma leading to drowning. However, the trauma was inconsistent with all the usual culprits. The victims were being found in a large man-made pond divided in two by a vehicle bridge. Vehicles routinely injure animals of all types, but they certainly weren't the issue this time. There was no evidence of fishing lines, litter, watercraft or mother nature causing these injuries. Many victims had damage to their heads and, oddly, their feet. Often the nails on the ends of their digits were literally torn out or worn bloody where they had tried to escape from a prolonged assault. I think we all expected to discover some despicable human, attacking swans for reasons known only to themselves. Perhaps they were using a dog or something, maybe training them to fight? But the dead swans were never found with any bite marks consistent with a dog attack. Truly, we needed the help of Sherlock Holmes or perhaps Ace Ventura, Pet Detective.

In the absence of such sleuths, the attacks and deaths went on unchecked over the summer. I dealt with more than one victim, but the mystery continued and perhaps a dozen swans died before the unexpected perpetrator was witnessed in the act.

I was called out to the pond by the RSPCA to care for the first victim to be found alive. Eyewitnesses had watched the brutal attack and were readily able to identify the murderous attacker. He had a long slender neck and a distinctive facial prominence.

It was …

… another swan.

I'd never heard of or witnessed such a thing, but it was unquestionably the case; numerous people had seen it happen. One swan had cornered another against a metal gate guarding a steep set of medieval steps rising out of the pond. Trapped between the bridge and a stone building, prevented from escape by the gate, the victim had been battered by the attacker using his head and wings to rain down blows on his fellow avian. For his part, the victim had been desperately trying to claw his way out of the water and up the steps, tearing out nails and, in this case, breaking at least one bone in his foot. Witnesses had managed to drive away the killer swan, but the victim could not be rescued as he was badly injured and could not climb out by himself. No one could assist him, as the gate was locked and the stone walls prevented access from elsewhere. Unless a boat could be found and deployed, the injured swan would likely die. Unable to fend for himself, he was vulnerable to a follow-up attack or simply lapsing into unconsciousness, being swept into the nearby sluice gate and drowning. If nothing else, a combination of shock and infection would probably do for him in less than a day or two. None of the fifty or so people present could effect a rescue and neither could the recently arrived RSPCA inspector, who had evidently failed to keep up a personal fitness regime.

This was the situation I was confronted with on my arrival at the scene of the crime. The RSPCA inspector had called me in the hope of a rescue. I mean, they had no idea how this might be attempted, but felt comfortable announcing to the crowd that all would be well now that the vet was here. I climbed out of the car under the watchful and expectant gaze of my audience. I didn't really see how I could be anything but a disappointment, as I had, to date, no superpowers. I was treated to a tour of the scene, vivid descriptions of the preceding swan battle and shown the facilities and equipment with which to conduct my heroic rescue – i.e., none. Things were not looking good. There were several attractive women around my age in the audience, dressed for the glorious summer weather. If I were to later exploit my reputation as 'Swan Rescuer to Her Majesty the Queen', I needed to have a brainwave, and quickly.

This is where my pastime of being an avid, but useless, pursuer of all activities outdoors actually paid off. I had a garage full of equipment for almost any outdoor pursuit you could care to name. I had never progressed beyond mediocre at any of them, but I understood the principles if nothing else. The question was: what technique to deploy? I could get my canoe, launch it from the jetty a few hundred metres away, paddle over to the swan? But then, how to get a probably unwilling and potentially pissed-off swan on to my canoe and then keep it there while I used both hands to paddle back against the current? If he fell off, he'd probably drown in his current condition. No, that wouldn't do. Perhaps a surfboard could be employed? No, mountain bike? Wetsuit? Windsurfer?

Goddamn it!

The expectation of the crowd was almost too much to bear. I was starting to look like an idiot, definitely not boyfriend material and certainly not deserving of the attention of even a single summer-dress-clad, sultry young lady.

Then, eureka!

The bones of a plan began to form in my head. The bridge and the stone building were separated by the stone stairway, blocked by the iron gate, on the other side of which was my intended rescuee. In typical medieval fashion, the stairs were narrow, perhaps a metre or so wide with the walls of the bridge and building rising vertically on either side. I knew what to do; it wouldn't be easy, advisable or health-and-safety compliant. It also relied on the wounded swan being stuporous and cooperative. I explained the plan to the RSPCA inspector. She plainly thought I was mad and said as much.

'You're mad,' she said.

I was a proficient, if untalented rock climber. I could use a technique normally used to climb 'chimneys' in natural rock. This is called 'back and footing'. I'd place my feet on the stone building and my back against the bridge. By pushing with my feet against the former, I'd be jammed in place and avoid falling to my death on the steps below. To be fair, if I did slip, the unfortunate swan would likely break my fall. For my part, it would be pretty embarrassing to attempt a recovery, only to atomic-elbow the victim to death.

Once I was in place, the semi-clever bit could begin. I'd walk my feet down a bit, all the while tensing myself to avoid the death thing. Then, I'd push off with my arms behind me and move my back down the bridge a bit, before placing it back against the stonework and being once again jammed in place. I'd repeat the process, climbing down between the two vertical walls and descending on the other side of the iron gate. Then I'd get in place, wrestle the swan on to my lap, before reversing the same climbing manoeuvre. Provided the swan was content to lie still, I could get back up with him on my lap. Someone would have to lift him off me at the top. He'd have to be cooperative, or I risked him falling off and getting further injured, but I could think of no other way to effect a timely rescue.

And so, heart in mouth, I found myself climbing over the edge of the bridge, to the consternation of my audience. Perhaps they initially thought that I'd decided, having examined the situation and accepted my inevitable failure, to simply throw myself to my death in an act of contrition? In my memory there were gasps of disbelief, but that might well be my ego talking. I'll admit, the initial moves were tentative, but my confidence grew as I realised that the stonework was abrasive and grippy. I'd climbed much more treacherous surfaces.

As long as I kept adequate pressure on my back and feet, I wasn't going anywhere. I even began to enjoy it a little bit as I realised the technique might just work. As I got closer to the ground, I could see the swan's predicament in more detail. His head was tucked under a wing, and he appeared to be completely still. Could he be dead? There was blood on the steps and on his plumage. After perhaps five minutes of effort, I got my feet down on the steps.

The swan was curled up at the base of the steps on a flat area level with the surface of the pond. Swans can certainly be aggressive, especially if protecting young. They can famously break a man's arm with their wing, but I've never met a victim or heard of such a thing actually happening. Nonetheless, I was a bit nervous as I gently touched the creature and began to swiftly check him over. It was immediately apparent that he was definitely alive. In his injured state, he just tensed up and furiously tried to get his head even further under his wing. I think he'd had enough. Perhaps he was so exhausted he even welcomed a potential predator who would just end it all? At any rate, it was apparent that the plan was still workable. There was a fair chance he'd just sit on top of me as I struggled back up between the two walls.

I got myself in place, back firmly against the bridge and feet pushing into the stone building. Then I was able to reach out and drag him on to my lap. He was surprisingly heavy and, at arm's length, I couldn't easily lift him. I had to drag him a little closer before awkwardly manoeuvring him into place. Once there, he did exactly the same as before, tucking his head tightly under his wing and remaining completely still. I started the climb up. It wasn't too far; I'd probably have to do 12 to 15 shifts. Quickly, I realised that it was much harder with the additional weight. Damn my short-sighted, conventional training regime; I'd never thought to practise swan-encumbered rock climbing.

It was hard, but I was making progress. It took a little longer up, but, sweating profusely in the summer sun, I was soon back at audience height, though just under the lip of the bridge, so out of sight. On looking up for assistance, I made eye contact with a local. I knew he was a local because he was dressed distinctively. For some reason, despite being an unemployed Welshman, he insisted in dressing like a short-wearing, Vietnam-jungle-warfare veteran all year round. The RSPCA inspector, assisted by the comically dressed but public-spirited non-veteran, was able to lift the swan off me. It's a little difficult to reverse the start of back-and-footing, but I managed to acquit myself reasonably well. Now relieved to be stood firmly on the bridge, I was able to examine my audience. I'd either deluded myself as to its actual demographic breakdown, or people had simply drifted away once it became clear I'd opted for rescue rather than suicide. Needless to say, there were no women eyeing me with barely concealed lust. There was certainly no admiring applause. There may have been seven, middle-aged locals, who had nothing better to do. The Vietnam non-veteran stared awkwardly at me as he cradled the swan in his arms, over-watched by the RSPCA inspector. I asked him if he'd be kind enough to sit in my car holding the swan as I drove to the veterinary practice where he (the swan) could receive further treatment. I directed the RSPCA lass to meet me there.

I must admit, I'd seen the chap around town many times and never spoken to him. He was obviously seriously eccentric, but I admired him now. His clothes were covered in a combination of blood, pond water and swan poo. But he was uncomplaining. Once at the practice I took the swan off him and quickly got it through the back and into a walk-in kennel normally used for large dogs. The nurses immediately started preparing the other walk-in kennel, turning it into a temporary swan habitat. We'd transfer our patient as soon as it was ready. The inspector said she'd ring tomorrow for an update and jumped in her van, off to the next wildlife or pet saga. My short-clad, jungle-hat-wearing assistant was at reception. I thanked him for his service; he smiled and said he was glad to help, before sauntering off into the sunshine, back towards the pond. I'd be saying hello the next time I saw him, that was for sure.

After taking the time to get cleaned up and make a quick, restorative cup of tea, I got one of the nurses to assist me in examining the swan. She'd already called the local 'bird lady', who specialised in helping injured wildlife recuperate in her garden. Every area has one. He now had a place to go if he was treatable, but was he?

There appeared to be a lot of blood. I carefully began examining him in a logical and exhaustive fashion. On balance, he didn't seem to be too bad. Whilst the amount of blood looked alarming, it's deceptive stuff. A little can look like a lot when it's spread around. I'd expected a substantial injury, but all the blood seemed to be coming from his feet. His nails were torn and bloody, some absent. There was one significant problem: he had an open fracture of one of his phalanges, the bones of his feet. It had broken in two and was protruding through the skin of his webbed feet. Not only would this be very painful, but it was a perfect entry point for bacteria. We'd have to do something with it. I considered my options, but eventually opted for amputation. I'd simply remove the distal portion of the bone, tidy up the other end, trim any useless flesh and stitch him up. He did have another couple of broken foot-bones, but I had an idea what to do for those. Once we judged we could risk anaesthetic, I gassed him down using a mask and got on with the surgery.

I carried out the operation as planned, neatly stitching up his skin. Then, the comical part. I had to splint his feet. I placed each swan foot on a plastic collar we normally use for stopping dogs from licking themselves; they come flat and fold into a cone-shape. Keeping these flat, I drew round his feet with a marker, then trimmed his new footwear. These bits of plastic, with some reinforcement, would act as splints, supporting the healing bones of his digits. I gently dressed his feet, coating the wounded areas in an anti-bacterial cream. Then I placed the splints on and bandaged over the top using pink, cohesive bandage. He now had two enormous, pink and clown-like feet. It was impossible not to find it amusing.

We placed him back into his kennel and monitored his recovery while keeping him warm. Amazingly, he came round well and was pretty bright after an hour or two. The combination of pain relief and clown-splints meant he could immediately get around, though his attempt to compensate for his enlarged feet were hilarious. I chuckled to myself and then filled out his inpatient form. Under 'Name' I wrote, 'Stupid Swan'.

The next day, Vicky, the aforementioned 'bird lady,' came to take him away. I was in consults when she arrived, but made my way through to the walk-in kennels as soon as I had time. As I entered the room, I could see her reading the inpatient form and medical notes. She was frowning. She made it quite clear in no uncertain terms that she felt 'Stupid Swan' was not an appropriate term of reference. We settled on 'Trevor'. And so, Trevor went off to his temporary home. He did well and was able to be released a few weeks later. Hopefully he is still roaming the Welsh countryside, maybe with some cygnets of his own.

The killer swan made it into the local paper. There was much speculation about why he was evil. People speculated that he might have a brain tumour or perhaps be suffering from heavy metal poisoning. Maybe he was the victim of some sort of Satanic ritual and now required exorcism, having been possessed by the dark one himself. There were proposals to test the water, test him or carry out surveys on other swans regarding their feelings. No test, to my knowledge, identified a causative factor. No one wanted to accept what I thought was the most obvious explanation.

There are plenty of arseholes in the world. They may be human, feline, canine or other; some of them are swans!

15

KAHLEESI

I always marvel at the enormous diversity in attitudes to surgery that we see from clients. Some have clearly spent the last 72 hours interrogating Google for information and want to discuss every possible complication whilst they hyperventilate with worry. At the other end of the scale, we often see the 'husband'. This is usually a disinterested bloke holding the end of a lead or carrying a cat carrier. When asked what their pet is coming in for, they will often reply: 'Dunno, the wife just said to bring it down for eight thirty.'

Occasionally these two people arrive together and are actually married to one another, leading to an especially interesting conversation.

Neutering of pets is by far and away the most common surgery performed by vets in first opinion practice. I think the fact it is so common leads many of our clients to underestimate the gravity and seriousness of the surgery their pets are undergoing. The language we use doesn't help, especially for female pets. Often what is discussed is neutering or spaying. The technical term for a spay is an ovario-hysterectomy. In layman's terms, the surgical removal of the animal's ovaries and womb, chiefly to prevent unwanted breeding. The most-performed human equivalent would be a hysterectomy; removal of the womb for a variety of medical reasons, including endometriosis.

There are some major differences in the surgeries humans and animals undergo. Our human patient undergoing a hysterectomy can expect to pay around £5,000 if they are in a private hospital, and can expect to have a surgeon who has probably had five years of university and a further ten years of surgical training. According to a doctor friend, there's a minimum of six staff, including two surgeons, an anaesthetist, an ODP (whatever that is), a scrub nurse and a theatre aid. The patient is likely to be in hospital for up to five days afterwards, and given that it's a private hospital, I would imagine free toast is included. Recovery, according to the NHS website, can be a while. If the patient doesn't have a manual job, they might be able to return to work four to eight weeks later.

Compare that to our veterinary patient. In the practices I work in, an ovario-hysterectomy will probably be around £300, say £450 with pre-operative bloods and some other luxuries. We expect vets with five years of university training to master routine neutering in their first couple of years in practice. It is expected that one vet and one or two nurses can accomplish a routine spay, even with animals who might be human-like in size, such as a Bernese Mountain Dog. Most of our patients will be discharged the same day. We'll remove the sutures 10 to 14 days later and a gradual return to normal exercise is advised. Of course, the occasional owner doesn't listen and immediately takes the dog for a long walk or throws a ball for it for 90 minutes. It is testament to the toughness of our veterinary patients that we do not see more complications.

I'm not disparaging our human colleagues here. To be clear, all my colleagues are human; I mean doctors who deal with humans. It says more about the different value we place on human and animal life. It is also fair to point out that there are key differences. I have no doubt our human equivalents are held to higher clinical standards and probably tolerate a lower level of patient risk. But it is also reasonable to point out that the fundamental requirements of both surgeries are the same. The anatomy and surgical principles are all but identical. I'm sure a human surgeon could spay one of my patients. I'm sure if they offered to reciprocate, I could muddle through one of their operations, though I'm equally sure I wouldn't be asked back. It would only take one lady sent home with the lampshade-like cone of shame fitted round her neck and instructions not to lick her wound to ruin a hospital's hard-won reputation.

I was working for a regular client, just over the border in the beautiful English countryside. Just as I was about to clamp on an ovarian artery our receptionist Lorna stuck her head through the swing door to theatre and said: 'Mondays, eh? Got a question: man's got a French Bulldog called Kahleesi and she's due Saturday. Wants to know if we can do an elective Caesarean today?'

'Nope,' I replied. Lorna raised an eyebrow.

I'm not known to forgo the chance to talk to a captive audience, so Lorna waited for the inevitable follow-up.

'So ...' I began.

I explained that it was not uncommon for owners to get their dates a bit mixed up. There is a large disparity in the skill of dog breeders. Some are utterly professional. However, the money to be made from expensive puppies of certain breeds has encouraged opportunistic breeders who are clueless at best. Even if their records are accurate, pregnancy does not necessarily begin at the moment mummy dog and daddy dog give each other special cuddles. The male's sperm can survive for several days in the female, and it is only when the sperm and egg encounter one another that pregnancy begins. Although the average doggy pregnancy is 63 days, there is some variability. Counted from the day of breeding, there is a range of 56 to 72 days. Because of the short duration of canine pregnancy, a day of development for a puppy in the womb is hugely more significant than a day of human pregnancy is for a baby. If we think of pregnancy as a marathon, reaching full term is 26.2 miles. A baby born five days early is under half a mile from the finish line; it's in sight. A puppy born five days early still has over two full miles to cover, and he or she has only little legs.

Since the dog had not been scanned, it might not even be pregnant at all, instead suffering a pseudopregnancy that mimics some of the features of pregnancy but does not produce puppies. We needed definitive evidence the dog was about to give birth before I'd consider a C-section.

'Stick him in the diary for a phone call; I'll ring him this evening and have a chat,' I eventually concluded.

'You could have just said that,' Lorna replied, rolling her eyes in *faux* exasperation.

'You're lucky I'm talking to you at all. Here I am in the middle of surgery and you're hassling me with this trivia?!' I smiled under my mask.

I glanced down to begin placing a ligature near my clamp. This loop of suture would seal off the uterine artery. If it was placed badly or not tightly enough, my patient might bleed to death after surgery. I finished my last ligature and removed the ovaries and uterus. With a swab in my hand, I inspected my ligatures, near the left kidney, then the right, then the cervical stump, where the now-amputated uterus had previously joined the cervix. There was a little blood in the abdomen, but nothing worrying. I was satisfied that all was well. I dropped the stump out of the forceps I was using, set them down and reached for my suture materials. I turned back to begin stitching. There was a little more blood than before, sat in the wound. No worries, muscle and skin often bleed a little, and as it accumulates, a little can look like a lot. I dabbed it with a swab and started my first layer of stitches that would close the abdomen.

Nope, there was definitely blood coming from somewhere. Opening the wound with one hand and holding guts out of the way with a swab, I investigated the abdomen again. I couldn't see my knots any more; they were under water. Well, technically, under blood. It was probably a minor vessel that hadn't been bleeding when I'd checked before. My patient was a big dog; she could spare a few millilitres. I absorbed some red liquid with my swab. I needed to get rid of the blood already there to find the source of it. I was looking for a little fleshy tube, probably spurting bright red arterial blood. The trouble is the abdomen is made of pink fleshy tubes, all of which were bathed in my patient's fluids. Every time I dabbed blood away, more replaced it.

'Okay, I need some lap swabs,' I said. The nurse swivelled her chair. Still monitoring my patient with a stethoscope, she opened a drawer and reached for the large sterile absorbent pads I'd requested. Pat called for another nurse, who came and dumped the swabs on to my instrument tray.

'Lucy, start scrubbing.' I wasn't sure if I'd need help, but better to have someone ready. Lucy would go and get herself prepped for surgery in case I required extra hands.

They say all bleeding stops eventually. It's half advice and half dark humour. If your blood pressure drops low enough, you will stop bleeding, that is true. However, if your blood pressure is zero at that point, you're dead and the point is moot. I couldn't identify the bleeder – a problem I'd faced dozens of times. I'd assisted other vets. I'd taken over from less experienced vets when they admitted defeat. I'd opened up dogs presented to the emergency service to find and rectify a surgical error. I pride myself on being calm in emergencies; panic is contagious and helps no one – it only leads to degraded performance. I was still stressed.

The abdomen was awash with blood. I'd checked all my ligatures; they seemed fine. What the hell was going on? Lucy was ready and prepped. As she approached the operating table, I saw it, a tiny current of slightly brighter blood, a couple of millimetres across.

'I see it!' I exclaimed.

I reached into the abdomen with my tissue forceps and gripped the offending squidgy bit. Pulling it up I caught a brief glimpse of my cervical stump, before a jet of arterial blood hit me in the face. I directed the jet elsewhere whilst I recovered, only for Lucy to shout 'Woooaaa!' as I inadvertently hit her with the mini blood hose.

I blinked the fluid out of my eye and reached for a clamp. With a quiet crunching noise, I closed the clamp on the stump and the bleeding stopped.

'Jesus, Gareth,' Pat said, 'way to control bleeding!'

'Not ideal, certainly,' I replied.

I got Lucy to hold some of my instruments while I searched for the cause of the issue. My ligatures were good, there shouldn't have been any bleeding. I handled the stump, trying to figure out what was wrong. Eventually I figured it out. My patient was older; one of the vessels I'd tied off had become calcified. The calcium had turned a flexible tube (resembling a rubber hose) into a rigid pipe (like copper plumbing). I'd crushed it, but there was enough resilience in the pipe for it to re-expand slightly, opening for blood to flow. I had to crush the pipe again and place two more sutures into it before I was confident all was well.

'Phew!' Problem solved, we turned up the patient's intravenous fluids to support her blood pressure and monitored for further bleeding. After 10 minutes I went through my checks again and, content, began closing. While many of our day-to-day surgeries are routine, they are not necessarily minor. Complications can arise for all manner of reasons. Unexpected reactions to medication or anaesthetic, abnormal anatomy, clotting disorders and undiagnosed illnesses are only some of the issues that might complicate a 'simple' procedure.

That evening I phoned Mr Smith. He'd recently bought Kahleesi as a family pet. He explained his rationale for getting into the dog-breeding game.

'She's a proper pedigree. I wasn't going to breed her, but it's four, five grand a pup, innit? Decent litter and I'm up thirty grand.'

There was no denying he was right, if I was really in veterinary medicine just for money, I'd be much better off running a puppy-breeding operation. I explained the reasons we would not do an elective surgery at the moment. To be fair to him, he listened and seemed to understand. I explained that when Kahleesi showed the first signs of impending motherhood, we should examine his dog and closely monitor her. She might be able to give birth naturally, but if she was in second-stage labour, pushing hard, and puppies were not forthcoming, a C-section would probably be necessary.

I'd forgotten all about our chat when the dog arrived as an emergency on Saturday morning. We were just about to close, already an hour or so late, when I spotted a white Audi RS5 pull up in the car park. As I bade farewell to my previous and officially last appointment of Saturday morning, my heart sank. Whatever was in the car, I just knew I wasn't going to be finishing on time. It had been a long week and I was looking forward to listening to a podcast on the drive home, going for a run, firing up the barbecue and spending the evening with some friends.

Alas, it was not to be. An attractive young couple hopped out of the car. The bloke was wearing board shorts and sandals in keeping with the summer weather. He got out, opened the back door and lifted out a French Bulldog. My heart sank further as my long-term memory clanked into action. This had to be Mr Smith.

'Hiya mate,' he said as he carried the dog towards me. 'I spoke to someone here about my dog earlier in the week. Kahleesi?'

'Hi there. It was me you spoke to; how can I help?' I replied.

'Well, we think she's in labour now, so how about that Caesarean? We tried ringing, but it went through to the emergency guys. We don't want to go to the night vet; we've heard they're really expensive ...' he finished.

This is all too common. Vets must provide a 24-hour, 365-days-a-year service. When I first graduated, this was usually done in house with vets covering nights on call as well as routine day work. These days many vets sub-contract their out-of-hours work to specialist providers. The emergency providers usually charge a premium for the service, and clients are not daft, word gets around. If I stayed and did the Caesarean, I'd be here for at least another three hours, probably more. I was under no obligation; I could simply direct them to the emergency clinic. We had officially closed. But I wasn't going to do that without first looking at the dog.

'Well, look, let's get her inside and have a quick check. We're actually closed now, that's why you got redirected to the night service.' I ushered them inside.

I got them in a consult room, donned some gloves and gave the long-suffering Kahleesi a quick exam. She was very docile, almost depressed. I quickly went from nose to tail checking the colour of her gums, her capillary refill time, heart rate, respiratory rate and temperature. I gently pinched the skin on the back of her neck into a tent shape. She was dehydrated and a little cold. As I felt her abdomen she shuddered with the effort of a powerful contraction. A vaginal exam revealed a puppy stuck in the birth canal; it was still alive, but it needed to come out sharpish. I used a well-lubricated finger to have a feel around the puppy. It was way too big to be born naturally, a condition called relative foetal oversize: the baby dog is too big for the mother's skeleton. Sadly, it's very common in certain breeds and a product of human-imposed selective breeding. We have a lot to answer for.

'How long has she been like this?' I asked.

Silence and some awkward looks between the couple were pretty much already an answer. Probably too long.

'Well, see, she was pushing a bit last night, but not much. Then she was sick once this morning. We phoned a mate of ours, the guy who owns the stud dog; he's been breeding for years. He said just to starve her for 24 hours for the sickness. He reckoned she wouldn't actually be due until Tuesday. So, we thought we'd be all right to pop out to the shops …'

I briefly fantasised about getting Mr Smith in a headlock and poking him in the eyes for the sheer pleasure of it. However, no matter how pissed off I was at them, a rant would just delay Kahleesi's treatment further. I had to grit my teeth and stop myself from visiting the sins of the owners on the dog.

'Okay. How long, maximum?' I asked.

There were another couple of guilty glances exchanged.

'Maybe five hours? Six tops,' he replied. Honestly, I didn't believe him.

'Okay, here's the deal; she needs a Caesarean. Ideally, she'd go to the emergency service, but by the time you get there and get seen that'll be another hour and I don't think we can afford the delay. I don't mind staying. I'll quickly ask the nurse if she can work late.'

I did mind staying, very much so, but it was the right thing to do. I already knew what Pat was going to say. She would say yes. She'd probably miss her own birthday party if she had to. I walked through to the prep room; Pat was emptying bins and cleaning the floor. As soon as she saw the apologetic look on my face, she had a good idea what was coming.

'Come on, what have you found?' she asked.

'Caesar,' I replied sheepishly.

'There's just me. I'll text Nicky; she only lives round the corner.'

I quickly got a consent form printed off. It detailed the procedure Kahleesi would have, the risks of anaesthesia and the likely cost. I'd have to go through the form with Mr and Mrs Smith as fast as possible before getting our debutant mother ready for surgery. I went through all the medical bits, when she'd eaten last, any allergies to medication and so on. More or less the last bit is the cost.

'How much?' Mr Smith asked.

'Around a thousand pounds, but it is an estimate, not a quote; she's a living, breathing organism, not a piece of furniture. We'll try to communicate any possible changes to that as soon as possible, but if it's life-saving we'll obviously prioritise Kahleesi and phone you later.'

'That's ridiculous!' exclaimed Mr Smith. 'Would I still have to pay if the puppies are dead?'

'Well, yes. Look, I understand it's a lot of money, but let me explain.'

Rather than just end up at loggerheads, I decided I'd break it down for him. I explained that because of Kahleesi's condition we'd have to get her on intravenous fluids. That in itself is a skill. I recommended some bloods. Our patient was clearly depressed; no one would have recommended surgery until she was more stable, but there was no doubt that significant delay to surgery would likely lead to the death of the puppies and possibly the mother as well. I stressed that our lab machine cost several thousand pounds, our new multi-parameter device for monitoring anaesthetised patients, £10,000. We wouldn't make any money until it had paid for itself. Then there's the cost of the building, heating, lighting, council tax, waste disposal. Of course, we also like to pay staff.

'Could you put her down and save the puppies? That would be cheaper, right?' he asked.

I began to wonder if the Royal College had sent him, trying to find out what it would take to push me over the edge? He was like a caricature of all that is worst in irresponsible dog breeding. Judging by the labels and bling he and his wife were wearing, they could have sold their outfits and paid for the surgery.

'I don't think that's an option. Her motherhood is really important. Yes, you can use artificial milk, but it is no substitute for the real thing. Without her, their chances of survival are reduced. I recommend we try to save them all.'

He glanced at his wife. She'd said nothing throughout, but she was literally biting her lip.

'I'll tell you what, I'm going to pop next door and see how things are going. Take five minutes and think about it, but we really need to jump one way or the other when I get back.' I started to exit the room. As I walked past Kahleesi, I stroked her head gently and just said: 'Hey girly, you'll be okay.' I hoped I was right.

Nicky had arrived and was helping Pat prep. If Mr and Mrs Smith decided not to go ahead, the effort would be wasted, but we had to be ready. Already the nurses had equipment out for us to get fluids running into our patient. A bag of drip fluid was warming in the sink, an IV cannula and tape to secure it, and other bits and bobs lay neatly lined up. On the table were blood tubes for biochemical and haematological testing, along with syringes and needles to get a sample. Next to that, drugs to induce Kahleesi, and endotracheal tubes to secure her airway. In theatre the oxygen generator was on, anaesthetic had been topped up. In the corner was a puppy crèche of sorts, filled with warm bedding and with an IR heat lamp directed at it. As puppies emerged, they would be checked and placed in their first bed. On the instrument tray were sterile gloves and gown; next to them a raft of instruments. I was happy we were about as ready as we could be. The question was, would we need it?

I walked back into the consult room. Kahleesi was curled up on the bed I had put on the table. She was looking sorry for herself, but at least her straining had stopped.

'Okay bud, go ahead,' said Mr Smith simply. The consent form was already signed.

I glanced across at his wife and wondered what the conversation had been? I explained we might be a while and the best thing was for them to go home and I'd phone with updates as required.

Moments later I was carrying our prospective mother into prep. I got her on the rubber-topped table.

'Okay GS,' Pat instructed, 'let's get the blood sample, then Nicky can get that running and we can get a line in Kahleesi and start fluids.'

'Sounds like a plan,' I confirmed.

Within 10 minutes we had fluids flooding into our patient's bloodstream while we waited on results. I was already suspicious that there was more going on than met the eye. Kahleesi was swaddled in her blankets, tucked up on top of a heat mat. Nicky returned from upstairs with a hot drink for each of us, figuring we could use something to keep us going; my stomach growled with hunger. The machines churning away in our upstairs laboratory would transfer the data on to our computer system as soon as they'd finished their analysis. Sipping my tea, I refreshed the data yet again; this time the results were there. Kahleesi's white blood cells were elevated, implying infection; toxins that her kidneys should have been filtering out were accumulating. At this point it was hard to say why, but the increases were modest, and I thought they reflected dehydration rather than kidney problems. So far, our treatments were on the ball. Ideally, I'd have liked to delay surgery, but to have any chance of saving the puppies, we had to get to work.

Normally we'd be giving a dog going to surgery a pre-med. A mixture of drugs to alleviate pain, reduce the amount of anaesthetic needed and ward off cardiac arrhythmias. Unfortunately, those drugs might jeopardise the puppies' chances. Instead, we trickled in the induction agent, intubated Kahleesi and got her on anaesthetic gas. Before long she was out and stable. I did the only thing I could to help manage her incoming pain. I used a syringe and needle to place multiple injections of local anaesthetic along the middle of our expectant mother's abdomen. At least the pain of the incision would be numbed.

Almost as soon as I'd finished with the local, I was incising through the skin. Pat monitored Kahleesi; Nicky would take puppies off me as they emerged, care for and resuscitate them as required. As soon as I'd opened the abdomen, I could see the problem. Kahleesi's uterus had ruptured. She'd strained so hard that she'd broken her own body. One puppy was free-floating in the abdomen, already dead. The chances that the others were alive were rapidly reducing. I expanded the rupture in the uterus and gently milked puppies towards the hole. I pulled out the next one, a little girl. Puppies have individual placentas; fortunately, hers was still connected to her mother. As I worked to get her out, I could see the movement of a beating heart; she was alive for now. I passed her, complete with placenta, to Nicky.

I worked logically and as rapidly as I could, pulling out puppies as I encountered them. So far, we had one dead puppy and two live ones. Next, I'd go for the puppy that was in the birth canal. I gently manipulated him out; his head was swollen, but amazingly he also was still in with a chance.

In total we had six puppies, four boys and two girls. One boy hadn't made it, but the others were quietly whining for their mother, letting us know they were still alive. Puppies out, we gave Kahleesi much-needed pain relief; she was no longer pregnant. I would have preferred to spay her, preventing her from going through this again, but Mr Smith had declined that option. Probably, he'd breed her again. I could have lied. I could have found a reason to spay her, but it is perhaps the bedrock of professional ethics that we are truthful.

Last puppy out, my attention was now on the mother. We flushed out her abdomen thoroughly, getting rid of the fluid spilled from her ruptured uterus. Now it was time to repair the damage. Once I'd closed the uterus, suturing her up was just like any routine surgery. There's a strange phenomenon with surgery: sometimes I'm apprehensive beforehand, thinking about how long it will take or how hard it might be, but once I've made that first incision, I'm in a different mode and the next time I think about it is when I'm finishing up. It is like playing competitive sport when, at your best, you are in a 'flow state', fully immersed in an activity. Time can melt away and it's an oddly pleasurable sensation.

As soon as we'd finished and Kahleesi was waking up, Pat and Nicky went to work, transferring the mother into a bed and immediately trying to get the hungry puppies feeding off their mother. It requires a gentle touch and great patience to open tiny puppy mouths and latch them on to their mother's teat. This first milk, colostrum, is very important. It's nutritionally rich, but also provides antibodies. These can be absorbed by the puppy, ending up in their bloodstream and providing immediate protection while their nascent immune system develops.

I was just about to pick up the phone when Nicky came running in.

'We've got a problem.'

I immediately replaced the phone and returned to the kennels.

While trying to get the pups latched on to their mother, Nicky had been checking their mouths for signs of cleft palate. It is a congenital condition of varying severity. One of the pups was affected; a large hole connected her oral and nasal cavities, linking her respiratory and digestive systems. It meant she struggled to generate a vacuum to feed off her mother. Any milk she could get, she might inhale. Once the milk was in her lungs, it could cause a nasty infection, inhalational pneumonia, a potential death sentence.

'Bugger,' I sighed, 'the rest okay?'

'Yeah, they're all good.' Nicky's eyes told me she was worried for the puppy.

Good news, bad news is always a difficult delivery. There's a technique for delivering bad news called a 'shit sandwich'. This is where you put some good news up front, then the unpleasant filling, before completing the sandwich with another piece of good news. I didn't mind giving Mr Smith a shit sandwich; it's just a shame it wasn't literal.

I explained that the operation had gone well, mother and five puppies were alive, and Kahleesi had a good chance at a full recovery. We had lost one pup, and I had to recommend that Kahleesi go to the emergency vets overnight. That would be costly, but it was undeniably the correct medical advice. I also broke the news of the puppy with the cleft palate. Mr Smith was pretty unhappy; after all, potentially he'd just lost two puppies or somewhere between eight and ten grand. I delivered the second piece of bread as a summary. Although the situation wasn't perfect, he had four healthy pups, a fifth we could discuss, and though the mother needed further care, there was a good chance she'd be okay.

We continued to look after mother and pups. Pat got some milk from the mother and I gently stomach-tubed the cleft puppy, making sure it had some nutrition.

Mr and Mrs Smith arrived, and I went through the options and recommendations again. Then I took them through to Kahleesi and her pups. They were delighted to see the mother and glad she was well. We passed them the pups to say hello. It was all very wholesome, and I must admit I softened to them a bit. However, there was a hard conversation ahead.

'Would we have to tell someone?' Mr Smith asked about the cleft pup. 'You know, if we were selling it?'

'Mr Smith, perhaps I didn't explain very well earlier,' I said.

I explained that there was a good chance the puppy wouldn't survive at all. It might be unable to get adequate nutrition, or pneumonia might kill it. Its cleft would probably need specialist surgical correction. For it to have any chance, we'd have to stomach-tube it frequently to provide it with nutrition and stop milk going the wrong way. It would be unethical to sell it. In essence, we had a few options:

1. We could see how the puppy managed.
2. They could nurse the puppy, feeding it every few hours, 24 hours a day.
3. We could put the puppy down.

The first wasn't a real option; it was neglect, and I made that clear. The last was a terrible decision, but better than a slow death from pneumonia. I could tell by their faces the second wasn't something they were willing to do. I'd already talked to Pat; there was one final choice. She and her partner had adopted a similar puppy. They'd come into work pale and with shadows under their eyes for weeks as they took turns stomach-tubing the pup, 24 hours each day. Multiple vets treated it when problems developed, but ultimately the puppy had survived. Princess was still an occasional visitor to the practice and was now five. Everyone loved her and she was seriously mischievous. Given the chance she loved to escape and get attention from whoever she could find while we all tried to capture her. Pat was willing to adopt this puppy too.

'I suppose,' Mr Smith began, 'and then we could get her back when she's older?'

'No, I'm afraid that's not an option,' I clarified. 'I would have to ask you to sign ownership of the puppy over to Pat; it would be her dog. It wouldn't be fair for her to nurse the puppy for weeks or months, only to give it up, I can't ask her to do that.'

Pat would also end up spending some of her wages back in the practice, providing for the puppy; we were now owned by a corporate company and free treatment wasn't a service they provided. I decided to leave the couple with the puppies to make a decision. We all left the room and used the time to get tidied up. After a while I wandered back towards the kennels. Just before I opened the door, I couldn't help but overhear the conclusion to their chat.

'I'll tell you what you're going to do,' seethed Mrs Smith. 'You're going to take that dog to the emergency service; I don't want to hear about the money. You're going to give that puppy to the nurse. I told you not to breed her. Plus, if you'd taken Leesi to the emergency vets when I told you, she wouldn't have a ruptured fucking uterus. Plus, you can tell that mate of yours we're getting her neutered.'

It turned out that Mrs Smith's earlier silence did not represent a lack of strong opinions. I cleared my throat as I entered the room. Feigning ignorance, I asked if they'd reached a conclusion. I was unsurprised to find out that Kahleesi was headed to the emergency service for overnight care. The struggling pup would become Pat's, who would do her best to save it. It was about as good an outcome as I could have hoped for; I was grateful for Mrs Smith's intervention. As they were leaving, I didn't have much to say.

'I'm sorry it's not gone as well as we hoped, but thank you, you've made the right choices; good luck. Can you give us a call Monday and let us know if we can help?' I asked.

'Thanks,' said Mrs Smith. 'Please thank the nurses as well; you've all been great.'

Pat still owns Titch; she's spent a fortune on her over the years. But Titch is now best friends with Princess; she's happy and very much part of Pat's family. Kahleesi did fine, was a good mother to her pups and came in to be neutered a few months later. She can now enjoy her life as a pet. Roughly speaking, the debacle probably netted Mr Smith about twenty thousand pounds.

Dog breeding is an ethical minefield. I'm not against it. Our pets, herders of sheep, helpers of the disabled, sniffers of bombs and lickers of faces have to come from somewhere. I once stayed with a couple who bred Weimaraners. They had two breeding bitches. They lived in a cottage in the countryside and the dogs had great lives. Mothers and pups were screened for every disease imaginable. The couple would raise two or three litters out of each bitch over a few years, then the mothers would be spayed, retired and become household pets. Potential owners were carefully selected for suitability. If that's dog breeding, I take no issue.

At the other end of the spectrum, one of my jobs required me to visit a puppy farm. There were dozens of breeding bitches in a large agricultural shed. I didn't want to go there. None of the other vets wanted to go there. There was no physical cruelty. The dogs were well fed, warm and dry. Health isn't just physical though. When I went into the shed, mothers and their pups would bolt out of their kennels, run to the barrier at the end of their enclosure and climb over each other for a few moments of my affection.

Supposedly one of the most psychologically gruelling

punishments meted out to humans is solitary confinement. How much worse is it to breed animals, specifically to crave human attention, only to deny it to them whilst we breed more? It seems uniquely cruel.

Then there's health. Breed standards are effectively the traits that make one breed of dog distinct from the next. Humans, in our folly, have selected for genetic problems in many breeds of dog. Instead of aiming for health, some breeders aimed for ever more extreme physical appearances. I'll discuss only one, because I can speak to its unpleasantness. Brachycephalic dogs, those with short noses and flat faces, have become very popular. Dogs like Kahleesi. Unfortunately, they are prone to something called BOAS, brachycephalic obstructive airway syndrome. It's a combination of several physical characteristics; when these dogs breathe in, air must make its way through abnormally small nostrils, then a fleshy soft palate partially closing the back of the throat, followed by a collapsing larynx, further impeding proper breaths. If air manages to negotiate that obstacle course, it still has to get through a narrow trachea, like breathing through a straw.

Some people will tell you these dogs are fine. They are not, and it's no longer a matter of opinion. Recent studies have demonstrated that affected dogs are suffering profound breathing issues. They are literally low on oxygen: hypoxic. A normal healthy dog's bloodstream will have an oxygen saturation of at least 98 per cent and usually higher. Brachycephalic dogs may have much lower oxygen concentrations, even when at rest. Concentrations as low as 70 per cent have been found. I've had levels this low. Once, on a trip to the Himalayas, I used a pulse oximeter to measure the concentration of oxygen in my blood. It turned up 69 per cent as the lowest value; at sea level this would have your doctor in conniptions and reaching for supplemental oxygen.

At high altitude, low blood oxygen is par for the course, though over time your body can make some adaptations. I performed reasonably well, even up to 8,000 metres. However, I slept badly. I'd wake up multiple times a night, in a panic and panting for air. Chronic headaches were common, especially on moving to a higher camp. The slightest incline would reduce me to taking a couple of steps, then panting to recover, before I could manage to make another few metres of progress. A thousand metres of climbing, something that might take me an easy couple of hours at low altitude, meant a whole day of labouring upwards. The entire endeavour was an act of forging forwards despite your body crying: 'No more!'

In my case, it was voluntary. I could give up and descend at any point. The dogs afflicted by this are not volunteering. They are condemned to the struggle because they have been bred this way. At least historically, dogs were bred to perform functional tasks. Collies owe their intelligence and athleticism to selective breeding. Even Miniature Dachshunds, popular now as pets, were historically bred to hunt burrowing animals such as rabbits. Recently, the appearance of some breeds has more to do with cosmetic appeal than function. In other words, vanity, transmitted into another species.

This is only one of many illnesses imposed on dogs by our quest for the cute, the adorable or the 'cool'. Breed societies and institutions like the Kennel Club must accept much of the blame, but have improved in recent years. There are schemes aimed at improving everything from hip dysplasia to retinal atrophy. There are many good breeders, doing their best to provide healthy pets and companions to the general public, and workers to shepherds and the like. However, one of the main drivers of breeding is economics. Bad breeding will not stop until the public demand for badly bred dogs ceases.

More widely, I recommend anyone who aspires to pet ownership to consider their own circumstances and what constitutes responsible pet ownership. Is it fair to buy an Alaskan Malamute, a dog bred for dragging a sledge through the Arctic for hours a day, if you live in a city flat and suffer from exercise-induced agoraphobia? Is it right to purchase a Bulldog and expect it to run around with your family on a sun-drenched beach, breathless and struggling to cope in the heat? I would implore any potential pet owner to really research their choice of pet and select a companion who will bring joy to your life, but who will also have the life it deserves with you; and before you approach any breeder, please, please, consider one of the many deserving animals in rescue shelters, who deserve a loving home as much as any potential pet.

Dogs that suffer from BOAS can have surgical procedures to ease their symptoms. It's not a surgery I personally offer, though I have considered learning it. I'm torn; I want to alleviate the suffering of the dogs I see so afflicted, but I also want people to stop breeding them. Vets stand to make a lot of money from congenital problems, as these often require surgery or intense medical management. However, I've never met a single vet who wouldn't click their fingers and render all these dogs healthy if they suddenly acquired the power. I may yet learn BOAS surgery, but I think I might only offer it to animals if the owners agree to neuter them. I want my surgical intervention on an animal's behalf to be an essential rarity, rather than an inevitable banality, entirely preventable.

The long-term solution to these animals' suffering is research, education and responsible breeding. If we can prove beyond a doubt that they have real issues, inducing unnecessary suffering, we will be compelled to act. At the same time, public education may reduce demand. It's a generational issue. I'm seeing more of the brachycephalic breeds than ever, and I hope they all have happy, healthy lives as family pets. I would ask anyone considering breeding them to seek out veterinary advice, have their animals assessed and consider whether it's the right thing to do. If you're considering buying one, really look into it. Even for the most selfish of us, these animals often come with large veterinary bills on top of their expensive price tag.

16

STICKY, SALT AND PEPPER

Recently, my work had tended to be small-animal or emergency focused, mostly working around Wales's largest city. The offer of a locum job in a mixed practice was an opportunity for a bit of variety. I was working over spring, helping with the increased demand that comes with lambings and calvings. It was a good arrangement; it would allow me to get out around the countryside again without committing to a full-time job, relieve some of the pressure on the other vets, and buy the practice vital time to find a new recruit.

That day, little did I know, was going to be truly mixed. First of all, I had to get through the initial bruising of morning consults. Normally we'd have two vets each running ten-minute appointments. We had a third column for emergencies, which applied some extra pressure. Unfortunately, my companion in arms had phoned in sick and now it was just me. The receptionists did what they could and cancelled or rearranged as many appointments as possible. The workload was still a touch over the top. All three columns in the diary had been booked for eight thirty in the morning and it was too late to cancel them. Some quick maths should leave anyone with the realisation that one vet with three appointments in ten minutes is three minutes and twenty seconds per appointment. Since a perfunctory hello and some small talk takes at least a minute or so, I was down to something like 120 seconds per consultation.

By the time I got to my last appointment I was running an hour and a half late and my clients were no happier than I was. I clicked on the final one. Clearly the reception staff or another vet had decided a practical joke would cheer me up. The appointment's details revealed my patient to be a stick insect called Sticky. I know two things about stick insects:

1. By definition they must have six legs.
2. They resemble sticks.

I opened my consult room door, which led into reception. I was going to shout 'Stiiiiiccckkky!' as loudly as I possibly could, reversing the practical joke. Now it would be the receptionists' turn to be embarrassed. They'd have to explain to the clients waiting to pay why the practice had employed a crazy man. Oh, they'd be so mortified. Unfortunately, I opened my door and, before I could shout anything, I caught sight of a family of three. On the lap of their son sat my potential nemesis, a vivarium, a glass enclosure often containing the general practitioner's worst nightmare: something exotic.

As I locked eyes with them, I managed to get out a quizzical and slightly pathetic 'Sticky?'

'Yes, that's us,' the mother replied.

'Please come in,' I said and made a sweeping gesture towards my consult room. As the family approached, I could see the head receptionist behind them. She looked at me and shrugged with a wry smile, knowing full well what a predicament I was now in. I mock-scowled by way of reply.

Once we were inside, Sticky's enclosure was plonked on the table by the young boy.

'Hi there, I'm Gareth. How are you …?' I began.

Once introductions were over, I was careful to explain that I wasn't an expert on insects and therefore I could only perform the most basic of consultations. I was happy to take an initial look, but if it was anything other than the most obvious of problems, I recommended we refer Sticky to a specialist. The mum thanked me and admitted that reception had explained as much. Issues with exotics are often related to poor client education or expectation. Even a little knowledge, a few basic facts, and signposting clients to good information can have a hugely beneficial impact on the lives of more unusual pets.

'What seems to be the problem?' I asked.

'Well, we don't think he's very well,' came the reply.

I asked for a basic rundown of why the family thought Sticky was poorly. He hadn't been eating much, the various leaves the family were providing him seemed untouched. He hadn't been as active as normal. In fact, he hadn't moved much at all.

'How long has he not been moving,' I asked.

There were some glances and a bit of chat amongst the family. Eventually a definitive answer was agreed upon.

'About a month,' the boy admitted.

I began to think I might be able to diagnose Sticky after all.

I tried to appear wise. Gently stroking my chin, I said, 'Riiiggghht', as if this was a subtle but important detail.

'Well, let's take a look,' I said. I surveyed the vivarium – it was literally full of sticks – and realised that I now had an identification issue. Which one was Sticky? It would be mildly embarrassing to pick out a non-Sticky stick before going through the show of a clinical examination on a piece of wood. The kid saved my bacon by slamming his finger against the glass and shouting, 'There he is!' at the top of his voice. Given the clue, I could now see my patient.

I opened the vivarium and gently poked Sticky in what I assumed to be his face. He fell off his perch, landed on the base of the vivarium and rapidly rearranged himself into a number of smaller sticks and some dust.

I looked up into the eyes of the horrified family and, as straight-faced as I could, said: 'I've got some bad news. I think he might have passed away.'

'Are you sure?' asked the dad.

As a scientist I don't like to offer absolute certainties, so I went with, 'Pretty sure; like 99.9 per cent.'

No sooner had the grieving family left with Sticky than I was called out the back for a lambing. We had a small outbuilding that served as an examination and operating facility for farm animals. Kate was mid-Caesarean on one sheep and another lambing had arrived. I quickly nipped over to my car and grabbed my wellies and waterproofs.

As I approached the trailer, I nodded a hello to the farmer. His farmhand swung the gate of the trailer open, and I found myself staring into the soulful eyes of a Welsh Mountain sheep. Just as the guy was about to close the aluminium gate behind us, the expectant mother made a break for it. The last thing we needed was to be chasing her down the main street. I took a step towards the wall of the trailer to trap her between me and the wall. Unfortunately, she'd anticipated the move and lowered her head like a battering ram. I took the full force of her 50 kg frame to the shin via her bony head.

'Dammit, lass!' I managed to keep the accompanying swearies under my breath. It's always tempting in these circumstances to lash out at your assaulter, but it's hardly their fault; they are just obeying their quite natural instincts. Instincts that consider rubber-clad humans to be a threat. Once we'd restrained my attacker, I could carry out an exam. Two small legs were protruding out of the back of my patient. I applied some lubricant to my hand

and slid it into the unfortunate mother's vagina, past the lamb's legs.

'Baaaaaa!' she protested noisily.

I could feel the problem almost immediately. Instead of being in a nice, streamlined diving position, limbs outstretched and head tucked between them, the lamb's head was bent round as if looking over a shoulder. Rather than nose first, the mother was trying to shove out the head side-on. I'd have to push the lamb back slightly, then pull its head into the correct orientation. Before I did anything I had a good feel around to make sure I was right. With multiple lambs it's easy to mix up who's leg is who's. Trying to pull two baby sheep out at the same time will not work. Following limbs to torso and torso to neck, then head, I was sure I had all the right bits. I put some ropes on the lamb's feet so that I didn't lose them. Then I started to gently pull the lamb's head around. Once it was in the right place, I lightly pulled on the ropes. The lamb immediately pulled its head away as if rejecting the entire idea of being born; perhaps it was perfectly comfortable where it was?

'Come on, little one!' I said. 'Give me a hand, would you.'

Again and again, I got the lamb in the right position; again and again it would pull away. My hand was tiring. I swapped limbs, using my weak hand; no joy. I'd have to get a rope around the head as well. I nipped off and came back with a thin rope, a noose in the end of it. There are special wire tools for this, but I couldn't find one. The rope would be harder to get around the lamb's head because of its flexibility, but it would have to do. Imagine an orange in a sock: you've got to get the rope around the middle of the orange, but you can't damage the orange or rupture the sock. Oh, and the sock is full of jelly. If nothing else, this game will keep a determined child busy for hours. I put the noose of the rope around my four fingers, slid my hand in, then spread my fingers, sliding the rope over the lamb's head.

Simple! This is one of those tasks where determination pays dividends. Multiple times I was almost there, millimetres away, then the sheep would move, or the lamb would decide it had better things to do. I kept trying. Just about, just about, I pushed the rope another millimetre or two with my now-exhausted index finger.

'Come on, come on!'

All this struggle was utterly invisible to the farmhand. Well, mostly; I've got a weird habit of mimicking what my dominant hand is doing inside the sheep with my other, spare hand. If the lad had been watching my left hand it must have looked like it was possessed by an errant demon as it writhed around in mid-air.

'Gotcha!' The rope was over the back of the lamb's skull. I ran my hand over its head and teased each ear under the rope to prevent it from slipping off, then ensured it was running through the lamb's mouth like a horse's bit. I started to pull gently on all three ropes, pulling the legs and head into alignment and the lamb into a superman dive. Now that he was in the right shape, he came flying out. I pulled membranes off his face and was rewarded with a loud 'Bbbbbbaaaaaaa!' as Salt came into the world. I checked the mother and there was another sibling still inside, so I fished her out as well.

The mother received a few jabs to ensure she wouldn't be too sore or vulnerable to infection. Before long a satisfied client was driving out of the yard.

For me, it was back into the surgery to lend a hand with the routine operations. They were mostly done, but I had a cat to spay and a dental to do. As the day wore on, it became apparent that I'd forgotten an important detail: I was on call that night. I normally did a Thursday, but for whatever reason things had been swapped around and I hadn't checked the rota. As it was Tuesday, I'd come to work without my overnight bag. I lived an hour away, so I stayed in the practice accommodation when on night duty. Bugger! Well, I kept a toothbrush and toothpaste in the car, there was enough shower gel floating about in the bungalow to keep me going, and I could borrow a dog towel. I'd manage overnight.

That evening we had a few inpatients for me to manage, but nothing too demanding. I was tired and hoping for a quiet night. As soon as I could, I engaged in the guilty pleasure of a kebab from the nearby takeaway and settled in front of the TV. When I started to nod off, I retired to bed and asked Loki, the Norse god of mischief, to just fuck off for once.

Alas, Loki had found me to be insufficiently worthy of a full night's sleep. My mobile rang in the wee hours, and I answered it to Sandra, one of our receptionists and the wife of a local farmer. We were very fortunate to have people like her filtering out nuisance calls and answering basic queries such as 'Can I cancel my appointment for Thursday?', which for some people apparently necessitates an emergency call to the vet at 2 a.m. Unfortunately, she couldn't fend this one off.

'Andy Williams has got a cow with a prolapsed uterus; needs you out soonest,' she said.

'Right-ho, where am I headed?' I asked. I wasn't local, and satnavs and Google are still notoriously unreliable in rural areas. I was lucky to have Sandra on the other end of the line; she knew every nook and cranny on our patch. She could probably get me to the right field, never mind the right farm.

Directions in hand, I was out of the door and in the car in no time. The practice maintained an on-call box, with most of what was needed for farm emergencies. I'd restocked it and chucked it in the boot earlier. Twenty-five minutes later I was driving up a rough farm track when a torch being waved in the darkness caught my attention. As I drew closer, a boiler-suit- and wax-jacket-clad figure came into view. I pulled up alongside and wound down my window.

'Mr Williams, I presume?'

'Veterinary! You found the place alright then?'

'Yeah, you've got Sandra to thank for that. I'd still be driving around the lanes without her directions. Where's this cow then?'

'Just in the field; she's thrown out her calf bed. If you park here, we can take the quad over. I've got a couple of buckets of warm water on the back.'

I reversed my car up and parked against the hedge. Climbing out I got into my gear and grabbed the on-call box. It was both bulky and heavy; there was no way the farmer, the water, my kit and I were all fitting on the quad. I swapped the kit for the water. I'd carry the two buckets down; at least a bucket in each hand would balance me out. I opened the gate and Mr Williams drove through on the quad. Shutting the gate, I set off across the field after him, following his tail-lights. Even with my head-torch on, I still occasionally stumbled on the rough, uneven terrain. After a while I could feel my shoulders starting to burn from the weight of the buckets. I gritted my teeth a bit and kept walking towards the now static tail-lights.

'Well, that'll save me a trip to the gym!' I commented as I arrived. 'Let's take a look.'

I swivelled my head-torch towards tonight's main event. Pepper was a black Limousin crossed cow. Her real name was something like 00052, but I'm going to call her Pepper. She was a few metres away, laid in the grass and facing uphill. Her head was still up, and she seemed bright enough from a distance, but behind her was a large, fleshy object: her uterus. On the other side of her I could just make out a calf. She'd given birth the day before. Unfortunately, for whatever reason, she'd managed to invert the giant sack that is the bovine uterus. It should have been inside her abdomen with the base of the sack in the bottom of her tummy. Instead, the whole thing, swollen to a metre in diameter, was outside-in and laid on the grass behind her. If it was too badly damaged, we'd have to put her down. I'd check her over, examine her uterus, then decide what to do.

'She's wild, mind,' said Mr Williams. That was not great news. If she tried to run off, she could damage or tear her uterus beyond repair. It also made her dangerous. Cows with a calf at foot can suddenly become vicious as their motherly instincts kick in and they seek to protect their offspring. I made my way to her head. She was wild-eyed and as I went to grab her head she threw it around, trying to catch me with her horns. In a way it was good, because she was still strong. She lashed out again, but I was able to dodge her horns and this time grab her nose. I had a finger in one nostril and a thumb in another. I had to grip hard as she tried to pull her mucous-covered snout out of my grip. I held her, and the farmer managed to get a rope halter on; we had some control. Giving her head end a quick check over, I listened to her heart and her guts, then made my way round to her back end. All in all, she was not too bad, considering. She was a bit cold, losing heat from her prolapsed uterus lying in the cold night air. Hypocalcaemia, a lack of calcium in the blood, common in recently calved cows, was probably a factor: that in itself could kill. Calcium is vital for muscular contraction; animals deficient in it are weak and unsteady on their feet initially. Eventually they cannot stand up and, if it continues to worsen … well, the heart is a muscle; if it stops, they stop. Fortunately, her uterus seemed okay.

I looked around at the cow, the calf, the terrain and the farmer, then came up with my plan. The first thing we had to do was get the cow facing downhill. There was no way I'd be able to push the uterus back in against gravity. There were just two of us and even our combined weight would be less than a third of hers. I decided I'd give her an epidural now, then we could manoeuvre her. Once I'd given the injection, we agreed that Mr Williams would pull on the halter and horns, I'd grab the back legs and try to manage the uterus. Between us, we'd rotate Pepper 180 degrees.

We were lucky the grass immediately around her was damp and smooth; she slid round reasonably easily. We put the calf off to a side in case Pepper tried to get up and injured it. We now had her facing downhill and her pink, fleshy uterus spread on the ground behind her. Mr Williams' job was to hold the halter and sit on the cow to prevent escape attempts. That left me with the sweaty, bloody, shitty and god-knows-what-elsey job of getting Pepper's insides back where they belonged. The epidural would numb her somewhat. Various antibiotics and anti-inflammatories would do their jobs. I'd no doubt she was short on calcium, but I couldn't give her that yet. If she fully recovered, she'd be too strong to restrain and likely throw us off before making a getaway.

Mr Williams had even put lids on the old feed buckets, so the water was still warmish. Mixing antiseptic with the water, I knelt facing Pepper's bum, with a knee either side of her calf bed. I washed it off, getting as much grass and debris off as I could whilst simultaneously checking it over. Satisfied it was still viable, I began trying to replace it. I had to be both careful and firm. You can't just push on the fragile tissue; a human finger is sharp enough go straight through it. Instead, a closed fist must be used to force the pink mass of flesh back through the cow's vaginal opening. Lubricant helps to protect the uterus, but simultaneously renders everything slippy. I positioned myself right up against the uterus with it half on the ground and half on my lap. The whole thing, swollen and cold in the night air, probably weighed about 30 kg. I started near the vaginal end, firmly pushing the calf bed back inside. I'd move one fist, hold it in position, then move the other, hoping to make a little progress each time. It's a slow and frustrating process. Two steps forward, one step back. Initially, it looked like nothing was changing. I kept going, starting to sweat, even in the cold.

Okay, I was making progress now; maybe a quarter of the uterus was inside. However, the sensation of anything near the vulva often causes cows to push against you.

'Mmmmoooooooooo!' With a great bellow, Pepper strained her abdominal muscles and uterine tissue forced its way past my closed fists. Even in her depleted state, she could still win the pushing contest. Sometimes it's more like two steps forward, one back, three forward, then eight back. Sisyphus is a king from Greek mythology who managed to cheat death twice and for doing so was punished by having to roll a boulder up a hill. No sooner had he completed the task than the boulder would roll to the bottom again. He was condemned by the gods to carry out the task for eternity. Replacing a prolapse is the kind of task Sisyphus would have recognised and probably given a miss if he had the chance. There was nothing for it but to start again. I'd begun to make noises too.

'Nnnnnnnnnk!' I strained.

'Mmmmmooooooo!' commented Pepper.

'Arrrrgggggg!' I replied.

'Mmmmooo!' Pepper retorted.

If Attenborough had been lurking in a hedgerow, I'm sure he would have had a blast narrating the scene.

'Here we see the lesser spotted veterinarian. With his puny limbs he struggles to complete his Sisyphean task in the vain hope of one day earning enough money to work four days a week with no on-call …'

Eventually pink fleshy stuff started going in and staying in, I was definitely winning. Gravity was helping, slightly edging the balance of power in my favour. I slowed down. As circulation improved in the newly returned tissue, I didn't want all the cold, pooled blood in Pepper's calf bed to hit the rest of her circulation in one go. More gradually now, I started pushing everything inside. Before long, I was laid on my side on the ground, pushing as far as I possibly could inside her to return her uterus to its normal position. Finally, it was in. I placed a 'purse string' suture in the lips of her vulva. This would close the opening, leaving only enough room to urinate, and hopefully prevent her doing the same again. We had one last thing to do: I wanted to give her some calcium to get her up and on her way, but I didn't trust her not to attempt to kill us. The plan we came up with was simple, but risky. I'd give her one bottle of calcium subcutaneously 'under the skin' that would be absorbed slowly. Then I'd start giving her some intravenously, using a vein on her abdomen, that would act quickly. My kit was preloaded on the quad, the buckets secreted in the hedgerow for later retrieval. If we got all the calcium in, great; however, if she recovered quickly, she might decide to give us a bit of a charging/stamping. So, Mr Williams' job was to sit on the quad with the engine running. At the first sign of our potential assassin rising to her feet I'd hotfoot it to the bike and we'd bravely run away.

I was about three-quarters of the way through the intravenous dose when Pepper had an enormous poo, a sure sign her gut muscles were back in high gear and getting rid of whatever needed getting rid of.

'Come on, quickly, get on, get on!' cried Mr Williams.

I stood my ground a few seconds longer; I wanted to get as much into her as I could.

Pepper started to rise to her feet. Unlike before, she was able to get both front legs under her and push up. That was my cue to leave. I pulled the needle out and ran the few paces to the waiting quad. Climbing on, I grabbed my kit box with one hand and the metal cargo rack on the quad with the other. As we accelerated away from the scene,

Pepper gave half-hearted chase before accepting that she'd have to get us next time. Back at the car, I cleaned up as best I could. I washed my kit and my waterproofs off in a stream at the side of the road. Mr Williams lived some way off; this was rented land. As I splashed water over myself, I felt a cold, wet sensation spreading in the genital area. Bugger, my waterproof trousers had a hole in them. I stripped them off, only to find that my tan trousers were now stained a bright red from my earlier struggles. I just hadn't noticed in the heat of the moment. This is why you need an overnight bag if you're on call. It was already getting light; I needed another cunning plan.

Fortunately, my driver's seat had a waterproof cover, so I wasn't going to ruin the car. I drove back through the country lanes, occasionally squirming around in my seat a bit to alleviate the itchiness of wet, blood-soaked underwear against my skin. At least, with the heater on, it was warm, wet and bloody. My new scheme relied on stealth. I would pop into town and get into a clothes shop as soon as it opened. Since I looked like I'd either murdered someone or been partially murdered myself, I'd have to somehow avoid the staff. I drove into the town centre, parked, and got my phone out. I Googled clothes shops. As I clicked on each one, Google revealed that they were not yet open. Who's buying trousers at 9 o'clock on a Wednesday morning? Apparently not I; then, at last, I spotted that a major chain store was opening soon. I strode through the pedestrian area hoping anyone who saw me would either be too sleepy or in too much of a hurry to notice my appearance. There it was; the lights were on. I slipped inside and made my way to the trouser section. Rifling through, I tried to find something 'vetty'. For once, things went my way. Khaki trousers, 32, short leg, looked useful for safari. I glanced around; I was still unseen. I made my way to the changing rooms, picking up a two-pack of boxers on the way. My plan went without a hitch; the trousers fitted well enough. I rolled up my previous pair and made my way to the cashier's desk.

I passed over the labels I'd taken off the trousers and boxers.

'Hiya, I'd like to buy these please. They fit well, so I'd just like to wear them if that's okay?'

'No probs. Would you like a bag for the old ones?' replied the girl behind the desk.

'Yeah, that would be really handy actually,' I admitted.

One card payment later I was out the door and safely away.

I stopped down the street and treated myself to a bacon roll. As I happily chewed away, I couldn't help but think about the irony of it. I was running around the countryside, taking occasionally not inconsiderable risks to save animals, but also happily munching one down for breakfast. Still, I couldn't dwell on it too long. I fished out my phone and dialled the office. I was going to be late for morning consults, but I figured they'd understand why. Twenty minutes later, another day had begun …

17

DELILAH

On first analysis the chicken is a humble animal, underrated you might say. Domestic chickens, *Gallus gallus domesticus*, are descended from the red junglefowl (*Gallus gallus*) and spread throughout the ancient world from the Indian subcontinent, eventually becoming ubiquitous. They were a bit of an afterthought when I was at vet school. We did learn about chicken biology. However, it was almost exclusively in a commercial context. Which is not all that surprising when you look at the statistics.

In December of 2020, according to the UK government, over one hundred million eggs were 'set' in UK hatcheries. Eggs that are set are those that are expected to hatch out and provide a viable chicken at the other end. That's more than ONE HUNDRED MILLION EGGS, 100,000,000, in one month; December of 2020. These can be further subdivided into a few different categories, but I want to focus on two because they are most relevant to the person in the street. Commercial broilers are birds that are going to be raised, fattened up and then slaughtered for meat. That December, 103.9 million eggs were set, providing a not dissimilar number of birds to be raised for meat. A further 7.8 million eggs were set to become commercial layers.

These would hatch out to provide chickens whose future is to produce eggs for human consumption.

It should rapidly become obvious that chickens are an extremely important source of food for humans.

Those that are raised for meat and those that are to be a source of eggs lead quite different lives. Now, it is fair to say that there are different farming and management styles with different advantages and disadvantages when it comes to productivity and welfare. However, I'll briefly walk us through the common pathway for each.

In the case of broilers, after being laid by their mother, their egg is removed and incubated under tightly controlled environmental conditions. At around 21 days, the chick will break out of its egg using an egg tooth, a specialist addition to the beak evolved for just this purpose, which drops off or is resorbed into the beak once redundant. The chicks are 'precocial', meaning they can immediately get around and fend for themselves to some extent. They are still vulnerable and require a warm, humid environment, almost jungley you might think. Their mother will have been vaccinated for several infectious diseases; this may reduce the risk of exposure to pathogens and confer some immunity on the chick. In addition, they may receive a few vaccines delivered in drinking water, sprays or, in the case of Marek's disease (the only one I can honestly remember from vet school), subcutaneous injection.

Now they are transported to their final home, the chicken shed. Here they will be fed and watered until their heart is content, and then some. In intensive systems, sheds have tens of thousands of birds. They are generally dimly lit, the birds' faeces and urine are absorbed by a litter, which is only changed once the birds have gone for slaughter. The environment provides only for eating, drinking, defecating and sleeping, with minimal room to move around. Environmental enrichment is absent to minimal. Fortunately, the birds don't

have long to suffer. Their genetics along with the management regime mean that they can grow to their 'mature'
slaughter weight in as little as six weeks. Sadly, their rapid
growth can lead to a number of health problems, from lameness due to excess weight borne by immature bones, to heart
failure.

Prior to slaughter they are usually stunned using carbon
dioxide, causing asphyxiation and brain death from lack of
oxygen; alternatively, an electric current applied across their
head and brain causes a similar loss of sensation. In either
instance, stunning is followed by having their throats cut
and ultimately dying via exsanguination, loss of blood. In a
minority of cases, they are slaughtered without stunning for
religious reasons.

Commercial layers are the birds that produce eggs for our
breakfast tables, cafes, protein shakes and cakes. The wild
ancestors of our chickens, which can still be found in
Southeast Asia, lay perhaps sixty eggs per year in clutches of
around five at a time and may live for a couple of decades.
Modern egg-producing chickens produce around three
hundred per year. Genetic and environmental manipulation
has made this possible. As a result of the physiological stress
placed on them, commercial layers live around two years
prior to being culled due to lack of productivity.
Conventional battery cages were banned in Europe in 2012,
though enforcement has not been uniform across all countries. The UK has done well in enforcing the ban. However,
'enriched' battery cage systems are still legal and in use. It is
fair to say that since birds are legally required to have
around 600 square centimetres each, these are at best an
incremental improvement. According to the RSPCA, in 2017
48 per cent of UK eggs were produced in battery cages, 1 per
cent in barn systems and 51 per cent free range. Personally,
I would like to see an end to battery cage systems. A lot of
the birds' welfare depends not just on the system, but on the

operator, their staff and their skills and motivation. To paraphrase a friend who regularly works with commercial chickens: 'I'd rather be a hen in John's cages, than one in Bill's fields.'

I'm not a commercial poultry vet, but I have read the UK legislation for chickens and, in fairness, it's pretty good. People far more knowledgeable than me have constructed the rules and they describe everything from the expertise staff must have to the levels of ammonia permissible in sheds. However, there are, if you'll pardon the pun, always some bad eggs and enforcement is not perfect by any means.

Once a chicken loses its productivity or becomes ill, it is generally culled and then we are back to the CO_2 or the electrocution. Both broiler and egg production involve thousands of animals and the margin for profit on each one is tiny. There is little money or time to spend on ensuring the health of individual birds and virtually all health interventions are done at a flock level. If birds are dying or suffering ill health, any diagnosis is often done via necropsy, which we might more casually refer to as post-mortem.

That leads us to Delilah. Delilah's owner, Gemma, lived on a local smallholding. As someone passionate about animal welfare and having the room to do something about it, she decided to give a home to some hens that had previously been unpaid workers in the greater egg industry. There are a number of charities that facilitate this, including the British Hen Welfare Trust and Give a Hen a Home. Gemma had a small flock of rescued chickens that happily foraged on her farm for worms, berries and seeds to satisfy their omnivorous diet. They had plenty of interesting stuff to investigate, could come and go as they pleased, and could generally do chicken stuff such as establishing a literal pecking order. Crucially, they also had plenty of spots to nest and lay eggs. Eggs, unless the female has been fertilised and the eggs are incubated, are non-fertile and will not produce chicks. Delilah and her band of free-roaming chickens supplied Gemma and her family with a modest supply of eggs without the ethical conundrum of worrying about industrial bird welfare.

Delilah had recently become ill. Gemma had noticed her reduced activity levels, as well as her becoming less sociable with the other birds. A regular layer, Delilah could be relied upon to leave eggs in the same spot. There had been no eggs for a few days and Delilah could occasionally be seen straining as if trying to pass something. Backyard chickens are increasingly common, but they fall into an unusual category, presenting vets with a bit of a quandary. Traditionally, *Gallus g. domesticus* is a production animal and falls comfortably within the purview of specialist agricultural vets who tend to deal almost exclusively with large commercial flocks. However, the increasing popularity of pet chickens has brought owners back into small animal vet's waiting rooms as they seek individual care for their beloved chooks.

Delilah wasn't well. Gemma used us for all her other pets and had phoned us to see if we'd be willing to take a look. I stressed that we were not specialists in chickens, but that I'd be happy to have an initial look and discuss whether it was something we could treat, or perhaps something that would be better dealt with by referring Delilah to someone specialising in exotics. As we saw earlier, there are an increasing number of vets specialising in exotic species, which can be everything from rabbits to pythons. It's a relief to many a first opinion practitioner to have somewhere to send the feathery, spidery or amphibious in their time of need. However, these specialists often charge a premium and are not within everyone's budget.

An appointment was made and before long Gemma was sat waiting patiently in our car park. The standard chaos of a veterinary waiting room includes dogs attempting to run amok and cats noisily protesting against their imprisonment, whilst plotting an escape from their carrier. In summary, our waiting room was not likely to be conducive to good mental health in the average chicken. Wisely, Gemma had chosen to keep Delilah calm and comfortable in her own car.

As unwilling animals were loaded and unloaded, and clients came and went, our car park had become almost as chaotic as the waiting room. In amongst the commotion, identifying the right person could be tricky. I could see a conspicuously muddy four-by-four in the back corner of the car park. It immediately set off my spider senses, which oddly were saying: 'Chicken?' I stared at the four-by-four and could just make out its occupant. She looked back at me and with a quizzical expression held up a suspiciously wicker basket, pointed at it and shrugged her shoulders. There was a chicken in there, I just knew it. I walked over to the pick-up, by which time its owner had exited and was stood next to her basket. It was the moment of truth.

'Hi, I'm Gareth, one of the vets. Is this Delilah by any chance?'

'It is indeed ...' Gemma introduced herself and we chatted through Delilah's symptoms. I got the picture and suspected she was suffering from egg binding: difficulty passing her eggs. Although the patient was eating a bit less and displaying reduced activity levels, Gemma thought she was 'okay'. Promising a thorough exam, I carried Delilah inside and enlisted the help of the least chicken-fearing nurse I could find. We don't see that many birds, but I had a rough idea what I was doing in a general health assessment. I started at the beak and worked my way logically towards the messier end. I inspected the comb, the red, vascular appendage on top of Delilah's head, looked in her mouth, glanced at her beak. The best way to spot the abnormal is to see plenty of normal. Unfortunately, variations from the average can appear to be abnormalities to the untrained eye. My eye was half-trained at best; I just don't see enough cases. However, Delilah appeared to be reasonably healthy. As I got to her abdomen, I gently massaged it, feeling the structures inside, a type of examination called palpation. Towards the end of her abdomen, I could feel a normal-sized egg, which must have been ready for laying.

As I got to her rear end, I donned a glove and covered it in lubricant. I gently inserted a digit into her vent, causing a sudden 'Pawwwcawwww!' Delilah's complaint split the silence in the room; she was not impressed, and I didn't blame her. I would not be impressed if I turned up at the doctor's surgery only for them to insert a digit in me without any preamble or explanation. However, there are as yet no universal translators and so our poor patients must undergo this unexplained indignity in certain circumstances. Sometimes a stuck egg needs only some lubrication and a bit of massage to help it on its way. I gave this a go, but to no effect. I tried gently massaging her abdomen, trying to milk the egg out. It moved a bit, towards the vent. I had a glance, and I could see the problem; there was red tissue between the egg and the vent. There was some inflammation of the reproductive tract, salpingitis. I couldn't see the egg itself, so it was either behind a narrowing or stricture in the canal, or maybe even in the abdomen. If that was the case, Delilah would never be able to lay the egg, and it was causing her significant issues. I could do a variety of further investigations, such as ultrasound and x-ray, but while they would help me with the diagnosis, they wouldn't solve the problem. Specialists will sometimes use an endoscope to actually look inside the abdomen through a tiny hole, but we didn't have access to one. We were also talking about several hundred pounds' worth of tests. Personally, I preferred the idea of referring Delilah, but I needed to talk to her owner.

I left Delilah with my fearless assistant while I made my way back outside. Gemma and I discussed Delilah's predicament. Gemma wanted to help her, but the cost of referral and the difficulty of travel ruled it out. Gemma had kids to care for and home-school, as well as a smallholding to run. Her husband worked offshore and was away at the moment. We'd have to do what we could locally. I proposed supportive therapy, anti-inflammatories and antibiotics. I hoped that if we addressed the inflammation and got Delilah eating properly, she might yet pass the egg. The alternative was opening Delilah up to diagnose the problem and fix it if we could. It wasn't something I'd done before, nor had anyone else at the practice. If neither was an option, we'd have to consider putting Delilah down. We agreed to try a day or two's treatment and reassess. I went back inside and got the relevant drugs from our pharmacy cupboards, then replaced Delilah in her carrier and took her back outside. Gemma and I went through all the instructions and then I wished her good luck and asked her to call with an update in the morning. We agreed that if there was no change in 48 hours, we'd have another think.

Our treatment regime didn't work. Two days later I was again examining Delilah. She was much the same as before and it was now clear intervention was required. I'd already ordered a backyard chicken manual online. I'd been able to brush up a bit, and I was confident that my patient needed surgery. However, the book had only black-and-white photos and little information on the procedure I wanted to perform. Therefore, I'd hummed and hawed and eventually opted to order yet another textbook out of my own money. At this rate I was going to spend more on Delilah than Gemma would. We had to decide. I told Gemma we had three options:

1. Continue medical therapy.
2. Surgery.
3. Euthanasia.

I was confident medical therapy was unlikely to succeed. Realistically, I could really only recommend one of the last two. It was going to set Gemma back about £300, and only because we'd opted to do the procedure on the cheap. I felt it only fair to charge in line with my expertise, which was modest at best. Having given it some thought, Gemma made a decision.

'Let's do it. I'd do it for my dog, so why not her?'

I explained to Gemma that another chicken manual was on its way. I checked my phone, and realised delivery was expected tomorrow. I wanted time to study the task I'd set myself. Given it was Friday, we agreed I'd plan the surgery for Monday morning. In the meantime, we'd continue the current therapy. Delilah's owner was very clued up on husbandry. After our last discussion she'd already placed her poorly pet in a windowless outhouse. It would protect her from bullying by other chickens who might take advantage of her illness. Chickens lay more eggs with longer daylight hours, so placing her in the dark outhouse would also dial down her egg-manufacturing insides. There was already one egg stuck, we didn't want more.

Normally, Delilah's left ovary, located near her kidney, would produce the new eggs. The ovary looks like a miniature bunch of grapes. It is covered in eggs at various stages of development, each wrapped in a bubble-like follicle up to around 20 mm in size. As the egg is released at the moment of ovulation, it is caught by the oviduct or uterus. The baby egg travels down the oviduct through several specialised areas that add proteins, minerals and other ingredients to the egg in layers. During the last half-day or so in the uterus, calcium is transported from the chicken's bloodstream to harden the egg's shell and turn it into something we would recognise in the supermarket. During its journey the egg has increased in size; initially like a grain of sand, it is now table ready. During laying, the egg is pushed out of the vagina and exits the chicken via the vent or, more formally, cloaca. In Delilah's case, the egg was probably stuck in the uterus, near the vagina.

I spent much of my weekend reading, learning more about chickens than ever before. It was embarrassing to register just how ignorant I was when it came to Delilah and how her body worked. Anaesthesia would be a critical part of our operation. Our patients are normally rendered unconscious with an injectable drug, then kept asleep with anaesthetic gas. But chickens are not even mammals; their respiratory system is totally different from ours. According to one of my purchases, the BSAVA Manual of Backyard Poultry, avian lungs are around 10 times as effective as those of mammals when it comes to getting oxygen out of the air, due to several modifications. Unlike us, their lungs do not expand; they lack a diaphragm. Instead, about 80 per cent of their respiratory tract is made up of air sacs. The air sacs even fill portions of the larger bones and act like bellows. They provide the power in the breathing cycle and push air through the lungs in one direction only.

There are a myriad of other differences between avian and mammalian physiology. I would have to use different dosages of drugs. We'd have to improvise with the equipment we had to achieve something suitable for my patient. I couldn't learn everything in 48 hours, so I had to select my reading carefully, concentrating on the anaesthesia and the surgical anatomy of Delilah's abdomen, making sure I knew enough not to cause her damage through ignorance. My textbook was firm on one thing: if I wanted to remove Delilah's ovary, preventing future issues with egg laying, I would need a microscope. I shelved that for now. I had some confidence that I might be able to manage. I could always zoom in by simply moving my head closer to the patient.

Monday morning came all too soon. I'd photocopied bits of my chicken handbook to give to our nurses. I'd be overseeing things, but they'd have to handle most of the anaesthetics. Gemma dropped Delilah off first thing. We agreed that if I couldn't sort things out, we'd put Delilah down while she was unconscious; there was no point in waking her up only to have her pass away soon after, suffering unnecessary pain.

I got my conventional patients out of the way first. I had a couple of cats to castrate, two bitches to spay (ovario-hysterectomies), a tumour to remove and some plastic surgery to do on a dog's eyelids. They were rubbing on his eyes and causing painful ulcers. Mammals out of the way, it was ornithology time. My references didn't all agree on how best to knock my chicken out. We opted to put a little mask over her head, a bit like a chicken space helmet, and turn on the anaesthetic gas at a high percentage. After a few cross words and a bit of struggling, Delilah started to slump to the table. The nurses got her on her side, and we discussed how best to prepare her. A heat mat would keep her warm while we plucked the feathers off the left-hand side of her tummy. Then specialist washes would ready her skin for my incision. At the moment, my plan was to remove her ovary and oviduct along with the offending egg, but I had to be prepared to change my plan if I found the unexpected.

Delilah settled, and with the nurses and I prepared for surgery, we began. I unwrapped my instruments from their sterile pack, and spread them out according to my preference, the ones for my right hand on the right, for my left on the left. Lifting my sterile drape, I cut a window in it and placed this over Delilah, leaving only the area I was to operate on exposed. The drape would stop contamination from the rest of her body entering my wound site.

'Ready?'

'Yeah, happy,' replied the anaesthetic nurse.

I gently started to make my cut. It would run from roughly halfway up my patient's ribcage to her pelvis and allow me a small window to assess her coelomic cavity, the fancy term for her tummy. Her tissues were thin and delicate. Although she weighed 1.5 kg, the shape of her body meant my incision was tiny, even compared to what I might achieve in a puppy or kitten. Once I'd opened through her skin and musculature, I had to puncture one of her air sacs to gain full access. The tiny incision in the sac needed no repair; it would heal itself. Straight away, I could see the egg. It was lodged in her vagina. Following her uterus up, I could also see the ovary. It had stopped producing more eggs, likely a combination of illness and Delilah's restriction to the dark. I spent a few minutes poking around, deciding what was what and assessing what I could realistically achieve. My previous confidence left me. I looked at her ovary and realised there was no question of removing it. It was tightly stuck to her body wall, covered in large blood vessels. Even an error of a millimetre or two would probably be fatal. It was immediately obvious why removing it was not advised. Perhaps you did need a microscope after all? Her uterus looked fairly healthy, but a narrowing near the end meant the egg was never coming out. I had planned to remove her uterus, but I realised even this was going to be difficult.

Time was passing; I needed a plan. I could remove the egg through the wall of the uterus. However, as soon as Delilah went back to her normal life she would lay more and end up with the same issue. It wouldn't be fair. Unless I removed the ovary, she would definitely produce more eggs, and I couldn't do that without killing her. I had one option left. I'd thought about a backup plan if I ended up in this situation. I would remove the stuck egg from her uterus and then stitch it up. Then I would reassemble everything else. Lastly, I would insert a hormonal implant under her skin. It would slowly release a hormone called deslorelin, stopping our poorly fowl from laying any eggs for up to a year. We'd have to insert another in time, but it was an option I'd already prepared Gemma for. The implant was expensive, but I'd discussed the cost and Delilah's owner had agreed to its use if necessary.

I had a plan of action; now I just had to carry it out. I gently cut into the oviduct with my scalpel. I asked one of the nurses to reach under Delilah and apply gentle upwards pressure, bringing the egg towards me. I gradually extended the incision; I could get the egg out of the uterus. However, the hole in the body wall was so small compared to the egg, I was struggling to get it out. I began to sweat. What if I couldn't remove it? Maybe I should have used a different way into my chicken? I could have made a cut in the centre of her abdomen. But this was the one the book had recommended for this procedure! Goddamn it, the egg was right there! A few minutes of fiddling about went past. I couldn't grab the egg and pull it out; there was too little space. It wasn't looking good. I had one last thought. I placed down my instruments and gently reached under my bird. I was now non-sterile, but I could rectify that in a minute. I gently felt Delilah's insides, then started to push the other side of her body upwards, using each of my fingers as individually as possible to push the egg out of my wound, while stopping it from slipping away.

Nearly there, nearly there. 'Clunk!'

The egg emerged from the wound and fell on to the operating table.

I looked up at the nurse monitoring all things unconsciousness related, only to realise two of the nurses had swapped and I hadn't even noticed. Nonetheless, we were both relieved. Stitching up went well. Muscle is deceptively weak, and my sutures were barely holding it all together, but it *was* together. I finished the skin off quickly. Antibiotics, pain relief and anti-inflammatories were already circulating in Delilah from earlier injections.

'Just a minute,' I said. I made my way through to the fridge and got the hormone implant. Gently folding Delilah's skin, I used the outsized needle to insert the grain-of-rice-sized object through the skin. Soon it would get to work, switching off her egg-laying machinery.

Once off the table, she came round quickly. We transferred her to a cage on her own, away from cats and dogs that would no doubt stress her out. I phoned her owner and let her know the outcome. I'm not sure which of us was more relieved. Unfortunately, I was already late for consultations. I'd have to skip lunch and start dealing with clients, already a bit cross at their increased waiting time. As evening rolled around it came time to discharge Delilah. First, I had a routine spay to discharge.

'Did you manage to do her teeth at the same time?' the lady asked as I passed back a West Highland White Terrier.

'Yep, all scaled and polished for you,' I confirmed.

The lady took a couple of steps forward, grabbed both my cheeks and gave them a good chuckle.

'You're just so handsome!' she said.

I'm 40 and less good-looking by the day. I was embarrassed and concerned that she was driving whilst clinically blind. I also secretly enjoyed the compliment.

It was now Delilah's turn. I went through all the aftercare, highlighting the need to keep her safe, comfortable and warm. She'd be in the house tonight; after that Gemma planned to keep her in the outhouse with another trusted companion to allow her social interaction with minimal risk. As before, Gemma was a step ahead of me.

As the busy week continued, I realised I hadn't heard

anything about Delilah for a few days. Was she okay? I tentatively picked up the phone and dialled the smallholding. I'd made this type of call before, only to find out a patient hadn't pulled through, an awkward conversation at best.

'Hello?' I recognised the voice; it was Gemma.

'Hi, it's Gareth here. How's Delilah getting on?'

'Oh hi, Gareth! She's … deeshhhgwwtzzzzzzpt,' Gemma said.

'Hi, hello? Can you hear me?' I replied. 'Helloooowwww.'

'Yeah, hi?'

'You broke up there, I'm afraid,' I explained. 'How is our girl getting on?'

'Oh yeah, she is doing great thanks, back to normal.'

I sighed in relief. It turned out I'd just missed Gemma when she'd been at the practice earlier. We went through all the aftercare, but things were looking up and Delilah could soon go back out with the other chickens. Gemma had dropped off a box of chocolates for everyone to share, and a bottle of whisky that had my name on it. It hadn't been easy, but we'd got there in the end. I now knew more about the humble domestic chicken than ever before.

One more thought occurred to me. In the film *The Martian*, Matt Damon's character, Mark Watney, is stranded on Mars. In order to effect his own rescue he must make his way to another spacecraft and use it without the owner's permission. He realises that since he is not on Earth, or governed by any country, the law that applies is the law of the sea. Technically, entering the other spacecraft is an act of piracy. And since the events occur in space, he declares himself: 'Mark Watney, Space Pirate'.

Crocodiles are sometimes described as living dinosaurs. However, according to a Harvard study, chickens are even more closely related to *Tyrannosaurus rex* than crocodilians. I'm not saying anything. I'm just observing that if Mark

Watney ever had to introduce me, he would almost certainly use the words: 'Dinosaur Surgeon'.

As job titles go, it must be up there.

18

MEAT AND MISERY

Will future generations look back on our industrial meat production the way we look at slavery, concentration camps or the gulag? Well, unless you've actually been to a slaughterhouse, I'd suggest you cannot honestly answer that question. I have; they're grim – professional, but grim. What else can you say about a process that renders sentient animals into slabs of meat in the space of a few tens of metres?

The process I saw begins with live cows. They are herded in one at a time; the group deliberately stopped from viewing the demise of their companions. A shot in the head with a captive bolt gun (which projects a bolt, rather than a bullet, into the skull) disrupts the frontal part of the brain and stuns the animal. Then they are pithed: a rod is inserted into the wound in their skull and pushed backwards until it exits through the foramen magnum. This is the hole at the back of the skull, through which your spinal cord exits. As the rod passes through this area, the medulla is destroyed; this can be thought of as the life support centre for the body. Consciousness already gone from the bolt, life support is removed, and death follows shortly thereafter. Then the animal is attached by its hind legs to the line, a conveyor belt of sorts, mounted overhead, which transports the carcass around the slaughterhouse and facilitates the animal to meat transformation. Next the animal is bled, skinned, internal organs are extracted, various bits are removed, and the carcass graded before it can be sold for butchering. The animals must be clean-ish when presented for slaughter. But they are still filthy with bacteria and a careless cut with a skinning knife will contaminate the meat with potentially lethal bacteria. It's skilful, hard and frankly distressing work. The people working there have grown used to it and often have a rather dark sense of humour, in common with all who regularly encounter death.

I still eat meat, probably more than I should. It seems there are reasons to eat less:

Health: the jury is still out, but it seems likely that we eat too much meat in 'Western' society.

Environmentalism: the industrial raising of animals for meat is desperately inefficient. At most, 10 per cent of the energy expended in rearing animals is realised once they are eaten. In addition, their faeces are often difficult to get rid of. It is valuable as a fertiliser but spreading it excessively can contaminate water and degrade the environment in both watercourses and the ocean through a process called eutrophication. Excess nutrients in the run-off cause an overgrowth of phytoplankton in the water, and oxygen levels drop, killing aquatic life. In many areas land is being cleared to make way for more farms, changing the face of our earth, altering climate and further endangering rare species. In some cases, this land rapidly ends up useless, as without the natural, complex eco-system, erosion and loss of nutrients renders the new farmland infertile and unproductive. Methane is an extremely potent greenhouse gas and is produced in copious quantities by our grass-munching victims.

These are laudable reasons, but they aren't what got my mind going. That would be the ethics. In the past few decades many of the supposedly unique capabilities that make us human have been found elsewhere. Where sentience and the ability to truly suffer begins it is hard to say. It certainly isn't at the level of a single cell, but it is somewhere before pigs, sheep or cows. That we breed, rear and then kill animals on an industrial scale may well prove something our descendants find truly repulsive.

European legislation affords animals the five freedoms:

Freedom from hunger and thirst.
Freedom from discomfort.
Freedom from pain, injury or disease.
Freedom to express normal behaviour.
Freedom from fear or distress.

In New Zealand, beef, lamb and milk are often produced extensively. Large numbers of animals are reared on a large area of ground with the minimum of input. That's probably about as close to the meadow idyl as cows are going to get, although the cows in Switzerland look pretty smug too. However, extensive farming does come with some issues. It takes a lot of land, leading to deforestation as demand for meat increases globally. It may also seem like a high-welfare environment and perhaps it is for the healthy animal. Using huge tracts of land makes daily inspection of animals difficult to impossible. As a result, any animal that finds itself compromised is liable to wait some time for help. Animals reared this way routinely suffer the kind of fate suffered on the savanna by truly wild animals: extremes of weather, predation, disease, birthing problems, trauma and misadventure. How can an animal farmed extensively be kept from discomfort or fear, spared from pain, injury or disease?

Conversely, animals in the USA and Western Europe are often farmed in an intensive manner. In some instances, they barely go outside any more. However, they are afforded adequate (by our measure) space, individual attention, dietary supplementation as required, rubber beds, scratching posts and so on. It's a veritable cow hotel. They are unlikely to fall prey to all but the most mythical of predators, and illness is usually detected and addressed early. Intensification also allows fewer people to care for more animals. In either system the idea is to minimise the cost per animal, and therefore maximise profit. I wonder to what extent a cow housed all year round can really have the freedom of natural behaviour. I've seen young cattle housed in small pens over winter let out on the spring grass; the obvious joy they take in running, bucking and playing on release is undeniable

Globally there are now more urban dwellers than rural. That tipping point occurred very recently. Since the Industrial Revolution in the 1700s and 1800s, people have gradually, and then precipitously, migrated into our urban areas for work and in search of a 'better' life. With that came a disconnectedness from rural life and the natural world. A great many people, particularly in the developed world, have been born and raised without ever seeing an animal raised for food or encountering a farmer. I was once called out by a lady who had found a sheep in extreme peril. It was trapped in mud below the high-tide mark and was going to suffer a terrible death by drowning if it wasn't rescued, or so I was told. It was hardly my problem. Really, she needed to inform the relevant farmer. I agreed to come out, though, as I didn't want to see the animal suffer and I expected she would have trouble identifying the owner.

'Okay madam, where are you?'

'I don't know.'

'I see, that is going to make things difficult.'

'Humph ...'

'Where did you set off from?'

'The cafe.'

'Which cafe?'

'Eh, oh, well, it was next to the river.'

'Right … The Baker's Dozen?'

'No, that's not it. I didn't think there'd be all these questions …'

'Corner Cafe?'

'Eh, yes, it might have been that.'

'Okay, then where did you go?'

'Towards the river.'

'Okay, so you walked towards the river. Did you go upstream or downstream?'

'How am I supposed to know that?'

'Eh, okay, was the water flowing towards you as you walked or away?'

'I don't know!'

'Hmm, okay, when you hit the water/land interface did you turn right or left?'

'Right.'

'Then you walked along until you hit the estuary?'

'The what?'

'Estuary.'

'Eh?'

At this point I was for the first time glad I'd dropped English for Geography in high school. I gave a quick description of the relevant feature. Unfortunately, there wasn't time to get on to the features of a glaciated landscape. I'd have to wait for another opportunity to wedge that into a conversation.

'Roughly how far along the estuary are you?'

'Well, I can hardly be expected to know that.'

'Right, yes, good point. Can you see an old castle?'

'Yes.'

'Okay, I know roughly where you are.'

'How long will you be? The tide is coming in!'

'I'm on my way now.'

'Will I have to pay?'

(Long sigh) 'No, I suppose not.'

I'd been using an Ordnance Survey map to track her description and had identified a rough area for my sheep rescue. If you are a student intending to work out of your vehicle at any point, get on a reputable map-reading/basic navigation course. Glenmore Lodge and Plas y Brenin are the national mountain centres of Scotland and Wales respectively. They run excellent, enjoyable courses and have bars. Off I went. I managed to manoeuvre my elderly car down a farm track until I was perhaps a mile or two distant from my expected rendezvous. Then I set off in my wellies and waterproofs. I drew the occasional quizzical look from dog walkers as they wondered what this rather oddly dressed chap was planning on getting up to. Something rather unsavoury, no doubt. Why else would you dress top to toe in stuff that you can rinse DNA off? I suppose from an animal point of view I was technically a serial killer. After a half-hour or so I came across the lady in question, who immediately castigated me for my tardiness and called into question my dedication to the job. I bit my tongue whilst fantasising about holding her head under the water until she apologised.

'Are you sure the sheep's stuck?' I asked.

'Well, it hasn't moved, it's in terrible danger ... it'll drown!'

'It looks like it's having a nap to me.'

'Well, I've never been so ... are you going to rescue it or not!?'

'I'm not convinced it needs rescuing.'

'This is an outrage; how dare you!'

Long story short, I strode out on to the mud in which the sheep was 'trapped' in the glorious June sunshine. I got within about five metres, at which point it glanced up, stood and promptly ran off. I strode back to shore and managed not to state the obvious. The woman was contrite. By now I'd calmed down a bit and I assured her that it was a nice day, I'd had a walk and she'd had the very best of intentions. We parted on good terms. From complaints about the smell, to expectations that you can safely saunter through a field with a bull in it, many folk have known little about the countryside for many years. They have lived in, and experienced life through, cities. It's no one's fault, just a fact of modern life.

However, I feel we have started to come full circle. Increased leisure time and access to vehicles has allowed people to get out in the countryside. Access laws have generally opened the land up for the reasonable participant. The internet has allowed almost universal access to information. Economic growth has meant people have the time and energy to worry about where their food comes from. It is right that we seek to minimise the suffering of animals in our midst. But we must maintain a balanced perspective. There is plenty of evidence that humans tend to place more weight on evidence that supports the conclusions they have already come to; this is confirmation bias. We see this on both sides of many debates. If no amount of evidence can change your mind on a matter, you're not engaged in debate or argument, you're engaged in rhetoric.

Animal rights activists perform a vital function highlighting the horrific treatment animals sometimes endure at the hands of humans. Many positive changes to welfare legislation can be traced back to the political pressure brought to bear by campaigns for animal rights, or the shift in public opinion that has come about as a result of them. For example, with some exceptions, such as Arctic reindeer herders, there is little excuse for wearing fur. Where animals are reared in horrific conditions and subjected to horrific deaths in the name of fashion it makes me want to form up a firing squad and book flights.

However, I have seen some adverts from animal rights groups that are either misinformed or deliberately misleading. In one a man holds a sheep that is badly injured and bloody; the words 'have the rest of your wool coat' are put in his mouth as he hands it towards the reader. This is, at best, disingenuous. Sheep are shorn for their wool; it involves shaving their coat short, not cutting the animal itself. The people who shear sheep are very hard working and take great pains not to injure the animals under their care; it is unfair to demonise them. Occasionally activists receive their information only from other activists and lack a balancing, contrary viewpoint. It is especially easy to end up in an informational bubble with our increasingly online lives, and there is a risk of undermining your own argument if you are seen to misrepresent the facts.

Animal welfare standards in the UK are high and continue to rise. I've seen only a few farmers from thousands and thousands who were deliberately cruel; I've even argued with some. They usually go out of business. On the other hand, I've seen tears rolling down a farmer's cheeks as I treated one of his cows; most farmers are just as empathetic towards their animals as any pet owner. There is no market for cruelty in the UK. Modern cattle would, in many cases, be simply unable to keep themselves alive without farmers and vets. Admittedly, we've made them that way, but they are not wild and haven't been for a while. I've seen cattle standing at the gate mooing to get milked. Not a behaviour you see in the average wildebeest. The world is not as we wish it and never will be. We see the cost of living in nature; we are part of nature. We are uniquely innovative, but we will be unable to end all suffering no matter our technology. It is easy to criticise others when your food is readily obtainable from the local supermarket, and you never have to deal with the realities of providing sustenance to an enormous population.

For farmers, be prepared for change. Tradition is not a defence. It's nice to preserve tradition, but nice doesn't trump better. The fact that your father or grandfather engaged in a particular practice does not give you the right to continue doing it. They were people of their time, and you are a person of yours. Only those who embrace change can prosper. Life is change, in many ways. Nothing is constant. As our world alters in its climate and geography, society and human behaviours also adapt and change. One of the greatest changes in our time is the amazing access to information we are all blessed with. Embrace it. Where the debate lacks clarity due to a lack of information, fill the void. Where others misunderstand or misrepresent the facts, set the record straight.

In the last few years, I have occasionally caught myself ordering vegetarian food in restaurants and even attempting the odd recipe at home. I'm not going to try to make the case for vegetarianism or veganism. I suspect there are some for whom such practices are incompatible with optimal health; there may be others that get on just fine. The suitability of any diet for long-term health may take decades to establish and the details are beyond the scope of this book. What I have to say on the matter is more to do with respect for the argument and the validity of other opinions. We must eat. The question is how to do it with the minimum of impact on the welfare of other sentient organisms. It may seem obvious, but there are issues with some of the answers offered up.

Pescatarians are those who add fish to a vegetarian diet. However, fishing and aquaculture present another moral conundrum for humanity. Goldfish only have a two-second memory, right? In fact, a recent study suggests fish have meaningful memories. I mean, they're not reciting Homer's *Odyssey*, but then neither are most humans. The study I read about involved a rudimentary maze placed in a tank with food at one end. Once fish had learned how to negotiate the maze, they were able to do so faster, even after the maze had been removed and then reinserted sometime later.

The point is that, if you are eating fish because they are too dumb to suffer, you are mistaken, I'm afraid. If that makes anyone uncomfortable, good; comfort is not a driver of thought or change, unless you work for a sofa company. Modern industrial fishing bears little resemblance to the activity engaged in by our ancestors. It would also be disingenuous to discuss fishing as if that's all it is. What about the innumerable creatures killed or injured by our fishing industry? We must examine the whole process as it operates in the real world, not via a romanticised ideal. 'Efficiency' has unfortunately led many industries astray, as it is often expressed using narrow parameters, usually those easiest to measure. This is short-sighted at best, arrogant at worst. The ecological processes that keep our oceans teaming with life are enormously complex; we do not, and probably will never, completely understand them. The best way to preserve them is to leave them alone as far as is possible, using only what we must.

Veganism is the supreme moral high ground: no meat or animal products. I admire these guys; they have the courage of their convictions. Meat production and fishing have obvious welfare concerns. After all, you generally kill things prior to eating them. To start eating something prior to its death is both problematic for practical reasons and, I think, just rude. However, there are legitimate welfare concerns over milk and egg production as well. So, consuming no animal products is the place to be at, right. Right?!

Well, like everything else in science, it's more complicated than that. Plants can move somewhat; they follow the sun. They release chemical messengers in response to damage and interact with insects in complex ways. One study has suggested that plants exposed to the recorded sound of a flying bee were able to make their nectar sweeter within minutes, increasing the odds of pollination. They may close their stomata – holes in the leaves for transpiration – to preserve water, responding not to drought itself, but to signals from neighbours who are registering the dry conditions, much like a scream in a crowded theatre. Plants emit sounds and chemicals, respond to messages transmitted in a variety of modalities; pheromones and noises released in response to damage could be interpreted as … pain? Uh-oh! Well, this is awkward.

We readily acknowledge pain expressed by other mammals, as we recognise it easily. Other species may express their difficulties in ways we cannot easily detect. What is pain? What is suffering? Well, we're not quite sure. Anyone who is, is likely to be ignorant or disingenuous. It's a debate and the answer isn't going to be simple. It's likely that the ability to experience pain will involve a spectrum rather than a binary situation. Not yes or no; but kind of, a little bit, a little bit more, and 'Ow! That fucking hurt!'

What does this mean for us? I think we are probably going to have to accept that the reality of existing is that in order to do so we will deny existence, or cause damage, to other things that also, well, exist. Every living thing on this planet modifies its environment in some way. Even if it is only the absorption of nutrients or energy and the excretion of waste or by-products.

'No!' I hear someone cry. 'I won't do it, I won't cause suffering.' That's great: don't bite into that carrot, don't crush its tiny, helpless, carroty cells and trigger those pain signals to the other cells and carrots. Spare it. Instead, die of starvation next to it, morally pure. But know that you've been outmanoeuvred by a vegetable.

We must eat, and to do so we are going to modify our environment, we are going to cause some unpalatable side effects. We now have over 7 billion mouths to feed. So how do we best proceed?

Efficiently. Enormous amounts of food are wasted. It is estimated that around 30 per cent of global food supplies are squandered in some fashion. We will not be able to eliminate waste, but we must seek to minimise it.

In the last decade or so, scientists have begun to grow meat in the laboratory. The idea of growing meat in the lab seems somehow, just wrong. When we picture cattle frolicking in alpine meadows and eating delicious grass and grass derivatives, borne of only the sun's energy and the fruits of the earth, it all seems rather wholesome. Petri dishes and white coats do not have the same appeal, but what if meat from the lab can be made as nutritious, or even more so? There are several claimed advantages.

Although UK vets and farmers have together reduced the amount of antibiotics used in agriculture by about 40 per cent, there is no doubt that antibiotic resistance is a concern for human health, and meat agriculture is not helping. Every dose of antibiotics given carries the risk of generating a resistant bacterial strain. Meat grown from rapidly dividing cells in the laboratory is not prone to pneumonia or diarrhoea, and therefore won't require veterinary care. You'd like to think it doesn't get covered in faeces and the food-poisoning bacteria contained therein. The risk to human health may be substantially reduced.

We have just seen how a virus jumping from one species to another, whether via a laboratory or not, can be lethal. Industrial farming represents an enormous population of animals, in close contact with humanity, who provide hosts for all manner of micro-organisms. Our industrial meat production has the potential to be the end of us.

The big issue for now is cost. A hot dog (lab-meat seems to be very much at the hot-dog, burger stage rather than the sirloin stage) is likely to set you back several thousand dollars. But sequencing a genome used to cost millions of dollars. Now it can be done for a few hundred. I think lab-grown meat is here to stay. I welcome it. Not intuitively, but intellectually; in this case we may really be able to have our cake and eat it.

I have no issue with ethical, sustainable hunting. The health of the deer population in Scotland, in the absence of any predators, depends on it. I've hunted deer myself. A friend wants to rewild his estate, returning it to something approximating ancient woodland. In the USA, the world-famous Yellowstone Park has seen the reintroduction of wolves, lowering herbivore numbers; returning flora has in turn seen the return of insects, then birds and so on as the food chain re-establishes itself. Biodiversity has taken off. Without large predators in the UK, humans must play that role. I can't take any pleasure in shooting a deer. I can only take satisfaction from doing it professionally and ensuring that suffering is minimised. Putting myself in the hooves of the deer, I think I'd rather be shot than torn apart and partially consumed by a predator while I still struggle for survival. We should make full use of any animal killed. The meat, skin, bone, antlers and hooves, every last morsel that's useful or nutritious.

Insect protein is another source of potential nutrition that has a large 'Ick!' factor but that has considerable promise. There are already pet food manufacturers exploiting this and I spoke with one representative who outlined the production process. Insect larvae are unleashed on waste vegetable matter. In a few days or so the larvae have undergone massive multiplication and converted the food waste into harvestable grubs that are suitable as a protein source for dog food. Using vegetable by-products would reduce waste and make organic garbage an economically valuable product, rather than something to bury. It's also claimed that this uses, very approximately, a fortieth of the land area, and a twentieth of the water it would take to produce the same amount of animal protein. Happily, it also only produces a twentieth of the carbon dioxide. Should we be eating more Stickies? Fewer Delilahs, Salts and Peppers?

I'm not 100 per cent down with insects as dinner myself, but I know a Labrador who is. For me, this is a win all round. Provided the amino acid profile is correct, which it appears to be, we should be encouraging people to transition their pets on to these foods. Pigs and octopi appear to be just as intelligent as dogs. Cows and sheep seem to have complex emotions. How can we justify the rearing or capture of one sentient animal to feed another if there's an alternative option? There's no logic here, only convention and tradition. In the future, like lab-grown meat, insect protein has an important contribution to make to human and animal nutrition.

Then there are genetically modified organisms (GMOs). You could argue that we are already consuming them. Our modern dietary staples, whether vegetables or cereals, are quite unlike their ancestors. Modern peas are some ten times the size of the wild variety. Modern corn produces about fifty times the useable cob of its predecessors. Crops can be manufactured to be resistant to drought, parasites and disease. Other modifications can change their nutrient profile, helping to address dietary deficiencies. However, altering a genome with advanced techniques such as CRISPR, a technique for editing genes, is not the same as selective breeding; we should perhaps tread carefully, but tread we probably should.

There's even a company in Finland, called Solarfood, that uses algae and fermentation, along with air, electricity and micronutrients, to produce a protein-rich foodstuff. They claim their process is twenty times as efficient as the photosynthesis that powers arable agriculture and two hundred times more efficient than meat production. I hope they are right.

Some of these technologies have the potential not only to replace industrial meat production, but to free the world from hunger whilst decoupling food production from land use and allowing the return of nature.

Right now, we can take steps to address welfare in existing animal-rearing units. More space, greater ability to express natural behaviours. We must address slaughter. All animals including humans experience physical and emotional pain. We will all die. For myself, I want a good life and then, hopefully, oblivion when the time comes. It's often not death itself we fear, but the pain and distress surrounding it. If I want a peaceful, painless, and hopefully, surprising death for myself, I must support it for animals. It's imperative that animals live lives worth living until they are slaughtered. When they are killed, it must be with a near-instantaneous loss of consciousness and awareness in order to minimise both physical and emotional pain.

When meat is produced in line with some religious doctrines, however, they have their throats cut while conscious. This is no longer defensible when other options are available. In the UK we have a strong tradition of religious freedom, but we recognise the primacy of law. I think a new generation of people of all religions and none are going to endorse changes to ancient practices as they grow up educated on the realities of human and animal biology.

I've thought recently about how we might optimise our agriculture, whilst also rehabilitating nature. A form of zoning may be one answer. At the moment we have a countryside that is a poor cousin of real nature. Perhaps the answer is to move away from a system of 'average'; instead we split our landscape into three loose zones.

Zone 1: This contains our large cities and urban centres.
Hydroponics or aquaponics, combined with multi-storey
greenhouses, are a feature, harnessing every tool in our
modern arsenal. Drones may dart from plant to plant,
harvesting crops at the optimum time, recharging from
localised solar power or low-carbon electricity from
modern modular nuclear plants. This zone would also
contain land intensively used for agriculture, whether
that be cereal crops or high-welfare dairy, beef and pork
units. Insect-protein factories and lab-grown meat are
also produced here. In time, fewer animals may be raised
as societal norms shift. In this zone, nature is not
ignored, but it takes a back seat to the realities of food
production. It would produce the majority of waste,
making it easier to manage as it's already centralised.

Zone 2: This would look not unlike the countryside we see
now, but farm size would likely be reduced. The role of
zone 2 is to grow rarer plants and raise rare-breed
animals. Its main function is to provide genetic diversity.
The animals used in intensive units are increasingly
genetically similar. As a result, they are potentially
vulnerable to any pathogen that leverages genetic
weaknesses. Zone 2 provides resilience. These animals
provide a living repository of genetics that might be used
to restock zone 1 in the event of a veterinary or
botanical pandemic. Insect and plant life is encouraged.
Even weeds are valued; many are in fact edible but have
not become a routine part of the human diet. Stocking
densities are low; fallow land and the return of much of
the land to its natural state is encouraged. Robots,
drones and AI can all be harnessed to allow keepers to
achieve high welfare with lower labour costs.

Zone 3: This is, for the most part, nature itself. In the UK
and many other countries, this will require rewilding
and, in some cases, rehabilitation. There are already

cases of rewilding in the UK; it's a beautiful thing and nature can be deceptively quick to reclaim its property. However, there are landscapes that will require some planting, the reintroduction of species and so on, in order to accelerate the process. Wildlife corridors will allow free movement. Modular arch units can be used to make bridging over roads and railways cheap. Planting and natural propagation of plants as seeds spread would provide cover, concealment, habitat and noise insulation to species choosing to migrate through them. Ethical hunting and fishing are allowed, licensed and balanced by a Department of Conservation and Biodiversity.

This is a generational project; it's going to take a lot of effort. But something like this is, in my opinion, a functional and ethical compromise. We are already doing it to some extent, but it would be improved by being explicit, well planned and executed. We should do something similar with our oceans, protecting the majority and using what we must as ethically and efficiently as our technology permits.

Global warming, climate change and environmental degradation now dominate our collective consciousness. I think it is impossible to reasonably claim that anthropogenic climate change is not occurring. To what extent it's our doing and what we should do about it are up for discussion. On the face of it, the fact that we have changed our world so drastically can seem overwhelming and depressing. I think we can and should consider our situation differently. We have changed the quantity of greenhouse gases in our atmosphere, which has warmed and will continue to warm our planet until a new equilibrium is established.

We did that … by accident.

I'll make the case for rational optimism. Imagine what can be done if we do the science, make it good policy, stop letting the perfect be the enemy of the good, dial down the rhetoric and collectively get to work. We can make our world better. For myself, I'll take what steps I can; I think I'm going to eat less meat. The key to making this common practice will not be the shaming of meat eaters; it will be offering alternatives that are demonstratively better. Tesla didn't get where it is by screaming at people with oil-driven vehicles while selling electric golf carts. Instead, they have built vehicles that are now objects of desire, more sought after than the conventional alternative. From veggie burgers to lab-meat, if these are just as tasty as the alternative, and even healthier, who is going to insist on some suffering with their dinner?

19

PINK

There was a knock on the door of my consult room. Susie stuck her head in, glanced at my client, then looked at me.

'Gareth, can you come through to prep as soon as possible?'

To the untrained eye, her demeanour seemed utterly calm. However, I knew from one glance that she was merely trying to avoid distressing my client. It is possible to be saying goodbye to a much-loved pet in one room and welcoming puppies in the room adjacent. Sometimes it's the same vet or nurse performing both roles, trying desperately to manage each situation without one impacting on the other.

'Emergency, Emergency, Emergency!!!' was the real message.

'Excuse me for a moment,' I said. My client offered a polite nod in return.

Once out of the consultation room I followed Susie through to prep, half jogging to keep up. As we burst through the swing doors I could see a puppy on the prep room table, Grace was holding an oxygen mask over its face while using her other hand to listen to its heart with a stethoscope. Her eyes met mine and she gently shook her head.

'Nothing,' she said simply.

'Okay, get the crash kit.'

'It's here!' said Susie. They were one step ahead and the box full of emergency drugs was already open.

The nursing team had been replacing an intravenous catheter, but it had 'blown'; any medication given through it was no longer entering the vein. Unfortunately, the puppy had chosen this moment to go into cardiac arrest; his little heart had stopped beating after days of struggle. What it meant for me was that I couldn't give him vital drugs. His chances of survival at this stage were near zero, but they would drop even lower if I couldn't treat him properly. I could inject drugs subcutaneously (under his skin), or into his muscle (intra-muscularly), but in either instance the puppy would be long dead before the drugs had any effect. I had one choice left: I could inject drugs straight into his bone, intra-osseous. He wasn't as big as he should have been at his age and the last few days seemed to have shrunk him further; it would be difficult to hit the right spot.

'Clip the top of his femur!' I ordered. There is not always time to be polite in these situations. Professionals understand that the patient takes priority; hurt feelings are a distant concern.

At the same time, I started chest compressions. The puppy was small enough that I was just using one hand, pushing on his chest sufficiently hard to literally compress his heart. I was trying to keep blood moving around his body, supplying essential oxygen to his brain and vital organs. I needed to compress his chest at a high rate; for a puppy it's about as fast as you can humanly do it. Now and again a pause would allow Grace to give him a puff of oxygen via the mask covering his face. It wasn't as effective as an endotracheal (ET) tube, something we needed to address. Susie had managed to clip and prepare his right hip, over the end of his femur.

'Right, let's get a tube in,' was my next step.

Grace nodded, gave the pup one more breath, then held his head upright, facing me.

'Go!' she instructed. I grabbed the laryngoscope from the table; it would help me see inside the puppy's darkened mouth, down to his larynx and the top of his trachea, the target for my tube. As I manipulated the puppy's lower jaw and pulled his tongue out of my way with the scope, Susie passed me an ET tube. 'That's a six,' she said, letting me know the tube was 6 mm in diameter. 'Roger,' I said simply. I could see the back of the puppy's larynx, but not the opening to the trachea.

'Pull his head up, he needs to be higher!'

Grace said nothing, she just gently moved my patient.

Repositioning worked; I could visualise the opening to his trachea. I slid the tube in smoothly, years and years of doing the same task several times a day paying off. Grace had already laid the pup's head back down and was reconnecting the oxygen; I was gently inflating the cuff that surrounds the tube, completely sealing the airway. Working rapidly as a team, I held the tube in place while Grace quickly secured it with a bandage. We had definitive control of the airway.

'Susie, can you take over compressions?' It was phrased as a question but was really an instruction.

'Done!' she said. As I stepped away, Susie slid into place and kept up the rapid chest compressions. Grace and Susie now would work in concert. Consummate professionals that they were, I didn't have to worry. I could concentrate on my next task. I had to force a large needle in through the aseptic skin and into the hollow core of the pup's femur. Normally we'd prep more thoroughly and use some local anaesthetic, but time was crucial. I donned some surgical gloves and started manipulating the leg, working to precisely locate the top of the femur. I uncapped a 19-gauge, inch-and-a-half-long needle. Holding the bone firmly in my left hand, I advanced the needle with my right, gently working it through the skin, then approaching the bone. I increased the pressure and started to rotate. Suddenly the needle slipped, and the end came through the skin. I'd approached at the wrong angle and glanced off the bone. I couldn't see the bone itself and I'd misjudged the approach. I took the needle out and used a few, excruciatingly long seconds to re-evaluate the anatomy, then tried again. This time the resistance was even. I increased the pressure on the needle slightly and rotated it, using its sharpened end to bore through the soft puppy bone. Suddenly the resistance was gone, and the needle progressed an inch or so into my patient. I fiddled it about a bit, moving the needle from side to side slightly, ensuring it really was in the right place.

'I'm in!' Neither Grace nor Susie responded, they were just as busy. I drew up adrenaline. He needed a tiny dose, just a fraction of the syringe's volume; in fact, I had to add some drip fluid just to give me something to inject. I pushed the adrenaline and followed it up with a large syringe of Hartmann's solution. Fluids and drugs injected intra-osseously rapidly get into the bloodstream; it's the next best thing to intravenous and can still be used if the patient's blood pressure and veins have collapsed altogether. We worked in concert, taking turns at the compressions, which are remarkably hard work even on one so small. Every now and again, we'd momentarily pause to check for a response. After 10 minutes and repeated injections, it was obvious we weren't going to win.

I looked up at the clock and, in my best deadpan impression of the protagonist in a human medical drama, said: 'Time of death, 1435.'

'Jesus, Gareth,' said Susie, with a tiny, unconscious smile, 'is there anything you won't joke about?'

'Well, Susie, it's that or cry, isn't it?'

'Yeah, I get you.' As someone who had shed more than a few tears over the puppies' plight, I was sure she did.

I just shrugged. 'That's her last one, isn't it?'

'Yep …' began Grace, but there was no more to say. Pink had come in three days ago with a litter of five 10-week-old puppies. The mother and pups had started out with mild diarrhoea, which had quickly worsened. Before long the big Rottweiler and her energetic offspring were reduced to resting as best they could in between bouts of vomiting and passing huge quantities of foul-smelling, liquid diarrhoea. Unfortunately, the owner had tried a few home remedies first, before accepting the inevitable and making her way to the practice. As soon as we'd smelled the first bout of bloody poo, the nurses were reaching for a parvovirus test. Everyone knows and dreads the signs. The in-house point-of-care test had come back positive, and we rapidly had a diagnosis. We have very few truly effective treatments for parvovirus itself. Instead, the mainstay is supportive therapy, so replacing lost fluids and electrolytes, using drugs to alleviate vomiting, keeping the patient warm and so on, allowing their body to fight the good fight. Antibiotics are given to prevent any bacteria, absorbed into the bloodstream through the damaged gut, from causing sepsis. The disease can affect the heart, but it usually kills due to the severe gastroenteritis it causes. Dehydration, loss of fluids and electrolytes are its hallmarks. As water is lost in vomit and liquid faeces, the body absorbs fluid from wherever it can, borrowing from other tissues. Animals are usually so nauseous they don't want to eat or drink, but even if they do, they vomit it back up. Eventually the body cannot support adequate blood flow to the organs and, one by one, they fail, and the patient enters an irreversible decline. Collapse and coma follow; only death brings relief from the spiralling deterioration.

Once diagnosed, mother and pups were all receiving the same care. It had been a challenge in practical terms. Puppies with drip lines coming out of them clambered over each other and tangled things up. Not only did they need the vital fluids running into their veins, they also needed the fats, proteins and carbohydrates present in their mother's milk or puppy food, but their continual vomiting meant nothing would stay down. All these patients had to be barrier-nursed in our isolation room. We didn't have enough space for all of them, so we'd had to erect folding cages as temporary kennels. Anyone going near them had to wear a protective apron, gloves and shoe covers. Once treatment had been completed, everything had to be disinfected. Parvovirus not only has a high mortality, or ability to kill, it is also very contagious, and we had to take every step to avoid spreading it to other patients. We were fortunate that, although the owner was not insured, she had some means and was willing to pay for the rapidly mounting bill. The owner of the practice had already agreed to some discount due to the sheer number of patients from one household. Untreated, parvovirus in puppies is fatal about 90 per cent of the time. Treated early and appropriately, around 85 per cent survive; the delay in starting treatment cost us dearly.

As a team we'd nursed Pink and her puppies for the last three days. I'd been on call the night before and in a horrible irony had only been able to manage because four of the puppies had already passed away. In between other patients and a calving in the early hours, I'd done my best to clean up the seemingly endless supply of liquid vomit and poo. No sooner had I dragged poor Pink out of her cage and cleaned her and her puppy up than everything was covered in everything again. On one particularly notable occasion, I'd been bent over cleaning up one puddle, when Pink stood up inside her kennel and turned her back to me. I assumed she was repositioning herself, so paid her little mind. A jet of liquid poo shot between the bars of the kennel and landed squarely inside my shoe. Everything would have to be disinfected and put on a hot wash. I had to walk home in my bare feet. Luckily, I only lived 50 metres away, a few doors up from the practice. When I came to check on her in the early hours of the morning, she'd pulled her intravenous cannula out. It's usually a two-person job to replace. Our nurses weren't actually on call but would often volunteer to come in if they were needed. We frequently relied on the ones who lived close by or had responded in the past. Those who are willing to give the most are often rewarded by being asked for the most. Rather than drag someone in, I thought I'd try myself. Fortunately, Pink was so collapsed and so friendly that I was able to raise a vein with one hand and insert a new cannula with the other.

The puppy had been stable overnight, but that only meant he wasn't getting observably worse. He'd started the day close to death and just managed to cling on. With his passing, the last of Pink's puppies was dead. It had been heart-breaking to watch each one gradually fade, then die. Even more so when those that had been in with their mother became unresponsive to her gentle nudges, followed by pitiful whines of concern. We now only had Pink herself to worry about. Fortunately, she was turning a corner. Her diarrhoea was now a reddish-brown paste; her slight recovery, in combination with the drugs we were giving her, meant she was now keeping down a little bit of much-needed nutrition. She had lost a lot of weight. Her gut would take some time to mend as damage wrought by the virus was slowly repaired by her body. In the meantime, we'd keep her fluids topped up and feed her a highly digestible food; something she could absorb despite the damage to her digestive tract.

Veterinary staff, like their equivalents in the human medical world, are only too used to tragedy and death. No one can afford to take these things to heart on a daily basis; it's psychologically unsustainable. When running a marathon, especially in the latter phases, paying attention to each and every painful footstep in the moment would make finishing all but impossible. Only by drifting away from the immediate sensation of pain does finishing the race become mentally achievable. The same, I think, is true for those who encounter tragedy daily. We must find a way to care, but also to detach and let go; anything else is a dangerous path to tread. What makes the case of Pink and her puppies so tragic is that it was largely preventable.

You see, we have an effective way of stopping parvovirus before it starts: vaccination. Pink had done better than her puppies for a few reasons: she was older and had a competent immune system, and she had received a primary vaccination course against parvo as a puppy, although no booster shots. At six years old, she hadn't been vaccinated for a few years, but perhaps some vestige of immunity remained within her body's defences. It was also possible she'd encountered the disease since and fought it off, only for her waning immunity to allow her to succumb to it a few years later. Pregnancy can have a myriad of effects on the immune system. Perhaps the burden of carrying the puppies had left her vulnerable? She was fortunate; she would probably be okay. Rottweilers seem to be prone to developing the disease compared to other breeds, though I don't think we know exactly why.

Parvovirus, or more properly, canine parvovirus 2 (CPV2), is a single-stranded DNA virus of the Parvoviridae family. In most vet clinics it is simply referred to as 'parvo'. It came on the scene in the late 1970s, before spreading worldwide. We are not entirely sure of its origins, but it is very similar to feline panleukopenia virus, which affects cats, replicating in their bone marrow amongst other places. It also resembles several other parvoviruses found in mink, raccoons and foxes. The assumption is that the virus mutated and jumped species at some point, a scenario that should both prick up anyone's ears and raise the hairs on the back of their neck. In immunological terms, 'naive' refers to animals that have never encountered a disease and whose immune systems have not developed any specific response to it. When parvo first revealed itself, it emerged into a population that was entirely naive; the virus was completely novel. It rapidly tore through the canine population. Such was the desperation at the time that some vets resorted to using the only vaccine available to them: that for feline panleukopenia. There are still vets now who can vividly recall desperate owners turning up with family pets and working dogs, anxious to do all they could in the face of the outbreak. By the end of the 1970s, vaccines for parvo were more widely available and they are now part of the core vaccinations for canines recommended by the World Small Animal Veterinary Association (WSAVA).

Vaccines have had a bad press in recent years; the scare in the UK over the measles, mumps and rubella (MMR) vaccine being a case in point. The initiator of this scare, Dr Andrew Wakefield, authored a 1998 study linking autism to the MMR vaccine. His claims found fertile ground and controversy raged for a least a decade. The vestiges of that scandal can still be found in any conversation around the wisdom of vaccination. Ultimately, the Centers for Disease Control and Prevention (CDC) in the United States and the National Health Service (NHS) in the UK, two of the largest bodies processing epidemiological data in the world, concluded there was no link. The General Medical Council (GMC) in the UK eventually found Wakefield to have acted dishonestly and his right to practise medicine was revoked. The question isn't really whether or not Wakefield or indeed anyone else should question vaccination. We each have every right to ask questions. However, we must be moved by the data, and the core of the decision to strike Wakefield off the register of practising medics was not that he had proposed a link between autism and the MMR vaccine, but that he had no good reason to do so.

For those of us in the developed world who had perhaps either forgotten or never been exposed to epidemic contagious disease, we have had a horrific reminder of what a world without vaccination against disease might look like. As one commentator observed when referring to Covid-19: 'You want to see what a world without vaccines would look like? This is the world without ONE vaccine.'

It is impossible to discuss vaccination without mentioning smallpox. Smallpox was caused by *Variola* viruses. It would initially cause fever and vomiting, and later characteristic fluid-filled pustules on the victim's skin. Although it had several forms, the overall case fatality rate was around 30 per cent (for comparison, the case fatality rate for Covid-19 was initially estimated at around 1–2 per cent, though there were large disparities from country to country). Smallpox may have killed as many as 300 million people in the twentieth century alone. Inoculation or variolation was an early preventative regime used to combat the disease, and may have been practised as early as 1500 in China. One form of variolation involved using a needle to pierce the pustules of a sufferer. The same needle was then used to introduce the putrid material subcutaneously into a healthy individual in order to grant them immunity to the wild infection. In the process the variolated individuals sometimes developed smallpox itself or any one of the several diseases present on the inoculation needle. Syphilis was rampant and was sometimes passed on in this manner. It was dangerous. Despite that fact, desperation led many to engage in the practice and the children of many European royal families were variolated. That is how scary smallpox was.

The smallpox outbreak in Boston in 1721 affected around half of the 12,000 citizens. Cotton Mather and Zabdiel Boylston trialled inoculation by variolation. They also kept records. They recorded a fatality rate of 14 per cent in the untreated population. The death rate among those variolated in the face of the outbreak was 2 per cent. The procedure was so effective that it was rapidly adopted by the British military in order to maintain the fighting capability of its troops. However, a 2 per cent fatality rate is still unthinkable in a modern context. Help was soon on hand. In 1757 an eight-year-old boy was variolated in Gloucester. His name was Edward Jenner. Jenner the man was an avid scientist, working in fields as diverse as human blood and hot-air balloons. He became a fellow of the Royal Society, the pre-eminent English-speaking scientific institution of the time. It was 1796 when Jenner began his campaign against smallpox. He had heard that dairymaids were conferred protection against it after having suffered from the milder cowpox disease. In May of 1796 he drew fresh material from a cowpox victim, Sarah Nelms. Using this material, he inoculated eight-year-old James Phipps. Phipps suffered some discomfort and ran a mild fever. Nine days after the inoculation he lost his appetite and felt cold, but he recovered the next day. Two months later, in July of the same year, Jenner injected him with smallpox; he was unaffected. Jenner coined the term vaccination from the Latin for cow, *vacca*. It was by no means an easy road, but by 8 May 1980, the world was declared free of the scourge of smallpox. Vaccination underwent major changes during this time. It became *much* safer. In the latter stages of eradication, approximately 0.1 per cent of individuals vaccinated suffered serious, but not life-threatening disease. Roughly 0.0026 per cent of those vaccinated for the first time experienced potentially lethal complications.

Vaccines work by tricking the body into thinking it has been exposed to a disease, triggering the body's immune system to generate cells and proteins that destroy the invader and guard against future infection. Modern vaccines achieve this by a number of methods. In some instances, the vaccine contains only part of the disease-causing organism.

Either just its capsule or fragments of it, which are identified and attacked by the immune system. A bit like giving a police officer the description of a suspect's outer clothing. Some vaccines may even use the whole organism, but attenuated in some way, killed by radiation for example. This is, I suppose, like dressing up a mannequin that resembles the suspect in the suspect's clothes, then showing it to the police. I wouldn't try this; you may well end up either arrested or sectioned under the Mental Health Act. In the case of some Covid-19 vaccines, they are mRNA vaccines. They function quite differently. In our normal cells we have deoxyribonucleic acid (DNA). From that, our body makes messenger ribonucleic acid (mRNA). This mRNA, through a couple of intermediate steps, allows the body to use the information originally contained in DNA to make proteins via a process called expression. Proteins perform countless vital functions in the body, enzymes encourage chemical reactions, receptors allow hormones and drugs to have their effect. In fact, we are each entirely the construct of protein expression.

The mRNA used in some Covid-19 vaccines contains the information to make spike proteins, which are normally present on the outside of Covid particles. Once injected into the body, the mRNA works by entering a cell; the cellular mechanisms use the mRNA as they normally would, manufacturing the spike protein. When produced, the spike protein is presented on the outside of the manufacturing cell, where various immune cells from the body recognise the spike protein as a threat and manufacture B cells, T cells, and antibodies that will attack similar proteins, mopping up any Covid when it is encountered for real. To labour our earlier analogy, this is like finding a criminal with a distinctive hat. In his or her pocket, they have the knitting pattern for the hat. You 'borrow' the pattern, get a factory to produce copies of the garment in question, then hand the headwear over to the police with instructions to round up people in similarly suspicious hats.

That's all very well and good, but what about our pets?

Well, their immune systems work much as ours do. To circle back to Pink and her puppies, we are fortunate to have vaccinations available for parvo. They often contain live, attenuated viruses designed to stimulate an appropriate immune response by the dog's disease-fighting mechanisms without causing actual disease. The vaccines used by most vets, most of the time, usually contain at least two other components. One protects against canine distemper virus which, interestingly, is related to rinderpest. Described in the fourth century by the Roman writer Severus Sanctus Endelechius, and with a fatality rate of nearly 100 per cent in naive animals, rinderpest remained an enormous scourge of cattle until the last case was recorded in 2001. It was the second disease after smallpox to be eradicated from the planet via vaccination; it was declared gone from our midst on 25 May 2011. Speaking of scourges, when distemper encountered naive dogs, it would kill around half of them, with puppies dying at a rate closer to 80 per cent. It is now rare in the UK, largely because of vaccination. Another component is designed to protect against canine adenovirus 1, which causes infectious canine hepatitis (ICH). The mortality rate for ICH is 10 to 30 per cent and highest in young dogs. Again, this has become rare in some areas of the world that have things like fridges, syringes and needles ready to hand. I'm sure you can guess why. These are examples of vaccination's success, not its redundancy.

The components of the vaccine designed to protect against parvo, distemper and hepatitis usually come as a kind of powdered block in the bottom of a small vial, which is mixed with a fluid to allow it to be injected. Often the fluid itself is a vaccine, for leptospirosis. Lepto causes kidney and liver problems, and I've seen several dogs die from it.

Perhaps most importantly, it is zoonotic and so can spread to humans. It's also a significant disease of farm animals and basically every mammal you care to name. In humans it is called Weil's disease; it's often contracted from water, which gets its supply from animals' urine. If your skin and the whites of your eyes are yellow, and you're coughing up blood, do see a doctor. It might be lepto, and you could die; early treatment is vital.

Parvovirus is now considered ubiquitous in our environment; it is everywhere. The best way to protect against it is vaccination. Had Pink been recently vaccinated, it is unlikely her puppies would have got the disease. They would have been protected by the antibodies she would subsequently generate. The puppies suckle from mum and in doing so absorb antibodies contained in her milk. These antibodies can cross the gut and end up in the puppies' circulation, providing them with temporary protection while their own immune system develops. In addition, because she is immunised, she is unlikely to either catch it or shed it, preventing the puppies from being exposed. There is some debate about what is exactly optimal in terms of timing, but most of the practices I've worked in recommend two injections two to four weeks apart, with the second after 10 weeks of age.

You may have heard in the press about 'over-vaccination' in pets or read horror stories about entire litters of pups being wiped out by vaccine reactions. The most controversial vaccine currently being used in dogs is one for four strains of leptospirosis, called 'L4' for short. Excepting a mild fever and some pain or swelling at the site of injection, which are expected, it has a suspected adverse reaction rate just under 7 per 10,000 or 0.069 per cent of animals vaccinated. That's not fatalities, just registered undesirable side effects. I have seen a few vaccine reactions in my time; they are usually self-limiting or readily treatable. I've never seen a fatality in almost twenty years. Some of those possible reactions may not be the result of the vaccine, some others may go unrecorded, but we have a rough idea of the scale of the problem.

I thoroughly recommend that anyone with pets, or indeed animals of any kind, talks to their local vet about vaccination. Now there is one problem here. There is a clear conflict of interest. Vets are both the people recommending vaccinations, and the ones selling them. That, I'll grant, is not ideal. Unfortunately, until we have government-funded animal healthcare and vets are unburdened from worrying about the affordability of their recommendations, we are somewhat stuck with the current situation.

You may want to know if vets are being honest, if they care, or if perhaps they are getting backhanders from the drug companies? I *have* received backhanders from drug companies. Probably once a year or so, I'll get a sandwich and a doughnut to listen to a drug rep talk about their products. Perhaps the most notable pay-off I had was when a drug company rep drunkenly bet me that I wouldn't swim a length of a Glaswegian canal. Unfortunately, I was just as drunk, he lost the bet, and I had to spend the rest of my evening enjoying my free drinks in wet underwear. If you honestly think these are enough for me to recommend something I know to be harmful, then I'm afraid you have, as former president George W. Bush once put it, mis-underestimated me.

I've sat in practice meetings and been party to heated discussions among vets about whether we are following the guidelines. Are we over-vaccinating? Are we using the right vaccines, at the right time? What age should we start animals at? How often should we give boosters? What about kennel cough? What about rabies? Each vaccine is a risk, however slight, and it must be balanced against the risk and consequences of catching the disease being vaccinated against. What is common in each discussion I've been in is that money is rarely if ever brought up. Yes, the steady stream of income from vaccination is valuable to any practice. However, the core of any conversation is this: how do we prevent another case like Pink's?

Vaccinate your animals.

20

TRAPPED!

A 'house visit' is the concept of visiting someone's home in order to treat their pet. These are a minefield, figuratively speaking. I guess you could consider the average farm attendance a 'house visit', since you are visiting the home of the farmer, and technically also the home of the animal. However, farms are places of work and are usually, but not always, equipped with the means to handle correctly and, if necessary, restrain animals. Decisions made around animal care are largely dispassionate while remaining compassionate.

True house visits are an entirely different breed of problem, often fraught with difficulty. Unfortunately, the ageing population of the UK, combined with the decline in nuclear, multi-generational households and the movement of younger generations in order to find work, has left many older people with little choice but to ask the vet to come to them. Without doubt, some people will take advantage of the good nature of vets. However, I've witnessed the opposite on many occasions, with older or less able people going to extreme lengths to avoid burdening others with 'their problem'. While taxis, relatives and independent pet ambulances can help with some of these cases, occasionally the situation demands that a vet must get the bit between their teeth and take on the role of emergency responder.

One house visit that stands out in my mind occurred when I was working for an emergency clinic. Our company covered the out-of-hours (OOH) services for a medium-sized city. In essence this meant that at closing time the other thirty to forty veterinary clinics in the area shut their doors and turned over to us any inpatients, which would be transferred to our clinic via a dedicated pet ambulance. They would also divert their phones to us, and we would deal with any calls of an emergency nature that came in once they had gone home for the evening.

We were a pretty busy clinic and a week's work was fairly intense. Each block of work consisted of seven back-to-back 14.5-hour night shifts, usually leaving you somewhat spent. My personal burden was somewhat worsened by the fact that I lived too far away to commute safely. Thus, I would spend my time off during the day getting a bit of exercise in the local forest park, prior to attempting to sleep in my small back-packing tent in the same forest park. All this because my ancestors are from the northern portion of our island and have instilled in me an acute sense of financial frugality. I was not prepared to shell out for a bed-and-breakfast for something so frivolous as comfort.

Occasionally, unreasonably demanding owners could seriously try our overstretched patience. We were not infrequently called upon to visit clients' homes. However, we tried to discourage home visits as far as possible for a number of reasons. Some I've already mentioned, but there was an additional issue related to the manner in which OOH clinics work. They can really only function by centralisation. OOH services can be offered to a wide geographical area and allow for the care of many inpatients only by bringing all patients to one central location where a relatively small number of staff can deal with a relatively large number of patients and problems. Our clinic worked through the night with only one vet and one nurse. Between us we had to care for any inpatients entrusted to us for hospitalisation, in addition to dealing with any new emergency cases. We had a receptionist to answer the phones, but only until 10 o'clock. For the most part the nurse would run around giving drugs, monitoring drips and administering a few gentle strokes of affection as required. The vet would deal with any new cases. Between us we'd also answer the phones after we lost our receptionist for the night. In the background we'd cooperate as needed to take bloods, turn patients, clean out kennels, restrain birds of prey and carry out any emergency surgery. I've known a nurse hold a stethoscope to a patient's chest in order to get a heart rate, while answering the phone with her spare hand, and at the same time nodding in response to a vet's expletive-ridden rant as she or he attempts some life-saving surgery that requires more than the normal human complement of limbs. Usually, this moment of seemingly ultimate stress is put in perspective when one of the many monitoring alarms attached to the various inpatients goes off; a subtle reminder that it can always be worse.

However, tonight's dilemma wasn't really medical but practical. Susan answered the phone to an extremely distraught lady who informed us that her pet rabbit was trapped. Between sobs she managed to describe her problem. Her pet rabbit had been out for his evening constitutional in her expansive garden as normal. He would usually make his way back inside once he'd munched sufficient grass and toured his realm. However, this evening he hadn't returned. She'd gone out looking for him and eventually located him after hearing some scratching sounds. These sounds were coming from between her garden wall and her neighbours brick shed. Somehow the rabbit had fallen between the two and become lodged in place. The lady had contacted the Fire and Rescue Service, but apparently they had refused to attend until a vet could confirm the inextricable nature of the rabbit's entrapment. Susan wisely removed herself from the conversation by placing the client on hold, turning to me with a look of *faux* innocence and saying: 'It's for you!'

A look of ill-concealed glee passed across her face. I glared at her. It was a fairly quiet evening and we'd been having a cup of tea together next to the phone; thus I'd overheard the conversation and knew exactly the kind of metaphorical quagmire Susan had all too willingly dropped me into.

I spoke to the lady at length. She had apparently contacted her usual vet, who had refused to assist. I doubted that, but reluctance or resistance can be interpreted by a client as polite refusal. Technically, there is no room for refusal; her own vet really had to attend. This woman wasn't a client of ours, nor a client of one of the practices covered by our service. But that wasn't the bunny's fault. Basically, she needed a vet to attend, confirm the bunny's predicament and either carry out a rescue or facilitate one by the Fire Brigade. I was now in my own predicament. I had inpatients to attend to and a clinic to run. If I went out to attend to Bart the rabbit, I would be 45 minutes away. That wasn't really an issue for my current inpatients, but certainly would be one in the event of a new, genuine emergency. I also knew that my boss discouraged house visits. Like, really discouraged them. As in: 'I know I can't tell you not to attend house visits because you can be struck off the register (of vets) for that, but DON'T ATTEND HOUSE VISITS unless you absolutely have to. Send the ambulance to pick the animal up, get the owner to bring it in. Get them to hire a taxi. Whatever, just don't go out. If you do go out, and a patient in the clinic suffers or dies, it'll be your fault.'

This was also in the immediate aftermath of a high-profile case in which a vet had been struck off ... for not attending an emergency in a 'timely' fashion. The facts of the case were worryingly relevant. A local farmer had run down his own dog, severely injuring her. The farmer phoned the vet in question, who said that he could not immediately attend as he was the only vet on duty and had several inpatients to deal with. Instead, he asked if the dog could be lifted in a blanket and brought to the practice. The owner was unable to get the dog in a vehicle and the distressed animal had bitten a relative as a result of the pain of manhandling. Cutting a long story short, the vet had not been able to attend as quickly as anyone would have liked and the animal had allegedly died in a state of 'unnecessary suffering'. There was some suggestion that the Royal College of Veterinary Surgeons had been waiting for just such a case in order to make an example of someone. The case had become quite infamous; many vets disagreed with the judgement, which included a comment that the dog should not have been transported in a blanket in case of a spinal injury.

From my perspective there was a least a touch of ivory tower syndrome going on. Vets in general practice are often faced with difficult situations. I'm not saying the vet behaved perfectly, but he had been placed in a catch-22. If he didn't immediately attend, he was leaving an animal in pain. If he did, and another emergency developed or arrived, he'd be absent from his post and that patient might suffer as a consequence. The bottom line for me was that 'My boss said so' wouldn't be a defence. Each vet is a Member of the Royal College of Veterinary Surgeons (MRCVS) and must act like it, even under duress. This is particularly unfair on young or newly qualified vets, who might lack the confidence to challenge their boss on such a matter. In my case, my boss was a vet, but he didn't work in the practice, or, in fact, live in the UK. Any sanction would probably be levelled at me. In many instances vets now work for corporate practices or for non-vet owners. In this instance the Royal College has little power to punish managers or policy makers, so, again, any sanction is likely to fall on the individual vet. It's something our profession must address. An ambulance driver is not struck off for a delay in attendance due to excess demand. Instead, it is usually the NHS Trust that is censured, for it is they that are responsible for ensuring there is adequate cover.

Nonetheless, I had to make a call. In the end it was a no-brainer for me. I couldn't split myself in two and I had no facility to call on another vet. I wanted to attend, so I'd have to run the risk of something needing my attention more urgently at the hospital. I'd also have to take my own car. The lady had agreed to pay our discouragingly hefty attendance fee, so off I went. When I say, 'discouragingly hefty', I mean substantially less than you'd expect to pay a plumber for a visit at three o'clock in the morning. That's not to denigrate plumbers, rather to emphasise the failure to value vets.

I got a basic kit together containing some sedatives, antibiotics, needles, syringes and dressings, trying to anticipate any likely scenarios. After a quick chat with Susan regarding the current patients, off I went, following my satellite navigation system towards whatever bunny-entrapment scenario awaited me. The house was relatively easy to find, with the rabbit's owner stood outside waiting for me. Bart's owner was quite distressed, but managed fairly quickly to convey a summary of the situation to me. Without further ado I asked her to show me the problem. She led me out into the garden, up a set of steps and across to her garden wall, immediately adjacent to her neighbour's brick shed. I got a torch out and shone a light between the two walls to see two partially visible olive eyes staring back at me.

I mumbled some noises that I hoped were universally reassuring to rabbits and lay down on my stomach in the mud in order to reach down between the two walls. The gap was narrow, but I hadn't realised how narrow. I doubt it was more than 4 cm or 1¾ inches. I tried inserting my inadequately noodle-like arms into the gap in a variety of orientations, but I couldn't even get close to reaching Bart. He seemed remarkably calm, but he must have been distressed and I'd have been surprised if being trapped in such a fashion wasn't affecting his breathing. The sides of his chest were clearly flush against the walls, and he couldn't turn his head. I couldn't get a hold of him, nor get close enough to give him any sedation or treatment. Should the worst come to the worst, I couldn't even put him to sleep. I wasn't prepared to leave him there to die. I pushed myself up out of the dirt and told the owner the bad news. It wasn't really news at this stage, but it did give her a justification to get the Fire Service out. While she contacted them, I wracked my brains for a solution.

I had a eureka moment. I had some ski poles in my car. If I took the snow baskets off them, they'd fit down between the two walls, and I'd be able to get one under Bart and pull him up using the end. I made my way to the car via the poor woman's living room. Just as I was about to walk out the front door, a fire engine pulled up outside. Five fairly burly blokes climbed off, looking a bit disgruntled and dressed as if they were about to attend Armageddon. I bit the bullet and explained the situation to what appeared to be their leader. He was certainly the most intimidatingly handsome and manly one. However, I was able to assure him that I'd hit on an idea and would soon be triumphantly rescuing the rabbit from his terrible fate. Their leader looked sceptical, but still handsome and manly. I fetched my ski sticks and quickly made some modifications.

I made my way back towards Bart. I'd also fetched a head-torch so that I could see what I was doing but have my hands free. Once I'd re-established Bart's position, I extended my ski stick to the appropriate length and pushed it down between the two walls. I was easily able to slide it under Bart, right under his chest. This was going to be a piece of cake! I'd gently bring the ski stick up under his abdomen and chest, then gradually pull him up from between the two walls before grabbing him. Tentatively, I began to bring the ski stick up. It touched Bart and he gave a bit of a start, but then relaxed again. I made more soothing noises. Bart looked unimpressed. Awkwardly but steadily, I increased the upward pressure. He wasn't budging. I tried a bit more effort and he appeared to move ever so slightly, so I dialled up my effort just a whisker more. Bart looked very uncomfortable, and his head started to look a bit funny. More force wasn't an option, I'd injure him for sure. I tried a couple more times from different angles, but to no avail. The problem seemed to be that the ski stick was too narrow. It was getting between Bart's chest wall and his limbs. As a result, when I applied upward force on the stick it pushed his forelimb away from his body, effectively making him wider and jamming him in place.

This was not going to be a piece of cake. I phoned the emergency clinic. All the patients were stable and thus far there was no need to rush back. It was lucky we were having a slow night. I reported my lack of success to the gaggle of firefighters who had taken on the role of the audience in my one-man veterinary-themed cabaret.

I went back to the drawing board. Could we go next door and ask the neighbour if we could take a few bricks out of his shed wall, allowing us access to Bart? Bart's owner was adamant that this was not an option. Apparently, she'd fallen out with her neighbour for long-winded reasons. In short, it was all his fault, but she did not have the kind of relationship with her neighbour that would allow the partial destruction of his shed without also having to carry out a partial destruction on the neighbour himself. Since I had no licence to kill, or even maim, that was a non-starter. Fire and Rescue could perhaps get a specialised animal rescue unit, but that would be tomorrow at the earliest. They had the equipment to deal with such things as an injured horse trapped in a collapsing mine on a remote island that could only be accessed by hovercraft, guarded by a security system who's only known vulnerability is a penchant for chiselled good looks. But they weren't available until tomorrow. No one, and I mean no one, was allowed to interrupt their beauty sleep. Besides, there was also no guarantee they'd agree to attend; hovercraft are very sore on fuel and everyone has a budget these days. I doubted Bart would still be alive by the time they could reach us, and I had to point out my uncertainly as to how I'd leverage a hovercraft's capability to rescue him anyway.

The brain-storming session in the garden was going round in circles. It was rapidly becoming apparent that Bart might be beyond rescue, at least timely rescue. It was so frustrating. All I really needed was a pole of some sort, about 4 cm in diameter. If it was the same width as the gap between the wall, then I could scoop Bart up. It would be too wide to slip under one of his legs, so it would apply force to him evenly and avert the problem of forcing his limbs against the walls. Hopefully it would be less likely to injure him as well. I said as much aloud.

'This is so frustrating; all I need is a pole about 4 centimetres thick,' I said.

Have you ever seen an action movie where the heroes or heroines are stuck in a brain-storming session, and someone says: 'I have an idea …'? There's usually the reflection of a fire in their eyes, still burning from the all-too-recent explosion. The same eyes have a thousand-yard stare, they've seen so much, almost too much to bear …

Well, it was exactly like that except the fireman's name was Donald and he had a thick Somerset accent. He'd been lost in thought for a while as the rest of us argued about rabbit-rescue techniques.

'We've got a pole on the truck that's about that size,' he said.

'What?' I answered. I'd been talking about 4-cm-thick bits of pole for about forty-five minutes at this stage. Had he been thinking all this time? Perhaps he had been converting from imperial to metric.

'What?' said the Fire and Rescue leader chap simultaneously. He'd also been listening to me talk about 4-cm-thick bits of pole for forty-five minutes and I suspect he was fantasising about killing me for the earlier remarks I'd made about the utility of hovercraft in the current situation.

'There's a pole on the truck that's about that size,' said Donald.

'Well, go and get it then,' said the leader chap, before looking at me and rolling his eyes.

Clearly Donald was not in charge of strategy. Donald jogged off towards the truck. Bart's owner, having seen signs of activity, slid her patio door open, exposing herself to the cold night air for a few seconds. I informed her that we had an idea, but it would be a few minutes before we could try it out. She nodded in recognition and slid the patio door closed. It was, after all, cold outside. Donald returned with the pole. On first impressions it looked perfect, but it could be out by a few millimetres, in which case it might prove useless. We walked over to where Bart was trapped. I had a quick glance at Bart; he was still there and still breathing. Donald handed me the pole and I slid it between the two walls. It fitted almost perfectly. My heart started to beat a bit faster. This might work. If only we'd had a pole, about 4 cm in diameter, earlier. Still, we'd all been doing our best. I manoeuvred the pole under Bart and started to apply upward pressure. He immediately began to move!

'Yes!' I said, unable to conceal a grin. I realised that if I pulled Bart out, he'd probably hop away from the scary strangers. Knowing Bart, he'd either throw himself between two static objects or stray on to the road. I had a quick chat with Donald, showing him how I wanted him to use the pole, emphasising gentle, steady force. When I passed it over, Donald, to his credit, performed perfectly. Bart emerged from between the two walls, and I immediately grabbed him. The rest of the Fire and Rescue lads had been watching and, to be fair, they seemed happy Bart was safe. I gave the bunny a very quick check over, then took him down to the house. His owner was inside with her back to me, clearly on the phone to someone. I knocked on the glass, cradling Bart in one arm. As she turned round, she saw Bart, hung up and came straight to the door. She opened it and I immediately passed Bart to her, telling her I'd be back to check on him in a minute.

The firemen were already mounting up on the engine. I wandered over and thanked them all for their help. Clearly it wasn't how they'd planned to spend the evening, but they shook hands to a man and were all happy for Bart. As they departed, I made my way back around to the patio doors. I knocked again and Bart's owner let me in. While she held him, I gave him a more detailed exam. As far as I could tell, he was fine. I gave him some anti-inflammatory and asked her to keep him in and monitor him for the next day or two. Rabbits often conceal illness and it remained to be seen how the trauma and stress had affected him.

All of that done, there was only one final bit to do. Unfortunately, it is the least rewarding part, collecting the money. I told Bart's owner the cost. I can't remember the exact amount, but it was something like £250. She immediately started to rebuke me. I let her have her say for a minute or two, but eventually had to interrupt and explain things from my perspective. I wasn't even her vet. I'd driven here in my own car since her vet practice had refused and the Fire Service would only attend if I did. It was late, I'd been there for a few hours, and we'd successfully rescued Bart. On top of that, she'd known the costs up front and agreed to them. In her defence, she was contrite. She apologised, cited the late hour and the stress, but agreed to ring up and pay the practice over the phone. She offered me a cup of tea in the meantime, and I gratefully accepted. All sorted, I gave Bart a final farewell check over and said my goodbyes.

A week or so later the practice received a clipping from a local newspaper in the post. It was the story of Bart's rescue! If I had expected a starring role, I was to be disappointed. The article focused on Bart's entrapment and the heroic actions of the Fire and Rescue Service in his extraction. They were not only on a moment's notice to crash out to such incidents, but were handsome, manly and excellent husband material to boot.

The article recorded that a vet had attended, but didn't offer any opinion as to his handsomeness, manliness or suitability as a long-term life partner. I'm not bitter, really I'm not!

21

HORATIO

The arrival of Covid in the UK placed an already struggling veterinary sector under additional pressure. Travel restrictions, lockdowns and the requirement for isolation of exposed team members exacerbated our staffing issues. One of the clinics I regularly work with relies on other European countries to supply about half of its qualified veterinary surgeons. Covid meant that staff who might have travelled over for work either couldn't or wouldn't do so. We had to minimise contact with owners for both our own and their protection. That left us immediately short staffed. Animals' owners are vital in most examinations; they can help to control and restrain their pets. Without them we vets relied on a combination of improvisation, adaptation and invoking the assistance of whatever deity was responsible for the current situation. When that failed, we had to ask our nurses to assist, adding to their already busy workload. Social distancing, masks, visors and extra precautions made everything from surgery to conversation difficult. Everything took longer.

After a brief initial reprieve, lasting a few days, during which we triaged as best we could and managed to keep the workload sensible, demand for our services first returned to normal, then increased as people purchased pets in record numbers, seeking to fill the void left in their lives by the loss of their normal social lives, sports clubs, holidays and weekends away. We had to stop taking on new clients, cancel non-urgent procedures and ration our services to those truly in need. Emergency services, for the first time I'm aware of, had to close with worrying regularity; they simply could not get vets to work through the night, as the same vets had already worked all day and would be back again tomorrow. Many, myself included, *did* take on extra shifts. But I also turned down work, even at bumper wages, because I simply couldn't do any more in a working week and keep my sanity.

In the midst of all this, I met Horatio; the first I knew of him was when I bumped into my colleague in the corridor. It was all too common to make your way out of a room in a hurry, on your way to fetch medication or equipment, only to collide with another vet doing exactly the same. We made our apologies and I fell in behind her on our way down the corridor. She also needed something out of the fridge.

My curiosity got the better of me. 'What you got?' I asked.

'Melting ulcers,' Francesca replied. 'Would you mind taking a look?'

'Yeah, no probs, I'll pop in as soon as I can,' I responded.

I took my turn at the fridge and removed a vaccine; I'd been blessed with the relatively easy job of vaccinating a puppy. Having fully inspected him to ensure he was healthy and happy I now had the unenviable task of inserting a microchip under his skin. The needle in the applicator must be big enough for the grain-of-rice-sized chip to travel down its centre and into the animal. I gently held the scruff of my puppy with one hand and pushed the outsize needle through his skin. He let out a little heart-breaking yelp and looked at me with sad little eyes, as if to say: 'Why? We're friends?'

'Sorry buddy,' I replied, hoping that my apologetic look would somehow cross the species barrier.

At least he was now street legal and had a good chance of making it back to his owner if he ever got lost. Unfortunately, I still had to vaccinate him and apply some flea and worm treatment to his skin. By the time I'd finished he looked thoroughly dejected. Even the liver paste I offered him was not going to make up for this affront to his dignity. He looked at me with nothing short of contempt as I scooped him up to return to his owners. I ran through the vaccine schedule and best puppy practice with them before making my way back and knocking on Francesca's door. As I made my way in, I was immediately greeted by the sight of a cat perched on the examination table: Horatio. He was sat on the table and looking in my direction. Or I assumed he was because the surfaces of both his eyes were such a mess I couldn't tell where he was looking.

With the Covid situation, we weren't routinely letting people into the building. But, due to the difficulty of communicating in a busy car park and H's complex and ongoing case, Francesca had made an exception. Even in a quiet consult room, masks and social distancing made communication difficult. I introduced myself to Mr Wales, Horatio's owner. 'Hi, I'm Gareth one of the other vets. I'm just going to take a wee look so that Francesca and I can get our heads together and hopefully get Horatio sorted out.'

I gave Horatio a few strokes; he immediately started purring and nuzzling my hand. I was quite surprised, given the state of his eyes. The clear window at the front of the eye is the cornea, made up of multiple layers, much like a double-glazed window. The top layer is called the epithelium; below that is the thickest layer – the stroma – then a very thin layer called Descemet's membrane and, finally, the endothelium. In cats, added together, these layers are only about three-quarters of a millimetre thick. Once the epithelium has been breached, a lesion is officially an ulcer. I've had an ulcer in my eye, and it is exquisitely painful. After surgery, I'd been told to expect mild post-operative pain, but instead spent 24 hours wishing for a swift and merciful death. I could empathise with Horatio's plight.

Horatio, however, was far more friendly than I would've been under the same circumstances. Many patients, myself included, would have bitten anyone who dared to come near. As I gently stroked him, I was also covertly examining his eyes without immediately giving the game away. Both were covered in a thick discharge. A mixture of infection, damage and the body's attempts at repair. I could immediately make out large crater-like ulcers in both eyes, stained a deep yellowy orange. The staining was a direct result of a special dye, designed to make any ulcer obvious. It sticks tenaciously to the stroma, but not the epithelium.

Francesca handed me the ophthalmoscope she had been using. I turned on the inbuilt light; gently holding Horatio's head in my other hand, I went to work examining his eyes. The light and optics built into the scope allowed me to examine not only the surface of his eyes, but the structures within as well. Remarkably, Horatio's eyes were functioning normally. If we could heal the ulcers, there was a good chance we could save his eyes and retain his sight. It was a big if. At the moment he had not only ulcers in both eyes, but 'melting ulcers'. On top of the already-existing damage and infection, the collagen building blocks of the stroma were being broken down by enzymes called collagenases. These are made by the body and part of the natural turnover of collagen in the eye as it is continually renewed. However, that natural balance of destruction and creation can be upset by infection. Horatio's body was dissolving his own eyeballs, even as it attempted to heal them.

Horatio had initially been brought in a few days ago with what appeared to be a mild conjunctivitis, a condition usually easily treated with antibiotic eye drops. However, when he came back in for a recheck with Francesca, she had been horrified to notice that instead of the steady improvement she'd hoped for, the cat's eyes were a mess. She had acted quickly and decisively by swapping out his antibiotics and taking some blood from our feline patient before spinning it down in a centrifuge to make serum. It was being administered like eye drops, using Horatio's own blood to counteract the destruction of his corneas. He had been coming and going daily for the best part of a week, but things were not going well. There was a number of reasons, chief among them the fact that Horatio's owner was not applying his drops regularly enough.

Mr Wales was not a youngster, probably in his mid-seventies. As we discussed the need for regular drops with him, he asked if we could instead give Horatio tablets. Unfortunately, the treatment of eye conditions usually requires drops or creams for good reason. Very few things you can give by mouth will make it to the cornea in sufficient quantities to make a difference; any attempt to heal Horatio was going to involve something applied directly to his eyes.

Mr Wales was struggling to apply his cat's eye drops. He was alone at home and could only manage it when his daughter came round. On top of that he had health issues of his own and was going back and forward to the doctor's regularly. As if to demonstrate the nub of the matter, he held up a bandaged hand.

'He won't let me get the drops in, and I can't afford to get clawed; I'm on blood thinners. He scrammed me last night and it took half an hour to get the bleeding stopped.'

Francesca and I looked at one another; this was not going to be easy. For the moment we agreed to admit Horatio so that we could give him his medications. That would solve the issue for now. But we would shut at half six and then the treatment would stop. We could send the cat to the local out-of-hours service that provided our overnight cover, but they were expensive; it would cost a few hundred pounds just for the night. Mr Wales had the money, but …

'I don't mind the money, I really don't, but what if I spend all this cash and he doesn't heal? I'm out thousands and he is no better. If it comes to that, I'd rather put him down than see him suffer.'

Mr Wales was after a guarantee that if he took our advice, Horatio would be healed. I wish it were so simple. Even with an unlimited budget, no one could genuinely make such a promise. On top of everything else, Horatio was no youngster himself. He was now 19 and in a similar phase of life to his owner where things start to malfunction. He'd lost a bit of weight and we agreed that prior to us doing anything more we'd do a blood test to make sure he was fairly healthy otherwise. It would be unfair to put him through prolonged treatment if some underlying condition was going to carry him away in the near future.

With permission from his owner, we admitted Horatio. Our nurses did the hard part, combining gentle stroking and firm restraint to obtain a blood sample and apply Horatio's medications. Our blood sample showed that he also had very early-stage kidney disease, something that might kill him in months to years. This was not good news, but Mr Wales took it in his stride. As the day drew to a close, I took the opportunity to wander through to our cattery, made my way to H's kennel and opened it up to examine him. He immediately uncurled from a good sleep, stretched and made his way across the kennel to get some well-deserved attention. His attitude was incredible really. He'd fight us furiously to avoid the injections and eye drops we had to administer. He'd writhe, squirm, meow and even claw to escape our mistreatment, but each and every time he'd forgive us and go back to his usual affectionate self. It was heart-breaking to breach his trust again and again. But my job wasn't to be his owner. It was to cure him so that he could go back to his owner and enjoy a vet-free life. Right now, I wasn't sure I could achieve that.

Francesca had finished at lunch for her half-day, so it fell to me to discharge Horatio. I ran through the results and advice for his overnight care. I knew it would be a struggle for Mr Wales to get the drops in; I was also worried about his health. I said as much to him and got a surprise.

'Oh, Francesca's coming round later to pop his drops in for me.'

I had a little moment internally. I guess perhaps I wished I'd extended the same kindness, though there were good reasons not to. Technically it was allowable under the then-current Covid-19 restrictions, and whilst I knew Francesca would be wearing PPE and doing her best, there was a real risk to Mr Wales. Each of us vets interacted with dozens of people a day; anyone could be an asymptomatic carrier. Despite our precautions, we couldn't guarantee that we had not contracted the virus. He was not someone who could expect to shrug it off if he developed symptoms. I knew, though, where taking this course led. I travelled 45 minutes to get to work, and was already getting home after eight. Visiting Horatio would make this at least nine, if I was lucky. If I started doing this for everyone having trouble getting eye drops in, I'd have to start sleeping in my car. Francesca was a locum and staying above the practice. She had the spare time, and it was her choice, but I knew what would happen: it wouldn't stop with eye drops. Mr Wales was polite, but very determined.

'What can we do if his ulcers don't heal?' he asked.

'Well, one option is to perform a corneal graft. It's not something we could do here; we'd have to refer you to a specialist ophthalmic surgeon.'

'Like where? How much?'

'Well, my cat had one a couple of years ago; it was about three thousand pounds …' I ran through the location and other issues with him. He wasn't too worried about the money. In his own words, he was very comfortable. Mr Wales explained that while he could drive the 90 minutes to the specialist, he would be too tired to return the same day. I suggested getting accommodation overnight nearby and returning the next day. Unfortunately, Mr Wales had his own appointments and health to worry about; staying overnight was not an option. His daughter didn't drive, so she couldn't chauffeur Horatio either. For a moment I was tempted to offer to take the cat myself; I had a day off the following day, after all. No, I had stuff to do. I forced myself to keep tight lipped, feeling guilty all the while.

'Could someone here take him for me?' It was like he'd read my mind.

'Well, look, we're not there yet. Let's see what he's like tomorrow, eh?'

'Will you be here tomorrow?'

'No,' I replied, 'I'm not here tomorrow, but I'll ask the guys here to update me, so I'll be following his case.' I was careful not to say I was 'off' or I'd no doubt be first in line to drive Horatio to the specialist.

'Perhaps I could phone you and let you know how it's going?' Mr Wales enquired, his eyes expectant.

'Well, if you phone the practice, they'll let me know and I can ring you back.'

'It would be easier if I just phoned you, the lines here are always busy,' he countered.

We went back and forth. Ultimately, Mr Wales wanted to phone me more than I could bear to resist. I broke my own rule and gave him my number. The guy was an emotional ninja. If Francesca went round later that evening and found a lifeless Mr Wales, eye drops still in hand, in a pool of his own blood, part of me would actually be relieved.

The following morning, my phone went off at half seven. I would usually have been up but had been hoping for an extra hour or so in bed before going for a run.

'No rest for the wicked!' I thought, my brain automatically adding the rest of the Douglas Adams quote, 'not even the extremely wicked'.

It was Mr Wales; he was very much alive and keen to subject me to another ethical waterboarding. H was doing okay; he was going into the practice today so that his treatment could continue. I talked things through with Mr Wales and we agreed that I'd coordinate with Francesca and come up with a plan as soon as I was back in tomorrow.

Horatio's eyes were not good. His left eye had improved, but his right was still much the same, maybe a little worse. Both Francesca and I wracked our brains. A graft might solve his problems. We both wanted to refer Horatio to a specialist. Unfortunately, Covid, Mr Wales's driving and practical constraints had closed off that option. Francesca wondered if we could take out his right eye, alleviating his pain. I was reluctant. I could easily do the surgery, but what if we lost control of his other eye? If it also deteriorated, he'd be left blind, the surgery nothing but an extra helping of suffering to no avail. There was one option. I could attempt a conjunctival graft. Harvesting a portion of Horatio's healthy cornea was beyond my skill and our resources. It is performed by specialists, using a microscope to image the eye during the procedure. Instead, I could try cutting a flap in the pink tissue next to the eyeball, the conjunctiva. I'd carefully trim a piece of tissue and then relocate it over the ulcer, kind of like filling in a pothole. The base of the flap would still be attached to the rest of the conjunctiva. It was more like filling in a pothole by picking up the pavement and bending it into the road. The pothole is covered, even if the pavement is bent. The blood supply present in the graft would help deliver nutrients to the damaged cornea. White cells could migrate in and kill off the infection. Covering the ulcer itself would alleviate our feline friend's pain. Ideally, it was also a specialist procedure, but I felt I had a realistic chance of success. Harvesting the graft would be easy, suturing it to the cornea would be the challenge. I put it to Mr Wales, and he extended his trust to me. I explained my lack of expertise carefully.

'You seem pretty confident,' he said. 'If you say you can do it, I'm sure you can.' That made one of us.

Time was also an issue. Ideally, I wanted a few days to prepare, but tomorrow was Friday. We didn't really have the staff to carry out operations over the weekend. But I didn't want to leave Horatio in pain any longer than I had to. Tomorrow it would be then. I had already purchased an updated ophthalmology textbook because of Horatio. I put it to good use, making sure I understood what I needed to achieve. I'd have to prepare the site for my graft: imagine trimming the ragged edges of a pothole until you've got a firm edge of tarmac with sufficient integrity to allow the hole to be durably filled. Then I'd mobilise my graft or, to pursue my analogy, pick up my pavement. Lastly, I'd bend the pavement into the road, shape it to the pothole and fasten it in place. In a few weeks, once I was confident the pothole was filled permanently, I'd return the pavement to its normal position, leaving a small portion of it behind. To really labour the analogy, I'd also have to close the road, which would mean anaesthetising Horatio, a risk in itself.

Mr Wales dropped him off first thing in the morning. Poor Horatio wasn't even allowed breakfast. We agreed that I'd try the graft, but if I couldn't make it work, I'd remove his right eye and continue treating his left, hoping to save it. The latter was looking a lot better, largely thanks to Francesca's evening visits. I finished all my routine surgeries first; I wanted to clear the decks before committing to what could be a difficult procedure. By the time I'd finished, our nursing staff had already got him ready. He was sleepy from his pre-med and soon under anaesthesia. The nurses monitored his anaesthetic while preparing him for surgery. Once I had my gown and gloves on, I placed a drape over Horatio, covering everything apart from his right eye and the shaved area immediately around it. I opened our ophthalmic kit, a special set of tools for eye surgery consisting of tiny instruments that must be wielded with the utmost care, and laid it out on the sterile area of my surgical trolley.

'Happy with him?' I asked Pippa, the nurse who was monitoring Horatio's anaesthesia. She nodded and I began.

I've operated on corneas many times. In dogs, sometimes we will deliberately scratch the cornea with a pattern of tiny incisions in order to assist the healing of an ulcer. It's a procedure called a grid keratotomy. According to our current knowledge, it is not suitable for cats, whose corneal physiology differs somewhat from dogs. However, this was the first time I would be making deep incisions into the cornea. I had very little room to play with. If I went too deep I'd puncture Horatio's eye. I could probably afford to remove half the corneal depth, about a third of a millimetre. The truth is, with the naked eye and the fidelity of our muscular control, such surgery is more or less the limit of what we can achieve, no matter how careful we are. Have you ever told your hand to do one thing, before watching it do another, perhaps spilling a drink or painting over a line? Yeah … that, except I'd be stabbing an eyeball. Paradoxically, Horatio's swollen cornea was making my job a little easier, increasing its thickness and bulging some of the damaged tissue outwards. I carefully trimmed the edge as Pippa and I took turns holding our breath.

After 30 minutes, I was satisfied the ulcer was prepared. Generating a big enough graft would be difficult. Over the next half an hour, I carefully trimmed away the conjunctiva from the periphery of the eye until I had a finger-like piece of tissue large enough to cover the ulcer. Horatio wouldn't be able to see through it, but that didn't really matter; he could see a bit around it and he had one goodish eye. That would have to be enough. It was imperative that the graft had no tension on it. I carefully moved it into place, fiddled around with it and generally made thinking noises whilst I assessed the possibility of it working. I thought it might just do. I started to stitch it in place. Ideally, I would have used suture sized 8-0. That is unbelievably tiny. We didn't have any and we could only order it by the box. We couldn't afford to order a whole box at the cost of £600 for one patient, so I had to use 6-0. That is only slightly less unbelievably tiny. The suture was attached (or swaged on) to the needle. The cornea is surprisingly tough. I had to grip the edge of the ulcer with tiny forceps, then force the 5-mm-long needle through the surface of the eye. I could afford to penetrate about half the depth of the eye, but no more. Each suture was a challenge. How hard is too hard to push? How deep is too deep to go? Unfortunately, the sensation of surgery cannot be taught, it must be felt. Negative feedback could mean complete failure. Without an expert mentor, it is taxing both emotionally and mentally. I was getting there though. After a few stitches, the graft was in place. I'd keep adding more until I was happy that it was secure. My confidence grew. I could do this; it was going to work.

As I finished, and could breathe a sigh of relief, I assessed my work. I was slightly concerned that there was a little tension on the graft; my manual was specific: there should be none. I'd generated it as the textbook advised, but in retrospect, I should have done it slightly differently. Unfortunately, 20/20 surgical vision is only available through the retro-spectroscope. There was nothing I could do to improve it without jeopardising its blood supply and viability. We'd have to wait and see. The plan over the weekend was to continue treating both eyes with drops; Francesca continuing to aid Mr Wales and his daughter with our patient's treatment. Francesca had become close to the family and was heavily invested in the outcome. For my part I was working elsewhere over the weekend, but Horatio occasionally entered my thoughts.

Monday would be the moment of truth.

Mr Wales dropped him off and seemed pleased. Horatio was comfortable at home, eating, drinking and vying for affection as normal. I was glad to hear it and offered his owner a reassuring smile under my mask as I carried the cat carrier into the practice. Once inside, I fished my patient out and stuck him in a kennel. Since he was only getting drops and pain relief today, I put some food and water in with him and gently stroked his head. Looking at his graft, it seemed to be holding. Francesca congratulated me on a job well done and thanked me by buying me a couple of sandwiches for lunch.

We went through the same procedure on Tuesday. As I looked at my handiwork, I could see one of the sutures had failed. My heart sank. By Thursday it was apparent that the graft wasn't going to take as more sutures ripped through the corneal tissue and the flap of conjunctiva came unstuck. I kicked myself. I'd been too arrogant, imagining I could manage the procedure without a microscope. I'd followed the book but was experienced enough that I should have known better and adapted the technique accordingly. I'd registered the tension but done nothing about it. I'd failed.

I broke the news to Francesca and saw her expression, likely a mirror image of my own. We discussed the case and decided I would chat to Mr Wales. It was my responsibility, after all. I dialled his number with a heavy heart. We discussed Horatio at length.

There were a few options, and none gave us certainty of a good outcome:

1. We could try another graft. What if it failed also?
   Every day we continued treatment without full
   healing was another day Horatio was left in pain.

2. We could take out his right eye. This would remove
   the pain from his worst eye, leaving us his less
   severely affected left eye to deal with. But what if it
   deteriorated? Then he'd be left blind. He might
   manage with accommodations in his home
   environment. I had to ask myself if I could justify
   putting him through so much, only to leave him
   sightless as a result.

3. We could put him to sleep. Sometimes the least bad
   option is to admit defeat. We cannot, no matter how
   good our medicine or pure our motives, cure every
   animal presented to us. Perhaps it was time to accept
   that sometimes less is more and say goodbye to our
   elderly feline patient.

He was 19, with early-stage kidney disease. Was it fair to put
him through more? Despite his good nature I knew he must
be suffering. After a long heart to heart, we decided that the
right thing to do was to put Horatio to sleep. If Francesca
had been upset before, now she was distraught. Mr Wales
didn't want to put him down immediately. He wanted to
take him home over the weekend and thoroughly spoil him.
I wasn't keen personally. I think once the decision is made,
any delay is just prolonging the agony. However, I supplied
Horatio with plenty of pain relief to make sure he was
comfortable. Mr Wales still had plenty of eye drops at home.
Francesca was also going to visit over the weekend to say
goodbye.

For me the weekend was an unpleasant interlude. I lost
a few hours' sleep each night, going over the case in my
head. What else could I have done? Volunteered to take H
to the specialist? Perhaps. My own cat had had a graft at a

specialist a year or so ago. It had also failed, and a second surgery was necessary. It had worked and Loki just looked even cooler with his corneal scar. I'm sure the local feline females appreciated his apparent ruggedness. I knew these things happened, but I couldn't escape the fact that I'd known deep down the graft wasn't good enough, its failure was inevitable. Or was it? I'd done my best, but that was scant consolation. I dreamed about doing a second, successful graft one night, only to wake and find that it was fantasy.

On the Sunday, Francesca sent me a message: 'Do we really have to put him down?'

A crying emoji completed the message. I phoned her and reiterated all the logic. I didn't want to do it, but it was the right course of action, all things considered. She reluctantly agreed.

I arrived at the practice on Monday dreading what was coming next, but at least it would bring this chapter to a close. As I walked past our car park, I was surprised to see Mr Wales already there. I said hello and enquired as to Horatio's whereabouts.

'Oh, he's inside. Francesca's just saying goodbye.'

As we talked it seemed that H had thoroughly enjoyed his last weekend, having consumed more salmon, chicken, tuna and treats than was entirely healthy.

'It's such a shame, he just seems so happy; I just can't stand seeing him suffer,' Mr Wales finished.

'I know, I know ...' I let myself trail off.

The plan was to get Horatio ready with an intravenous line and sedation before Mr Wales was allowed in, then we'd gently put H to sleep. However, when I entered Francesca's room, she was completely absorbed in examining his eyes. No doubt his right one was a write-off. But ...

'I think it's healed!' she exclaimed as she examined his good eye.

'Really?' I discarded my backpack and coat. The eye was still picking up a bit of stain, but sometimes that can happen. As eyes heal, blood vessels and pigment make their way into the site of the ulcer as the body tries to repair itself. Francesca passed me the ophthalmoscope. As I looked in detail, I wasn't 100 per cent sure, but it certainly seemed possible. Horatio was happy and purring. His right eye was still a disaster. What to do? Early in the treatment I'd agreed with the office manager that if the graft failed, we could take the eye out for a reduced fee. He managed the finances but was naturally sympathetic. I could see the excitement on Francesca's face, but was reluctant to subject H to another procedure.

'Okay, okay, I'll ask Mr Wales if he wants to try.'

She grinned and hugged me; despite the fact I'd taken a step back to avoid just this sort of levity. Underneath my mask, I also wore a reluctant smile.

Mr Wales agreed. The procedure is called enucleation. In the past I'd found it to be painful and distressing for the patients. There were also significant risks. If I applied too much tension to Horatio's eye as I removed it, I could cause a life-threatening drop in heart rate called bradycardia. It might even kill him. The nerves from both eyes run through a central 'junction' called the optic chiasm; the same tension might render him blind in his other eye, leaving him sightless. Fortunately, I'd done the procedure many times and I was confident in my technique. Over time the profession has learned more and more about pain relief. I'd gone from watching animals suffer a distressing few hours after surgery to adapting my techniques and procedures. Now, with what is called multi-modal analgesia, including local anaesthesia around the eye and optic nerve, I've been able to have the satisfaction of watching my patients wake up with minimal pain and distress. Horatio was no exception. More or less as soon as he came round, he was enjoying head rubs and sardines.

Francesca was embarrassingly grateful.

'I was just doing my job.'

'Yes, but you listened, you changed the plan. Thank you.'

Horatio's case had been difficult. Sure, attempting the graft had been technically challenging. However, what really made Horatio's case harder to deal with was the ethical decisions. For a start, how to balance human and animal health concerns? Horatio was suffering horribly. Obviously, we wanted to get him sorted out. Unfortunately, the more physically involved we were in his treatment, the more chance we would have of inadvertently harming Mr Wales. Every time we met with him, passed over medication, handled Horatio or his cat carrier, we risked transferring a potentially deadly virus. Some might argue that the risk of treating the animal just wasn't worth it. That's a qualitative decision I don't think anyone can honestly say they definitely know the answer to. Mr Wales knew the risks, we explained them to him, and he chose to continue. Who was I to deny him that right? It was clear that Horatio meant the world to him, bringing daily interaction to someone who might be quite lonely otherwise.

Then there was Horatio himself. How much suffering is enough? We couldn't talk to him, so we had to make assumptions. Unfortunately, assumptions can be wrong. In his worst moments, would he have preferred to blink out of existence? Or was it all quite tolerable in exchange for some treats and a few gentle strokes? Was the surgery, the drops, and the days spent in the vets restricted to a cage, worth it? How long would he live? If he lived five more years, was it okay? What about five months? Five weeks? Five days? The truth is we don't and can't know. We can take comfort only in the acceptance that we were doing our best.

I don't know how long Horatio has left. What I am sure of is that I'm glad we gave him one more chance. He is still on the go, still as friendly as ever, and I'm always glad to see him.

22

TIME TO SAY GOODBYE?!

This is the age-old question. Our pets, for the most part, can rarely be expected to outlive us. There are obvious exceptions. If you are already 100 years old, well done. However, statistics would suggest that if you were to purchase a Jack Russell puppy at that age, it would outlive you. Life expectancy is increasing, especially for those who are health conscious. But, no matter how long life becomes, it's going to finish at some point. If you adopt your first dog when you're 18 years old, and always have one thereafter, you're probably going to have six to eight dogs over your life span. What does that mean? Well, you are going to lose them. Unfortunately, dogs, cats and most domestic species have life spans considerably shorter than those of their human companions.

The loss is inevitable, but many factors can have a bearing on its impact.

I once had a lady bring her dog in under rather odd circumstances. I was in my consult room and viewing the waiting list. On it was a 10-year-old Spaniel scheduled for 'PTS', veterinary shorthand for 'put to sleep' or, in technical language, euthanasia. There were no specifics on the screen I was viewing, only the reason for the visit. I switched screens and had a look at the dog's medical record. We hadn't seen it for several years. Unfortunately, this is often a sign that the animal's health has been a bit neglected. Not necessarily deliberately; people are frequently just maxed out keeping their family halfway organised. I wondered what was ailing the dog. Arthritis, cancer, heart disease? Anyway, I stuck my head out of the door and asked the lady to come in.

'Mrs Oxbridge with Penny please!' I bellowed across the waiting room.

Mrs Oxbridge got out of her seat and started walking across the waiting room, Spaniel in tow. I couldn't immediately make out any obvious problem with the dog, but it's not always staring you in the face. I held the door for her, closing it once she was in and had sat down. After the requisite amount of small talk regarding the weather, her health and so on, I asked: 'So, why do you want to murder Penny?'

No, I wouldn't have lasted long in veterinary practice being as blunt as that. Instead, I tried to broach the subject more subtly.

'I see that you've booked Penny in for euthanasia today. Can I ask what seems to be the matter?'

The woman looked at me quizzically, as if this was an extremely stupid question.

Perhaps I'd missed something or the appointment had been incorrectly annotated?

I elaborated. 'You see, Penny's appointment appears to have been booked for us to put her down, but she seems quite healthy on first impressions. I was wondering what's going on with her. We haven't seen her for a few years. Has she been diagnosed elsewhere? Is there something you're worried about?'

Mrs Oxbridge sighed. Clearly, she considered me to be rather dim.

'Oh, no, there's nothing wrong with Penny!'

'Right?' I raised an eyebrow.

'It's the kids,' she continued. 'I've told them again and again that if they don't help look after the dog, I'm having it put down.'

'Ah, ha?' I said, eyebrow raised and twitching slightly.

'Well, they haven't helped, so here we are.' She gestured towards Penny as if Penny might offer some sort of agreement as to the inevitability of her fate.

I glanced at Penny; her tail wagged slightly as our eyes met, but she didn't say anything.

'So,' I said, 'in summary, you've had the dog for a while—'

'Ten years,' interrupted Mrs Oxbridge.

'Yes, ten years, and your children haven't been helping recently—'

'Never,' she interrupted again, 'they've never been helping with her and enough's enough!'

'Okay, okay, but the dog's healthy as far as you know?'

'Yes, yes, she's fine,' she said dismissively.

How do you just say: 'No!'? In veterinary medicine you take your oath to all the furry things, but you deal every day with their owners who pay the bills and do the complaining. It is usual practice to try to avoid outright contradiction, argument or assault. However, this lady was trying my patience. I was honestly astonished. It's not so unusual to have owners come in and request that their animal be put to sleep on somewhat spurious grounds. Sometimes owners will claim that their dog is aggressive and has bitten them, even when it's obvious the dog doesn't have a bad bone in its body. It's often a sign of some other issue in that person's life. Financial trouble and relationship breakdown are probably two of the more common problems. Sometimes, it's for purely selfish reasons. However, even the grimmest of individuals will usually go to the bother of creating some semi-convincing pretext to put the animal 'out of its misery'. You rarely hear people just come out with the truth.

Certainly, it's unusual to say that you've basically grown bored of looking after the dog and since the kids won't help, you've decided on dog-a-cide.

I refused. She seemed quite surprised. I didn't leave it there. I asked her what she hoped to achieve by putting the dog down. She was clear that she wanted to teach her kids about consequences. If they'd been asked to help with the dog's care and refused, then been threatened with the dog's death and still refused, well ... there was only one thing Mrs Oxbridge could do. I don't think ill-considered threats are a good idea. What if someone calls your bluff? That's how you find yourself at the vets trying to get your dog killed. Mrs Oxbridge was hard to read. Looking back, maybe she was a sociopath? She didn't seem bothered whether Penny lived or died. I've seen people angry at the refusal, but she seemed unfazed either way.

Anyway, I explained my logic. There was nothing wrong with Penny. I'm obliged to prevent unnecessary suffering, but not to put animals down on a whim. I also went as far as to suggest that maybe this lady wasn't teaching her kids what she thought she was teaching them. I mean, what kind of message are you sending if you display willingness to end the life of another sentient being in order to teach your kids a lesson? Or worse yet, if you exact vengeance on a third party for lack of help around the house. You would be hard pressed to describe such an act as reasonable or proportionate. There was also additional pressure. If I put this dog down, the nurses would quickly have me in the freezer next to her. It would be unforgivable in their eyes.

I eventually suggested that instead of death, an alternative could be found. There are many rescue centres and plenty of kind-hearted people who might take an older, friendly dog. If Mrs Oxbridge could give me a week or so, I could look into such possibilities. She reluctantly agreed that she could labour on for a few days, but said she would call the practice next week. I agreed that, if no other option could be found, I would reluctantly put Penny down. I doubted I'd actually honour that; I'd probably end up fostering her until I could find a long-term home, but Mrs Oxbridge didn't need to know that.

She never came back. About a year later, I saw Mrs Oxbridge cheerily walking Penny down the main street. She did not seem to have murder in her eyes at the time. What brought her to the vets that day? Who knows? But sometimes it's worth asking some hard questions.

I have had a similar situation, with the opposite outcome. A couple had brought in their middle-aged, male cat. Gordon was an overweight, black-and-white moggy. Once out of his basket and on the examination table, he gratefully received a few strokes to his head and began purring. He was booked in for urinary problems. There is a stream (pardon the pun) of questions that are appropriate in these circumstances and some tests you might want to perform. I began with what, by this stage, was a relatively routine question set, designed to get to the bottom of Gordon's wee-wee problems.

'Does he seem to be straining to pass urine?'

'Does his urine look normal?'

'Is he urinating more often, or a larger volume, or both?'

'If not, is he using a litter tray or bit of the house you would rather have urine free?'

'Is he drinking more than usual?'

'Do you think you could—?'

'We'd like to have him put down.'

'Oh, erm, I see. There's a good chance we might be able to get him fixed up you know?'

This was, a bit like the previous incident, the first time Gordon had been to the vet's for quite some time. As the conversation went on it became apparent that he had been urinating in the house for a good number of months. To be fair, cat urine stinks and it's one of the last things you'd choose to soak your carpet in prior to a visit by the Queen. Not only does it reek, but the smell is remarkably resilient and often takes a good while and a lot of effort to get rid of. I sympathise with anyone in this position. I was brought up in a household that, at its high point, had 13 cats. I can assure you that means a lot of puddles of feline wee-wee in places you'd rather it wasn't. I currently own a cat who views my bed as a giant litter tray, to which he has only occasional access. Otherwise, he's forced to use the much smaller and less comfortable one, full of actual cat litter and located in the utility room.

However, I digress. Back to Gordon. I side-stepped the request that he be put down and tried explaining that, though his problems might be complicated, they could also be quite simple. A sample of urine would allow us to get some idea of what was going on. Feline Lower Urinary Tract Disease (FLUTD) is quite a common presentation. It is multifactorial, and genetics, environment, stress, diet, crystals in the urine and infection are just some of the contributing issues. However, a simple urinalysis might yield enough information to treat Gordon. The inflammation associated with this condition can lead to the cat constantly feeling the urge to urinate. Critically, the constant straining requires a veterinary exam. It is possible that the cat is straining because it feels as if it needs the toilet, even though there is little urine present. However, if the urethra – the tube from the bladder to the outside world – is blocked, that is a true medical emergency. Affected cats are in terrible pain and their bladder keeps expanding. Unrelieved, the pressure can be so great that tiny amounts of urine dribble past the blockage; these can easily be mistaken for the constant small puddles of wee caused by FLUTD. If he did have FLUTD it might be manageable by treating any infection, transitioning on to a special diet and increasing his water intake. Admittedly, a transitional cell carcinoma (TCC), a tumour of the bladder wall, might also be the problem, in which case the outlook would be grim. Sometimes investigation and treatment run up against the limits of finances or medicine and we must admit defeat, but at least an investigation allows us to accept the inevitable with the knowledge that we have done our best.

The owners wanted no investigation, just an end to things. I tried various tacks, but the couple were quite resistant to persuasion. In the end, the husband couldn't stop himself from elaborating.

'Look!' he said, 'we could have been cruel to this cat, he's ruining our house, but we haven't touched him. If you don't put him down, well, I can't guarantee the same in the future.'

Or words to that effect. It was certainly clear that if the cat continued to pee in the house, then he'd get rid of it. And it was clear that he didn't mean re-homing. I don't know exactly what he had in mind, but nothing nice. I didn't know quite what to say. I'd very rarely had anyone directly threaten an animal. Even some of the more unpleasant characters I've dealt with made some effort to hide their intent. What to do?

I could take the cat myself, but I knew that if I did that in every instance, I'd rapidly become personally overwhelmed. I thought about charity intervention, but charities have limited resources and the cost of investigation might run away. I knew our local cat charities were already straining at the seams. I asked if maybe we could try cheap therapy, based on some assumptions: a therapeutic trial. Maybe they could get a kennel and Gordon could live outside? The couple were not willing to look after the cat for even another day, or to try any alternative options. I could accede to their request, though I hated the thought of putting down an animal that might be saved. But if I refused, what would happen? At best, another vet would be putting him down soon. At worst ... who knows?

In the end, I put Gordon to sleep. He was friendly, even when I sedated him with a small needle and an intramuscular injection. After 15 minutes or so, he lay down, sleepy. I find that cats hate having their limbs interfered with; placing an intravenous cannula, therefore, can result in their final memories being a needless wrestling match, so, unless there's a reason otherwise, I usually pre-med or sedate all animals for euthanasia. Cats, I usually give the lethal injection intrarenally or into the kidney. So, with Gordon sleepy, comfortable and lying on his side, I slid a hand underneath his abdomen. With the muscle flaccid, I could rapidly identify his kidney. I pushed gently upwards, cupping it in my fingers. With my other hand, I slowly introduced the 23-gauge inch-long needle. It's quite easy to tell if you're in the right place. I won't bore you with the details; it's a sensation identified by experience. With the needle correctly located, I depressed the plunger on the syringe. Within 30 seconds, Gordon's eyes glazed over, his breathing slowed, then stopped. I could still feel the activity of his heart. It went from regular, to fibrillating, to nothing. He was dead.

I had explained the process to the owners in advance. I checked his heart with a stethoscope, mostly for show.

'He's gone now,' I said to the owners, who had opted to stay.

The hardest decision had been made. At least for Gordon, it was over. However, the decisions weren't over for me. In the immediate aftermath of an animal's death, it is the vet's job to step into the role of priest, counsellor and confidant. Something for which many young vets are woefully ill prepared; I know I was. These were difficult circumstances. The inevitable loss of an older and beloved pet, though heart-breaking, is an easier set of circumstances to deal with from my point of view. What did I say to this couple? Admonish them for their decision? Lecture them on the sanctity of life?

No, and I'll tell you why. This couple were visibly upset by Gordon's passing. They loved him but chose to put him down. I couldn't know their precise circumstances, but I could look at them. They were in their early sixties, but time had not been kind. They were both obese. The husband walked with a stick, the wife with a walking frame. It may be unfair to judge a book by its covers, but they did not appear well off. I put myself in their shoes: the house reeking of cat urine constantly, the difficulty of cleaning it up, multiple times a day when you are not very mobile. Then there's the money. What if you have none? Or some, but you need it to eat and pay the bills? And what if there are no promises? It could all be a waste?

What was more telling was that, as the lady gently stroked Gordon's head, tears in her eyes, she said: 'He would never have been happy with someone else ... or outside. He just loved us too much for that.'

I could have made the point that he might have preferred it to the alternative, but I didn't. Instead, I found myself telling them that, under the circumstances, they'd made the right choice. All things considered, taking a holistic view, it was the best of a bad lot. I'm not quite sure I meant it, but I had another thought in mind. What if I did admonish them? Stood there and lectured them while they bowed their heads and realised what awful characters they were? It would probably have made me feel better in the moment. But they'd never be back. The next cat wouldn't make it to the vet's. This way, the door was open.

The decision to put a beloved pet to sleep or not is extremely complex. Most vets will take a holistic view that is not often expressed well in scientific literature. All aspects must be considered. For me the most valid reason for euthanising an animal is intractable pain. If the animal is constantly suffering to an unbearable degree, the gig is up. Even here, though, there are complications. What is unbearable? You may often hear someone state that they have suffered 'unbearable' pain, yet they are telling you the story, so they must have borne it. Many of our fellow humans suffer pain daily; in many cases it's quite severe. Only the very few would choose to end their life. Philosophically, you might argue that the ability to suffer is synonymous with life.

I feel there is a fundamental difference between the pain borne by humans and the same in animals. The difference is derived from our capacity for logical thought. As far as we know, no animal has displayed the complex, nuanced appreciation of the link between current circumstances, behaviour, and the future that humans do. A human may hold out in the knowledge that tomorrow may be a better day or that a novel therapy may appear. We can assess our own quality of life and come to a conclusion. Not so animals: we must do that for them. Our answer is unlikely to be perfect. Occasionally you look into an animal's eyes and they just say, 'kill me'. Excepting that, it's always a judgement call. Neither you nor the owner are likely to be happy about it, but the important thing is that you are both satisfied that it's the best option available. One of the most important things I urge owners to do is set parameters. Have an end state in mind, then stick to it. It may be the first time the animal cannot get itself outside to the toilet. It might be when they are no longer interested in human affection. The danger in not having a clear cut-off point is the movement of goalposts. Every time that things get a little worse, the owner adjusts and normalises it. Eventually, they're accepting circumstances that, had they appeared overnight, would undoubtedly have had them knocking on your door and asking you to help their animal slip away.

I've occasionally allowed someone to leave the surgery with their animal, when I knew the right thing to do was euthanasia. At the time, the owner just could not face it. I firmly expressed my opinion but left the ultimate decision to them. After offering them all my sympathy, I then let them leave. Obviously, I could not have legally stopped them doing so. However, I could have sought the intervention of the RSPCA or police. Such people sometimes just need a little time to think and process things. They almost always come back soon after, having realised their mistake. The danger in pushing them too far is that they do not return for fear of your disapproval. I think it's better to acquiesce to a little more time, as it's often the best of poor options. Where that is the case, ensuring the animal has adequate pain relief is paramount.

Vets are occasionally wrong. I know I have been. Animals you assess to have little or no chance go on to a remarkable recovery. If you've been that vet, I sympathise. As long as you've given someone the best options that your training and logic allows, coupled that to ethical considerations and reached a logical conclusion, you've done your best. Animals aren't lawnmower engines, and nothing is certain. If you are the owner who has lost faith in your vet after a similar episode, know that they almost certainly did their best. No one has a crystal ball.

Sometimes owners will go home after putting an animal down, have time to think, then feel the urge to ring up for reassurance. It's a hugely awkward situation. I've had a similar, but not identical problem. A lady rang me up out of hours. She was extremely upset, and it took a bit of cajoling even to figure out what was going on. I admit, it was early in the morning, and I was a bit cross. Eventually she managed to get out that her cat was dead.

I told her that I was uncertain as to what she expected from me, given that I was a vet and not a sorcerer. Eventually, through sobs, she got out the story. She'd tumble-dried her cat to death after leaving the tumble-drier door open in a moment of distraction. Not knowing the cat was inside, she'd come back and closed it; it had automatically come on. She only discovered the cat when she opened the door to retrieve the contents. In addition to some dry clothes, she found some dry vomit and a lifeless cat. I passed on my condolences and made sympathetic noises. By now I had fully woken up and was in a more humane mood. Once she had calmed down, I asked her what I could do for her. She could bring the cat in if she wished us to dispose of the body? We could arrange cremation and the return of the animal's ashes? No, she would bury the cat in the garden. Instead, what she wanted was reassurance. What she wanted to know was: 'Did he suffer?'

'W-w-what?' I stuttered.

I could hardly imagine a worse way to go. Imagine being put in a large metal drum, then being whirled around and slowly cooked. I'm not sure I'd wish it on my worst enemy. Perhaps a punishment reserved only for those who drop litter in national parks? That is not what I said. I told her that given the disorientation, centripetal force and heat, unconsciousness would have come quickly. After that, the moggy would have been unaware and suffered no more. Who knows, maybe I was even right? Nothing I could say would make her feel worse than she already did. She wouldn't be making that mistake again.

Those owners who re-examine their decision to put an animal to sleep need similar reassurance. It's done. It's certainly not reversible afterwards. No one is going to be happy about such an outcome; the best we can hope for is confidence that it was the right choice. We can also take reassurance from the fact that while there is overwhelming evidence that animals fear danger and can anticipate pain, they do not, as far as I can tell, fear death as an abstract concept. Their experience of euthanasia may be little different from their experience of a general anaesthetic. The only difference being, they will wake up from one and not the other. Therefore, the only logical approach in my mind is to talk through the decision with the owner and help them reaffirm their course of action. They will thank you for it later.

I've found with most people that reassuring them they ultimately gave their pet the best possible life is some comfort. Their animal's life may not have been perfect according to some utopian ideal, but none of us are perfect ourselves; we lead complex lives. We each have the capacity for selfishness, laziness and all manner of vices. However, most people are doing the best they can. At the same time, if I were to die, I'd like the people left behind to remember me fondly, get pissed together and then move on with their lives. I like to think our animal companions would want the same. I don't think your faithful pet would want you to suffer crushing guilt or permanent anguish.

I'll leave it thus: we owe it to our companions to give them the best life we possibly can. When the time comes, there is one last kindness we can offer them. That is, to weigh up their quality of life as dispassionately and objectively as we can. If they are no longer living a life worthy of the name, our duty is to quietly ease them into the great unknown. I'm an atheist; I've never found the evidence for anything after our current consciousness to be convincing, and I find the workings of our world to be incompatible with a benevolent deity. However, it would be a mistake to assume I wouldn't like it to be the case. I hope there is something after this where we are all reunited with our loved ones, where the sick are well and the damaged made whole, and I sincerely hope there is a place there for our furry friends. A lot of people lose a pet or companion and get another one. They are going to need and want more, good, humane advice.

23

VETS

I've spent all my time in veterinary medicine working in first opinion practice of one type or another and I'm still a general practitioner, jack of all trades, master of none. I've tried to accurately convey what life is like for those of us treating and caring for the nation's pets, companions, workers and soon-to-be steaks. I've given it a lot of thought. If someone asked me to sum up the average GP vet's day boiled down to its essential elements, I'd define it thus: high-consequence decision making in a complex environment, with imperfect data, on a budget.

Many careers have some of these elements, but few have all. NASA make high-consequence decisions in a complex environment, but they have a budget of over $20 billion; no one is making astronauts chip in for the rocket fuel for re-entry. The reality of veterinary practice is quite different from what's imagined by most people. The same could be said of many professions, but I think the gap between what's imagined and what's true is especially large for my profession. I've done other jobs, so I'm not entirely without perspective. It's worth discussing some of the details and dichotomies.

Who are vets?

Places at vet school are in high demand. The academic requirements mean that anyone who gets a slot must be fairly bright. Veterinary schools prize practical experience; I think I was 12 when I first started making my way into the local vets to begin learning my future trade. To be in with a shot, any candidate must also be driven, and self-imposed high standards are almost ubiquitous. They often have a wide range of options open to them; why choose veterinary medicine? Most vets find themselves empathising with animals from a young age. A more general interest in the natural world is common. Anyone brought up on nature documentaries can't help but imagine themselves coming to the aid of an orphaned orang-utang or an injured gazelle.

The extent to which we can aid an animal is limited by our knowledge, amongst other factors. While many injuries are obvious to the casual observer, much of both human and animal illness is concealed within the body. A knowledge of complex and interdependent systems is key in diagnosing and treating disease. There's a common misperception among clients that a 'blood test' is a case of taking a sample from the poorly animal and running it through a *Star Trek*-style medical analyser, which makes a few robotic sounds before helpfully spitting out the answer along with the solution. Unfortunately, that technology is some way off. What vets actually receive from their machine is a list of parameters. These must then be put in context. The appropriate response may be further tests, trial therapy, specifically indicated medication, surgery or even euthanasia. The diagnosis and the treatment options require the gathering of information, logical deduction and then rational decision making. This generally appeals to those who enjoy problem solving.

We've discussed who might become a vet and why they might do so. Now let's overlay some realities of the job to gain some perspective.

The empathy that most vets, and most people, have for animals is laudable. However, it can be an enormous burden. It is terrible to see your pet or livestock in pain or suffering.

Pain and the distress it causes are probably right at the top of owners' or keepers' concerns. It's often what makes euthanasia tolerable. In the previous chapters are only a few of the situations I've been in: ones that involved intractable pain, horrible trauma or emotionally wrenching decisions. Whilst an owner or keeper may face these challenges once in a while, all these cases are centralised at the veterinary practice or veterinary practitioner; we may deal with them daily or hourly. I have cases, years old now, that will occasionally deny me sleep or trouble my emotions in my waking hours. Could I have done more? Was I right? Maybe I should have tried harder, stayed later, worked *pro bono*? Who could refuse to work through lunch, stay late, foster an animal, provide care cheaply or for free? What kind of monster could decline? It's only a little longer, one meal, one night, a few quid. Many examples could be argued and won on their individual merit. It is their individual merit that makes us and others ask it in the first place.

A few years ago, I found myself on Makalu, the fifth-highest mountain in the world at 8,485 metres. We were attempting to climb a new route on the south-east ridge. On return from Camp 1, it was apparent that one of our team, Tony, was missing. He could have tripped and plunged to his death. Falling rocks could have cut the rope, severing his link to the earth and casting him down the mountain. He could have been hit by passing debris, and now be hanging injured on the rope and awaiting rescue. Altitude sickness or exhaustion could have immobilised him. Tony might already be dead, but if he was injured, it was critical that we find him quickly. Any rescue would involve considerable risk and back-breaking labour. My two companions were the expedition leader and our doctor. Both were exhausted from our 12-hour day carrying heavy loads in the thin high-altitude air. They were unable to help; they simply didn't have it in them. It may seem callous, but it isn't. If a member of the rescue team collapses, the rescue fails. I wouldn't be able to help Tony alone. Fortunately, a friend of mine, CJ, was about to arrive from base camp. Like me, he'd had a long day already. I quickly briefed him and one look in his eyes told me what I needed to know: he was in. We rapidly reclimbed our route in the darkness, pushing ourselves hard in the oxygen-depleted environment and hoping to find Tony alive. If one or both of us developed altitude sickness or got hit by a rock falling, unseen, out of the night, we were probably beyond help. It was unlikely a helicopter could reach our altitude. It definitely wouldn't fly at night, and even if it could the face was steep, and the chopper might not have a winch. The Sherpas couldn't get to us until tomorrow at the earliest. Two of us might manage Tony, but neither of us would be able to rescue the other alone. A strenuous eight-hour journey at a normal rate had taken six at maximum effort. As we came to the end of our fixed ropes, Camp 1 was in sight. We'd found no trace. He was either here, or he was gone. I could see the green nylon tent in the light from my head-torch.

'Tony? Tony?' I shouted. 'You there mate?'

Silence.

'Tony!' screamed CJ.

'Toooonnnnnnnyyyyyyyy!?' we shouted in unison.

Nothing … then a rustling.

'Yeah? What do you want?' came Tony's reply from inside his fabric shelter.

'What do we want? We thought you were fucking dead, you eejit!' I said.

'Nah, just dropped my belay device, realised I was a danger to myself and others, and came back up here.'

'Well, never mind that; get the bloody kettle on!'

I hammered my axe into the ice adjacent to the tent door and began unzipping it. Meanwhile CJ let base camp know we were okay. As the nearest thing we had to a doctor, I checked Tony over and declared him below average. I recommended immediate castration to stop unwanted breeding from an individual of low genetic merit. Tony declined. After a couple of cups of tea and some well-deserved piss-taking, we settled in for the night. I slept the sleep of the truly spent.

Mountaineering may seem only distantly relevant to veterinary medicine, but I think there are many parallels. The teamwork aspect is obvious, but what is attempting a new surgery or procedure against the clock other than a rescue bid? Who could refuse to go out into the storm to save another? Rescuing someone is one of the most life-affirming things a person can do, but failure can be crushing. And what if the storms are daily? It cannot be sustained. If every owner only needs a few extra minutes? Collectively that's impossible to deliver in a working week. Most vets see a case every 10 to 15 minutes. Let's say they start at 0830, finish at 1830 and have an hour for lunch, an unusual luxury in itself. Let's allow 15 minutes for appointments, more than the average. If we stick to consultations, no surgery, that adds up to 36 individual animals with 36 individual problems a day. If they each need 'just five more minutes' that adds up to 180 minutes, or an extra three hours per day. Even if you give up your lunch hour, you still owe two. Like my team-mates on Makalu, we must consider self-preservation or there will be no rescue team.

Human medics deal with similar issues. The parallel is obvious, more accurate in this recent outbreak, but false. For the most part, human medics are highly specialised and operate in teams. Decision making is collective, and individuals are usually very experienced before they are required to wield the authority to stop treatment in the face of insurmountable odds, allowing the patient to finally rest easy. No one is asking their GP if they could manage a splenectomy at lunchtime. This is not the case for vets. Most of us work either alone or are at least siloed from other vets throughout the day, working on different cases. This can lead to all sorts of unique mental strains.

Although there is increased specialisation, most of us are still general practitioners. In my early career I've spent the morning with my hand up a cow's bottom diagnosing pregnancy and addressing fertility management, only to drive back to the surgery and start an orthopaedic repair of a cat's leg. I've been presented with most species that the average UK citizen can imagine and some that they probably cannot.

'Why don't you know this? You're seriously telling me you don't know what the ideal diet for a Bearded Dragon is?'

'What do you mean, you can't do this surgery? Maybe you should have spent your money on a course, instead of holidays?'

The internal voice is ever the critic. I've gone from neurologist to dermatologist, orthopaedic surgeon to obstetrician, from assassin to saviour, all in one day. The range of competencies the average vet, or indeed vet nurse, maintains is an order of magnitude greater than that expected in human medicine. Consequently, the depth of the knowledge in that competency is, well, not deep. If you think you're disappointed at your vet's lack of knowledge, trust me, it's not a patch on what's going on in their head. I can distinctly remember listening to a podcast on the drive to work. It was about *Angiostrongylus vasorum*, lungworm. I was listening to a world-leading expert on the worm discuss her research. As the podcast neared its end, she mentioned another parasite, one that infests ant's brains and causes a behavioural change. Then she wondered if perhaps she was making it up, maybe she'd imagined it? She was talking about *Fasciola hepatica*, liver fluke. Her highly specialised research had left her dubious as to its very existence, yet it's commonly treated by farm vets throughout the UK.

We have the modern issue of 'Dr Google'. There's a lot of information out there for the discerning owner, and research can yield likely diagnosis and treatment. It does occasionally place vets in an awkward position. It's like being in a competitive quiz, except the other side has access to Wikipedia. We are eventually going to lose. Fear not though, the solution is honesty. If there's a chance it's right, we should include whatever is available in the list of possibilities and thank the source for their help; we're on the same side after all. Once familiar with the information, vets are in a much better position to understand the science and research involved than the vast, vast majority of owners. We can then decide how relevant it is and guide the owner. It can feel intellectually threatening, but the issue is not insurmountable.

I think it's just as hard to be a good generalist as a good specialist. However, it can leave generalists with 'imposter syndrome', as we tend to feel embarrassed at our lack of knowledge in niche areas, forgetting that if we compare ourselves to the leading light in any and all human endeavour, we can only view ourselves as inadequate. The vet's inquisitive mind naturally wants an answer to what's wrong. The empath in them wants to return the animal to health. What tests must be done and how might we work up the case? How do we balance that against …?

The elephant in the room is money. I would estimate that 90 per cent of the stress of my job would be removed if I could just think about the medicine, with no regard to cost. I have, in a different life, treated human casualties during war. I never had to worry about the money. Our NHS is incredible, if not perfect, rightly envied by many. Vets are the unintended victims of its delivery of healthcare, which is free at the point of use. Our clients have rarely been exposed to what medicine costs. I've often heard a client tell me a particular procedure is ludicrously priced. x-rays are a good example, let's say £70 for each. Since the average pet is unlikely to oblige us by sitting still for the procedure, we will need sedation or anaesthesia on top. Say £350 to £500 for a set of three? Ridiculous! Until you understand that the digital X-ray machine was £50,000. Plus, maintenance, running costs and the usual ancillary expenses. Over seven hundred x-rays must be taken and paid for just to break even, without a penny of profit. Seventy-five pounds just to nurse an animal overnight? Crazy, except that 'night' is 14 hours and the minimum wage is close to £9. So, even if you're happy with an entirely unqualified member of the public staring at your animal with no clue what to do, you're still in the hole for £126. Many procedures in veterinary medicine are charged at a fraction of what they are in human medicine. I'd argue that the human medics are held to a higher standard, but veterinary medicine is advancing quickly.

I have lost count of the number of times I've been told, 'You must be rich', in response to admitting I'm a vet. Vets are paid more than the average citizen in the UK. In 2020, the average vet in the UK earned about £33,400 per annum. The average full-time vet earns £42,000. The average full-time employee in the UK earns about £30,000. These figures are approximate. So, vets do just fine, but compared to careers with similar training burdens? The average UK GP doctor earns around £100,000, the average lawyer makes about £60,000. Any vet in it just for the money has made a mistake, especially so these days. I was lucky enough to graduate with modest student debt. Veterinary students nowadays are paying £9,000 per year to train, plus all the normal outgoings that life requires. The course requires that holidays and weekends are spent either studying or taking part in extra-mural studies, working on farms, volunteering in shelters, or gaining experience with those already working in the profession. This work is mostly unpaid. Unfortunately, this all makes pursuing a veterinary career a financial as well as academic challenge. It may be a point for another day, but it probably stops some eminently suitable candidates from ever applying.

Thus, vets are faced with a relatively rare triumvirate of competing demands: Empathy, Knowledge and Resources. We empathise with owners, keepers and their animals. We are placed or place ourselves under enormous pressure to know our stuff, work up the case logically, do the right tests, at the right time, in the right order. If necessary, we must be willing and able to perform the correct surgery. It must be delivered in challenging circumstances, with minimal staff compared to a human equivalent. A Caesarean section on a cow might be performed in a darkened field, illuminated by head-torch, alone or with only the farmer to help. A thoracotomy on a cat might be your only hope to save it, but rather than evacuate her to expert care, you must put yourself to the challenge if you dare. You may have all the empathy and knowledge in the world, but still be unable to save a patient. Further investigation is not economically or ethically rational. All we know is that the suffering cannot be allowed to continue.

It may seem that a refusal to offer further treatment on financial grounds is immoral. Let's analyse that. In the case of any practice, there's no anonymous donor. The bill isn't sent off into the ether. Any treatment offered for free is coming straight out of the boss's pocket. An owner who wants an operation for free is asking the practice owner to pay their bill. An uncomfortable fact is that if an owner is paying, say, £50 a month in media subscriptions, but doesn't have insurance for their dog, that says more about their priorities than any vet's. I've once had a couple refuse to pay their bill because, and I kid you not, they needed their spending money for Disney World. What if I want to go to Disney World? Although, no doubt I'd end up reattaching Mickey's ear after a preventable industrial accident, *pro bono*, of course. The vast majority of owners are understanding when faced with economic realities. Unfortunately, a minority are not, and I've had strips torn off me by desperate and traumatised owners before now. Granted they are often very emotional and may not even mean what they say, but none of us can just shrug these things off, even if we'd like to claim otherwise. That many practices do quietly absorb some costs and help where they can is testament to the humanity and kindness of those running them. Unfortunately, accusations of money grabbing are unfairly thrown at individual vets with irritating regularity.

About half of practices in Britain are now owned by large corporate chains. Corporates have brought many improvements. Better IT, improved human resources, reduced hours, access to education and much-needed investment in equipment. But they have also brought a heightened profit motive; in some cases, corporates are publicly traded companies, and it is ultimately about shareholder value. In many practices, there is no longer any point in complaining to the vet, or indeed the manager, about prices; they are not setting them. I think vets and particularly veterinary nurses are undervalued, but I also worry that we are pricing some pet owners out of much needed care. Having a pet is a privilege, but one I'd like most families to have access to. Hardly a day goes by when I don't hear colleagues worry about rising costs to owners. At the same time, we all need to make a living and I don't have an easy answer.

Unfortunately, the hard choices vets are forced to make may result in moral injury: a cognitive paradox between the desire to help and heal, and the necessity of euthanasia or limited treatment due to practical or economic realities. I've had to carry out three euthanasias on a Boxing Day morning. All were justified. The owners had each chosen to give the dogs one last family get-together as presents were opened, belly rubs were given, and the family celebrated before saying goodbye. No doubt each owner was experiencing heart-wrenching guilt and deep sorrow. While I was not close to the owners or the animals, I can report that it was a hard morning and certainly affected my mental state. I'd consider myself at the upper end in terms of mental robustness, but it still had an undeniable impact. If you're an owner, spare a thought for the vets; they are not impervious or immune to tragedy. If you're a vet, know that the emotions you feel on these occasions are perfectly natural; you would be inhuman otherwise. However, we must all find a way to leave it at work.

Social media and our increasingly online lives also represent a significant threat to our psychology. The polarity in arguments is, at times, startling to me. It seems that online is not a place for nuance. Issues that are far from simple are quickly reduced to binary positions, with each side assuming the motive of the other. Instead of considering another viewpoint, we are quick to judge. Even if we disagree with someone, we must maintain perspective. It seems to me that humanity loves goodies and baddies; simple narratives are appealing to us – you have only to watch our most successful movies. Unfortunately, what this leads to is demonisation. If we are good and we hold one position, someone holding a differing or opposite opinion is not merely mistaken, they are bad. I've seen vets accused of terrible things online and in some instances the situation rapidly spun out of control until death threats were made and the police contacted. No one making the threats seemed to stop and ask if the accusation was well founded. Vets, by the way, are not immune from these instincts. I've been left awestruck by some of the things said by members of our profession after someone in a veterinary group offered an opinion, asked for help, or posted a funny photo to inject a little humour into everyone's day. The most astonishing thing is that many of the worst perpetrators are self-declared 'lovely people'. I'm extremely cautious of anyone who considers themselves to be lovely.

I'm certainly guilty of checking on my cases via messaging app on my days off. Another feature of our lives is the ubiquity of mobile phones. What it means for many is that the working day is never really over. It may be an innocent message to warn of a difficult case coming in tomorrow, it may be a reminder to order a drug or phone a client, but it keeps us at work well after we should be leaving it behind. I recommend setting up strict rules. No messages on work groups before, say, 0800 or after 1900, for example. If you need cat memes in your life that much, I'm sure you can find them yourself. Emergencies are obvious exceptions, but we should place a value on our time away and act accordingly. One of the reasons I love expedition life is its purity: the objective is simple, the focus complete and distractions few and far between. For me, I'm in the moment, not removed from it by a million conflicting online messages, adverts and news I can do nothing about. Unplug when you can.

Presentee-ism is rife in the veterinary community. In the last permanent job I had, over a two-year period, between six vets, we had one day of absence. That was half a day each, for two different vets, both of whom were sent home because they were vomiting while still trying to treat animals. For comparison, if vets were off sick at the same rate as the average worker, you'd expect 88 days of illness in the same practice, over the same period. Veterinary medicine generally requires you to be present to do your job. Veterinary staff are only too aware that a day of absence for any reason means extra pressure applied to other staff, staff who simply do not have spare capacity. The practice can cancel appointments, but there's always the worry an animal suffers because a surgery wasn't done, or a service provided. Perhaps regular exposure to poo and infection means vets have better than average immune systems? But it would be naive to think that self-induced pressure to do right by our patients and colleagues isn't a big factor.

This leads me to mention a tragic fact of life in my profession. Many vets struggle with their mental health for the reasons above. In addition, we have the knowledge and access to drugs required to take our own lives relatively painlessly. Veterinary surgeons take their own lives at four times the rate of the general public. There are a myriad of pressures on vets, but perhaps there is another factor. From the very start of our careers, vets are trained to take a pragmatic attitude towards life itself. Euthanasia of a patient due to an unacceptably low quality of life or intractable pain is not only an option, but a logical and all-too-frequent conclusion to cases we see daily. If we assess our own quality of life, deem it poor, register our own pain, physical or psychological, and decide it is simply unbearable; well, there's an obvious conclusion.

I have, on a number of occasions, nearly lost my own life to what might be politely called misadventure, or more accurately, stupidity. Once, I was washed out of my kayak in big breakers. I had chosen not to wear a buoyancy aid, because I'm way too cool to need one. As I tried to recover, successive waves pushed me deep underwater. Each time I fought my way, breathless, to the surface, another wave would crash over me, I realised I was drowning. As I swam for my life, a small part of me wished to simply black out, for my seemingly eternal ordeal to end. Another part of me was at peace with it: I was going to drown, right now ... oh well. But something deep inside wasn't ready to surrender, not yet. I gave it one last go and swam like I've never swum before ... suddenly my feet touched the sand and I struggled ashore. I survived, and I'm glad I did; I have had so much more life since. The only advice I can offer to anyone who feels like they are drowning is: swim for shore, you'll be glad you did.

No one should be embarrassed to ask for a lifeline. No one should feel guilty if they need to stand on the shore for a while, and perhaps only get back in on the days when the ocean is calmer or there is some help to hand. As your own capability increases, then you can consider going out in rougher seas. There is much more support out there than there has ever been, and mental health is front and centre in many conversations about the veterinary profession. I wonder if we could do more. I wonder if perhaps we might have to look at our selection criteria for vet school. Academics are great and necessary; true academic brilliance is not essential. Perhaps we have paid too little heed to selecting for mental resilience. It can be learned, for sure. However, it's impossible to deny there is some natural inclination. There's no use having great, exceptional vets who last three years then burn out, or worse. Perhaps we need to look at including the big five personality traits in our criteria:

Openness (inventive/curious versus consistent/cautious).
Conscientiousness (efficient/organised versus easy-going/careless).
Extraversion (outgoing/energetic versus solitary/reserved).
Agreeableness (friendly/compassionate versus challenging/detached).
Neuroticism (sensitive/nervous versus secure/confident).

These are sliding scales, not binary states. I don't want to take away anyone's opportunity, but I don't want to pull the wool over their eyes either. Whether we use these as a filter for applicants for vet school, or perhaps use this or a different model to help future vets decide where in the profession they may be most happy. There are many roles available to those who become vets. The public image tends to focus on clinical practice, but actually vets may work in research, science communication, academia, industry and numerous other capacities. Is it really fair to let someone who scores highly in neuroticism, who is highly introverted and obsessively organised, go forward into general practice without even discussing it with them? Maybe they'll bring order to the chaos; maybe the chaos will come for them.

It would be easy for my generation to point out that modern vets have it better than we did. Many no longer cover nights on call. Hours are shorter, support more readily available, online resources provide instantaneous access to information that previously had to be memorised, and mental health is at the forefront of the profession's collective mind.

However, I think there has never been a more challenging time to be a vet, especially a newly qualified one. The information, clinical interventions and data available have increased exponentially during my career. Client expectations have also risen, far faster than the average client's ability to pay for it. Gold standard medicine is taught in the veterinary schools, the need for informed consent, good note taking and the possibility of professional or legal ramifications emphasised. I've seen young vets almost paralysed by the fear of getting it wrong, watched them give up their lunch hours to typing out exquisitely detailed clinical notes, and seen waiting rooms fill with a backlog of angry clients as they struggle with one complex case. At the same time, our society has become increasingly intolerant of our humanity. Farming is more and more about efficiency; any misstep is lost revenue. Our companion animal clients, in many cases, now see their pets as literal family members, referring to themselves as pet parents and their adopted family as fur-babies. Some clients expect human standards of intervention but delivered within their wallet's constraints. Mistakes should not happen, right?

It is said that to err is human, to forgive, divine.

This gets the cart before the horse. It would be more accurate to say that to be human is to err, and that given this, forgiveness is essential and should be ubiquitous. We are not robots. The Turing test, postulated by Alan Turing, who was made famous in modern times by the film *The Imitation Game*, refers to a machine's ability to express complex behaviour, similar to, or indistinguishable from, that of humans. A good analogy would be a conversation carried out by text message. If you cannot tell whether you are texting a computer during a conversation, it might be said that the machine has passed the Turing test. Here's the thing: if we were to programme such a machine, we would have to build in errors, or it would be an unconvincing facsimile of a human.

We often see in the media people who have made a mistake immediately asked if they will resign. I've seen clients suggest that the fallout of an alleged clinical error should be the permanent removal of a vet's right to practise. Well, that way madness and dysfunction lies. If everyone who ever makes an error is forced out of an organisation, there are two issues. First of all, no member of staff in any entity would survive the day. Second, the organisation will rapidly be stripped of its institutional experience, doomed to repeating previous mistakes. Each of us would like some understanding when we get it wrong; we should be just as willing to extend it to others.

The very fact that most vets will say, 'I am a vet', instead of, 'I work as a vet', in response to being asked what they do for a living is telling. It implies a vocation, a calling and pride in the fact. Vets are still generally trusted and held in high esteem by the general public. That trust and esteem is earned, and we must not lose sight of that. It's not earned at admission to vet school, nor at graduation, but every day, and we should not forget it. If lost it will not be easily regained. We must learn to balance excellence and access, remembering that pursuing one at the cost of the other may not be in the best interests of our patients when we take a holistic view. We have to find a way to best deliver affordable care, now and in the future, for our non-human companions. Collectively, we humans must learn to share our world with other sentient beings, doing the least harm to them that we reasonably can, consistent with our best understanding of their needs and within the constraints of our economics and technology. At the same time, we must take care of ourselves.

I don't have all the answers, but I'm confident we can do better.

However, I cannot leave you on that note.

Perhaps, just one more story ...

24

BILL

It's not often you can bring something back from the dead, but when you do the sensation is worth all the effort, I can assure you. A young couple rang me up to say that their normally boisterous Lab wasn't himself. Normally he was very excited to see his owner home and made a great show of it. However, this evening he'd seemed subdued and then wandered off to the garage and lain down. They had tried to encourage him out, but he refused to move. He didn't seem to be in pain, but something was definitely up. Listening to their account, it didn't sound overly serious, but certainly worth checking out. When they turned up, it was around 9pm, but I was still at work dealing with our inpatients for the evening. They'd actually had to carry Bill to the car and then into the surgery. He was a 10-year-old, black Lab and quite subdued. Once in the door he did manage an untidy walk into the consult room, but he immediately sat down against a wall. I skipped the formalities as something was clearly up. He didn't seem distressed or in pain, but when I checked his gums they were white. Uh-oh! I had a feel of his abdomen and it felt 'fluidy', the same way a water balloon does. He was panting a bit with a respiratory (or breathing) rate of 60 and a heart rate of 160. There was no history of trauma. I told the owner that their dog likely had a bleeding tumour in his abdomen; he would require immediate surgery, and survival was not guaranteed. There was another option: we could put him to sleep; it wouldn't take much in the circumstances.

They looked stunned. Not just by the illness I'd described, but also by the rapidity and certainty of the diagnosis.

'How do you know?' they said.

Well, how do you describe 'just knowing'. Experience, that's how. If you see enough of something, sometimes you just know. Much of medicine is pattern recognition. I did, however, suggest one more test: an abdominal tap. This involves inserting a small-gauge needle through the abdominal wall and into the peritoneal cavity. Then light suction is created by drawing back on the syringe. It's not a perfect test as clotted blood or other tissue can block the syringe. You may hit a small vessel and suck back blood, which may give you a false positive. However, if you select the right site and get back a large quantity of blood with little effort, it's a pretty good indicator that you're dealing with an abdomen full of blood. It is quite painful, so sedation is recommended in an ideal world. However, do you want to sedate an animal that's bleeding internally? Nope, me neither; that may be sufficient to kill them, rendering the test moot. Local anaesthesia is the ideal answer. I hadn't access to local immediately and he seemed like a nice dog, so I stabbed him with a 1-inch, 21-gauge needle and drew back. Blood, lots of it; that was enough for me. I could have performed an ultrasound, I suppose. In this instance, that confirmatory test, largely to reassure me, would have been a mistake. Now, he may not have had a tumour – other things were possible – but when you hear hooves think horses, at least initially. Then look in more detail for donkeys, zebras and only then someone playing the maracas, or using coconuts.

The couple were visibly distressed. I like people to make informed choices where possible, so I gave them an estimate of £800 to £1,000 for their dog's surgery. Critically, this is an estimate, not a quote. A living, breathing organism is not a set of tyres. There was a lot of information I wished I was able to share with them. Was it really a tumour? What type? Had it spread? How long might Bill live? The trouble was that any time spent trying to garner this information prior to surgery would reduce his chances. They were clearly torn, but I had to push them. If the dog was to survive, every moment counted. The on-call nurse, Ruth, was already inbound, and while they thought about things, I gave the dog antibiotics and started to shave the skin on his abdomen. This allows us to surgically prepare the skin, as it must be cleaned and treated with surgical washes in order to render it aseptic prior to surgery. I then excused myself while I went out the back, switched on the oxygen, got the Bairhugger (a large blow-up blanket that is inflated via what is effectively an equally large hair-dryer to serve as a warming device) ready and prepared intravenous (IV) fluids. I also checked to make sure we had enough gaseous anaesthetic in the vaporiser, got out the correct-size endotracheal tube, drew up the induction agent, turned on all the lights, and stuck the IV fluids in some hot water to warm.

That probably took 10 minutes. Where was Ruth? I couldn't start without her. She lived on a farm, so it was going to take her a little while to get in. I'm sure she was going as fast as she could, but I struggled to control my frustration. Anyway, I had to get an answer from the owners. At this stage I might find myself putting the dog to sleep and tidying everything away again. I approached the consultation room with some trepidation. Ultimately, my evening would be a lot easier if they decided against surgery. I'd be done in 10 minutes and poor old Bill would be in cold storage. I realise that sounds incredibly selfish. It is, but I guarantee all but the most rabidly enthusiastic vet has thought the same thing at one time or another.

I slid the door to the consult room open, and Bill looked at me sadly.

'Hi guys, I know this isn't easy, but I need an answer,' I said.

They briefly looked at each other and then the lady spoke.

'Do it, do whatever you can.'

'Okay, let's get him through to surgery. If you can just sign his consent form, it just formalises our permission to carry out his procedure.'

She signed the form. In the background I could hear the back door go, indicating the timely arrival of Ruth. The couple said a quick farewell to the dog, knowing it might be the last time they saw him alive. They had earlier requested to be by his side during surgery, but I couldn't allow that. Health and safety were the reasons I cited. That was technically true, but the main reason was that I didn't need an untrained, potentially hysterical person in the room during surgery. It applies extra, unnecessary pressure and may well prove too much for the owner.

Once they were out I managed to coax Bill to his feet, then I was able to gently cradle him and carry him through to the prep room. Ruth was busy checking my preparatory work. It was imperative that the dog undergo surgery immediately; I was already unhappy with the unavoidable delays and didn't want to add to the problem. We got him on a table; I inserted an intravenous cannula, allowing me to get drugs straight into his system; then I pierced the resealing port fitted to the cannula with my needle-tipped syringe and began giving him propofol, the intravenous agent we commonly use to induce anaesthesia. I gave it slowly, adding a millilitre or so at a time. I wanted to give just enough and not a fraction more. Bill's head gently dipped, and he rested his chin on the prep table. As soon as his eyes were down and his jaw muscles had relaxed their tone, Ruth scooped up his head and gently held it in position as I slid in an endotracheal (ET) tube. In large dogs, the larynx is often visible and they can readily be intubated without a laryngoscope, which may be necessary to visualise the entrance to the trachea in smaller animals. He coughed gently as I inserted the tube.

He was only just out of it, exactly where we wanted him. As soon as the tube was in and cuffed (a small inflatable cuff completes the seal around the ET tube, fully protecting the airway from fluids such as vomit), we connected him to the anaesthetic circuit and he was immediately breathing a mixture of pure oxygen and 1.5 per cent isoflurane, the gaseous anaesthetic agent. Normally, we'd allow an animal to settle for a while prior to doing much of anything, but time was of the essence. We got him on his back and Ruth completed the process of shaving his abdomen that I had started earlier. While I monitored his vital signs she cleaned his hairless abdomen. She would complete his surgical scrub in theatre, while I was scrubbing myself. Quick prep done, we wheeled him into surgery. His IV fluids were up, but not running. These days I don't give loads of fluids to an animal bleeding badly; it dilutes clotting factors, increases blood pressure and accelerates bleeding. The time for aggressive fluids is after you've controlled the haemorrhage. Bill was hooked up to the monitoring equipment, Ruth was scrubbing him and monitoring his vitals, I was scrubbing myself. Suddenly, the expression on Ruth's face changed to one of alarm.

'I can't hear his heart; he's not breathing either!'

I paused mid-scrub. She didn't look certain.

'No, definitely, he's gone!'

This was it; we just hadn't got in quickly enough.

I had probably five seconds to think about it …

'Right, let's just get in there and see if we can get a clamp on whatever is bleeding.'

Bill was not yet sterile enough for surgery, but he was also technically dead, so I decided post-operative infection wasn't too much of a concern right now. I made a large, midline incision in his abdomen, holding the scalpel in my ungloved, incompletely prepped hands. Immediately a large quantity of blood spilled out. I couldn't see anything, but I knew where the spleen is located. I felt around and grabbed the object in question. I fished it out through the abdominal wall; as blood ran off it, it was immediately apparent that it did, indeed, have a large tumour on it and had ruptured, causing Bill's catastrophic loss of blood. Normally I'd take more care, but I simply got the largest clamp I could and clamped all the vessels running to the spleen in one coarse motion, applying it as close to the spleen as practicable.

'Right, push adrenaline; let's tip his legs up and I'll start CPR. Get some fluids going as well!'

Now, with bleeding definitively stemmed, fluids were imperative to re-expand his blood volume. Tilting him head down would redistribute blood towards his brain, heart and lungs. Adrenaline would hopefully give his heart a severe talking to, but I had to get involved, manually. Dropping my instruments I moved to Bill's chest. He was on his back and I couldn't roll him sideways without his abdominal contents spilling out. There was only one thing for it: I'd have to man up (sorry, person up). With a hand on either side of Bill's chest I rapidly compressed his ribcage about as fast as I could manage. It was like using the pec deck at the gym, but hairier. I'd do 30 compressions, then Ruth would give him two lungfuls of oxygen using the anaesthetic circuit and its reservoir bag. Intermittently, Ruth would listen for a heartbeat. Each time, she made eye contact with me and gently shook her head. We'd only been going for a couple of minutes, and I was already dripping with sweat and covered in dog hair. Suddenly, Ruth looked up … then nodded.

'I can hear it; it's faint, but his heart is beating.' She was struggling to stifle a grin of satisfaction.

'Okay, okay … eh,' I managed, still out of breath from the compressions. 'Right … eh, let's just monitor him for a bit, keep the fluids going in – 500 mils at least. I'll go get scrubbed up again and we'll finish off.'

While I went next door and got cleaned up and prepared, Ruth kept monitoring Bill. Once I got back into theatre, I received the update. Bill's heart was regular and seemingly stronger by the minute. The rate was still high at 150, but under the circumstances, not bad. I tied off the vessels running to his spleen, removed it and then searched the rest of his abdominal cavity for other evidence of tumours (technically, neoplasia, 'new growth'). I found none. That was a relatively good sign. Approximately two-thirds of dogs with a blood-filled abdomen, without a history of trauma, have a hemangiosarcoma. One of the most common tumours affecting the spleen in dogs, it is a malignant mass derived from the blood vessels, which readily spreads to other organs. By the time the mass is large enough to rupture and cause catastrophic bleeding, it has often spread. Cure is very unlikely, and animals survive on average about eight weeks from surgery. Roughly 10 per cent of afflicted dogs who survive surgery are alive a year later without further intervention. One thing to bear in mind with statistics is that though they give us some idea of likely outcomes, they say little about the individual in front of you. Bill might be in the 10 per cent, or not …

These days chemotherapy can significantly increase both quantity and quality of life, up to about eight months on average, and the possible treatments are constantly evolving. If Bill lived, we could consider referring him to a veterinary oncologist, a cancer specialist, for further treatment.

The tumour on the spleen hadn't spread as far as I could tell, but even a single malignant cell seeded elsewhere in the body could become another mass. I closed him up. While we had been operating, his gums had become pinker and he now had a heart rate of 130. His blood pressure was stabilising, and blood was getting to all the places it should be. Blood loss might be survivable in the short term, but if organs have been deprived of blood, and therefore oxygen, for long enough there may be damage such that they fail shortly thereafter. Only time would tell, but I thought he had a good chance for now. Given that he was stable I could give him something for the pain. I gave him a NSAID (non-steroidal anti-inflammatory drug) and an opioid, methadone. We had him wrapped in the Bair-hugger. He was cold at 34°C; normally his temperature would be about 38 to 39°C, but he had started out cold due to his blood loss, lying still and being in shock. Hypothermia is detrimental in recovery; it also inhibits clotting. It would be important to monitor Bill's temperature as he recovered. We'd turned his anaesthetic off even as I completed the last suture. While Ruth monitored Bill, I took off my gloves and gown, binned them and made my way upstairs to perform the next critical stage in the dog's recovery. I made myself and Ruth a lovely cup of tea.

Brew in hand I phoned the owners.

'Hi, it's the vet here; it's mixed news I'm afraid. Bill's made it through surgery, but he did have a tumour on his spleen. It had ruptured and that was what caused his internal bleeding. I've removed his spleen and he's fine for now. However, the tumour may have spread microscopically, which I would not be able to see. That said, I saw no sign of metastasis (secondary tumours, which have spread from a primary tumour), so fingers crossed. We'll send his spleen off to the lab; they'll be able to tell us more and give us an idea whether or not it was malignant. In the meantime, he's going to be with us for a day or two recovering. Now I can't promise anything. The loss of blood may mean that he suffers organ failure, but we'll monitor that. For now, he's sleeping and we've done all we can.'

They were grateful, but I'm sure they didn't get much sleep that night.

I came back down and passed Ruth's tea over. We chatted while we monitored Bill. It took about thirty minutes for him to show any signs of true consciousness. His temperature had come up a bit to 36.2°C; hardly a miracle. But he was still here. We got him through to the kennels, padded one out with blankets for him and transferred him, complete with hi-tech inflatable blanket. Occasionally he would gently whine; I'm sure he was sore despite the drugs. I gave Ruth a hand to clean up and we worked through the remaining inpatients while checking in on Bill from time to time.

I was a locum in the practice, staying in the practice accommodation. Ruth had a young family, so as soon as I could, I let her get off home. I wrote up Bill's notes on the computer and priced up his treatment. I was tempted to go off to bed for a couple of hours, but I really needed to monitor Bill's temperature. So I resigned myself to the inevitable, laid out a fluffy dog blanket next to his kennel and lay down on it, setting my watch alarm for 30 minutes hence. It was not comfortable, but I was tired and soon nodded off. I intermittently slept and checked on Bill, repeating his medications as necessary and occasionally checking his gums, heart rate, respiratory rate and temperature. About 5 a.m. I was satisfied that he was stable and sufficiently warm for me to climb into bed for a couple of hours. I needed to be back down at 7.30 a.m. to start going through the inpatients. Bill was awake, so I gently stroked his muzzle and despite myself said: 'You're going to be all right mate.'

I was rewarded with a long sigh and the gentlest of tail wags.

Bill got stronger almost by the hour. Typical Lab, his appetite was largely unaffected. On the first morning he seemed a bit disinterested in breakfast. Until I rolled the dog meat into a ball, sat him up and offered it to him. He wolfed it down, covering my hand in a mixture of dog food and saliva. This had clearly whetted his appetite. I pushed forward the remainder of his bowl of recovery food and he made short work of it. By day two he was able to get up and around, and then he went from strength to strength. The same day I invited his owners in for a visit. The instant he saw them his tail wag went straight to hyper-speed. They were quite emotional and it was a truly rewarding thing to witness. Once Bill was safely back in his kennel, I got them through and chatted about recent events. We hadn't yet received the histopathology, so I couldn't add much about his long-term prospects. However, I just wanted to update then on the plan for the next few days.

During the discussion the owners asked: 'You mentioned it was a close-run thing; we were wondering how close. I mean, could we have waited until the morning?'

'Eh? No. At one point Bill was actually dead, and we had to resuscitate him; it couldn't have been any closer.'

I realised I'd completely forgotten to mention that Bill had technically been dead for about five minutes.

'What do you mean, DEAD!?' I steeled myself for a complaint.

'I mean, he had stopped breathing, his heart had stopped and he was technically dead. Without adrenaline, chest compressions, ventilation and so on, he wouldn't be here.'

'So … you saved him?'

'Er, well, I suppose.'

'That's … amazing … thank you so much. I just don't know how our son would cope without him; they're like best friends.'

'Er, thanks, I, er, well, uhm … Cheers, yeah.'

I'm not good with praise, but I'd be lying if I didn't admit to a moment of pride. For now at least, a family was whole again and a little boy had his best friend back.

And that, ladies and gentlemen, is why I'm still a vet.

ACKNOWLEDGEMENTS

There are simply too many people who have helped me throughout my life for me to thank them all here. However, there are a few who deserve special mention. First of all, I would like to thank my family and friends who have both put up with me all these years and afforded me opportunity, friendship and advice.

I'd like to thank my agent, Ariella Feiner, and my editor, Kelly Ellis, for helping me make this spark of an idea the book you see before you.

If vets are the unsung heroes of animal welfare, then nurses are the unspoken. Far too often we see praise and thanks levelled at vets, when much of the gratitude should be directed elsewhere. That veterinary nurses are underpaid and under-thanked for the gritty work of delivering animal care is a massive understatement. It is easy to assume veterinary nurses are merely the holders of puppies and the therapists of particularly difficult cats. In fact, the average veterinary nurse is an anaesthesiologist, phlebotomist, lab technician, wound-care specialist, radiographer, microbiologist, confidant, nurse and saint all rolled into one. Of course, there are the bad ones as well, but you get the point.

This book is dedicated to each and every one of them, but with one stand-out candidate. In the interests of full disclosure, I must reveal that my wife, Siân, is a veterinary nurse. She is also my greatest supporter and many of my modest achievements can be traced back to her seemingly limitless patience and friendship. We can only presume that her predilection for small hairy things has influenced her choice of both career and husband.

To my wife, thank you, this is for you.